50 Secrets of Magic Craftsmanship

SALVADOR DALÍ

Must Have Books
503 Deerfield Place
Victoria, BC
V9B 6G5
Canada
trava2911@gmail.com

ISBN: 9781774641378

Copyright 2021 – Must Have Books

All rights reserved in accordance with international law. No part of this book may be reproduced or transmitted in any form or by any means, electronic or mechanical, including photocopying, recording, or by any information storage or retrieval system, except in the case of excerpts by a reviewer who may quote brief passages in an article or review, without written permission from the publisher.

Contents

Clear and Brief Prologue   5

Chapter One   8

Chapter Two   28

Chapter Three   75

Chapter Four   117

Chapter Five   190

DEDICATION

At the age of six I wanted to be Napoleon—and I wasn't.

At the age of fifteen I wanted to be Dali and I have been.

At the age of twenty-five I wanted to become the most sensational painter in the world and I achieved it.

At thirty-five I wanted to affirm my life by success and I attained it.

Now at forty-five I want to paint a masterpiece and to save Modern Art from chaos and laziness. I will succeed! This book is consecrated to this crusade and I dedicate it to all the young, who have faith in true painting.

Salvador Dalí

CLEAR and BRIEF PROLOGUE

in which it is explained that the beginning of this book is to be found only at the end.

"The two most fortunate things that can happen to a painter are, first, to be Spanish and, second, to be named Dali. Those two fortunate things have happened to me."
S. D.

SALVADOR, AS his very name indicates, is destined to nothing less than to rescue painting from the void of modern art."

This categorical affirmation, though it would seem at first sight, by its egocentricity, to have been written by Dali himself, is from the pen of the famous Catalonian philosopher, Francese Pujols. In 1937, in the midst of the surrealist chaos when he wrote this, I admit —modestly, for once—that I myself, in spite of my ambitious imperialisms of very kind, did not place much faith in it. Today I realize, however, that I have become, little by little, firmly convinced of it.*

This is due essentially to the fact that my intelligence has never ceased to grow in the course of my ambition which, as everyone knows, has always been lofty and majestic since my tenderest childhood. I like to compare my ambition to a century-old oak tree, and my intelligence to a loving vine which climbs round its bark to reach its top. And if this oak tree seems to me to be immemorial and immobile in its growth, so august and harmonious is its lofty height, the vine of my intelligence, on the contrary, appears to me to have a biological exuberance, to grow by leaps, inasmuch as each time I observe what is happening to me at the moment of beginning or of completing a work, I am always surprised by the bursting forth of vigorous new shoots.

And this is so true that I can say right now that in the three or four days since I have begun to write this book I already feel myself more intelligent than before. Fortunately so! For in order to be capable of writing this book—a kind of culinary initiation to the Eleusinian mysteries of painting—and in order to make translucid the most obscure technical secrets, which would seem to require the art of magic in addition to the practice of painting itself, it does not suffice to be terribly intelligent. Indeed I would go so far as to have the deeply rooted suspicion that all the greatest intelligences combined would not suffice to succeed in such an undertaking, and that consequently the writer who should undertake such a task would have to possess, in addition, some other supra-essential thing, and this other thing, this "quintessence" of the essential, which happens to be exactly what is required to paint a beautiful picture, I must say at once—and for the exclusive benefit of my readers—this other thing I also possess. But I do not wish to say at once what this thing is: in the first place, for fear of discouraging my readers by wearying them through a too great presumption on my part, and in the second place because I have the catholic habit of always beginning at the end. Is not "beginning with ends" the essence of catholicity?

That is why "this thing" which I am not revealing, and which normally would be announced at the beginning of this clear prologue, will be found by the reader, as he has been forewarned, only after he has read the entire book and is overwhelmingly convinced: he will find it exactly in the last two lines of this book.

END OF THE CLEAR AND BRIEF PROLOGUE

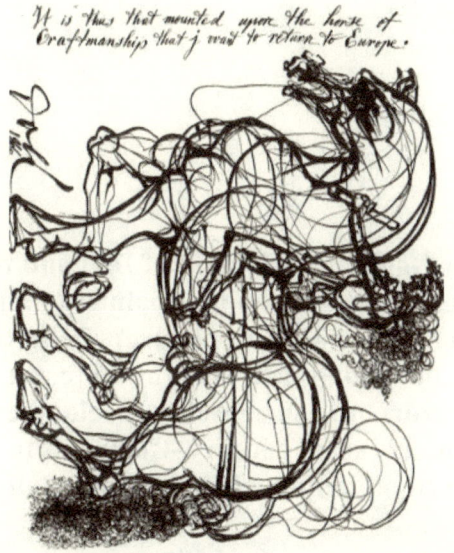

[*] Quite apart from my intrinsic value as a painter—which I am one of the first to be ready to discuss—one thing is certain: that if "painting" is to survive our epoch of barbarous mechanical progress, this continuity of painting will have its starting-point in Salvador Dali; and it is for this reason that this book is destined to have a daily-growing vital interest. For no person, whether directly or remotely interested in the real phenomenon of painting, will be able to avoid consulting it.

CHAPTER ONE

The ear of Van Gogh, the left hand of Dali and the foot of Cézanne–Modern painters, house painters and the ancients–What is a well painted picture?–Definition of painting–Advice to the young art student to contemplate philosophically the azure of an absolutely cloudless sky, preferably in a Mediterranean country–Comparison of the head of the painter to an oil lamp which illuminates all realms of knowledge.

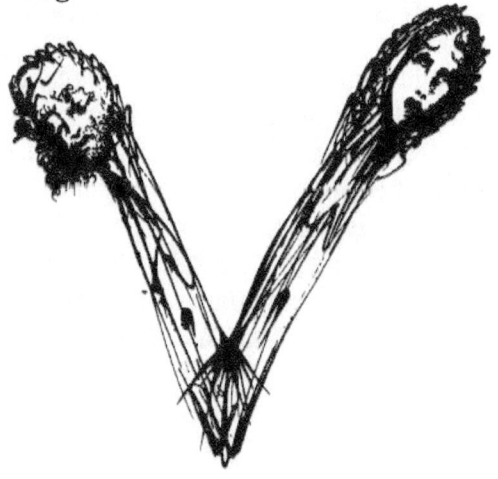

VAN GOGH was mad, and unconditionally, generously and gratuitously cut off his left ear with the blade of a razor. I am not mad either, yet I would be perfectly capable of allowing my left hand to be cut off, but this under the most interesting circumstances imaginable: on condition, namely, that I might for ten minutes be able to observe Vermeer of Delft seated before his easel as he was painting. I should even be capable of much more than that, for I should likewise be prepared to let my right ear, and even both ears, be removed provided I might learn the exact formula of the mixture, which composes the "precious juice" in which this same Vermeer, unique among the unique (and whom I do not call divine because he is the most human of all painters), dips his exquisitely rare brush; which, I have no doubt, was in his time as common, daily and usual as in turn must have been the "precious juice," the current coin of the ingredients of the studios of the golden age of the arts, but which has become in our dull and scatological days of artistic decadence a mysterious liquid gem which all the gold in the world could not hope to ransom, for the simple reason that the formulae of the "media" with which the painters of former times painted their immortal works do not exist. All the hypotheses of the greatest experts in this regard lead only to violent polemics and to flagrant contradictions which become aggravated day by day.

This might seem merely another typical Dalinian exaggeration, yet it is a rigorously objective fact: in 1948 a few persons in the world know how to manufacture an atomic bomb, but there does not exist a single person on the globe who knows today what was the composition of the mysterious juice, the "medium" in which the brothers Van Eyck or Vermeer of Delft dipped their brushes to paint. No one knows—not even I! The fact that there exists no precise recipe of that period which might guide us, and that no chemical or physical analysis can explain to us today the "majestic imponderables" of the "pictorial matter" of the old masters, has often caused our contemporaries to assume and to believe that the ancients possessed secrets which they jealously and fanatically guarded. I am inclined to believe rather the contrary, namely that such recipes must in their time have been precisely so little secret, so incorporated in the everydayness of the routine life of all painters, so much a part of an uninterrupted tradition of every minute of experience, that such secrets must have been transmitted almost wholly orally, without anyone's even taking the trouble to note them down or, if so, only by means of that elegiac charcoal pencil with which the masters traced so many unknown, effaced and often angelic ephemerides.

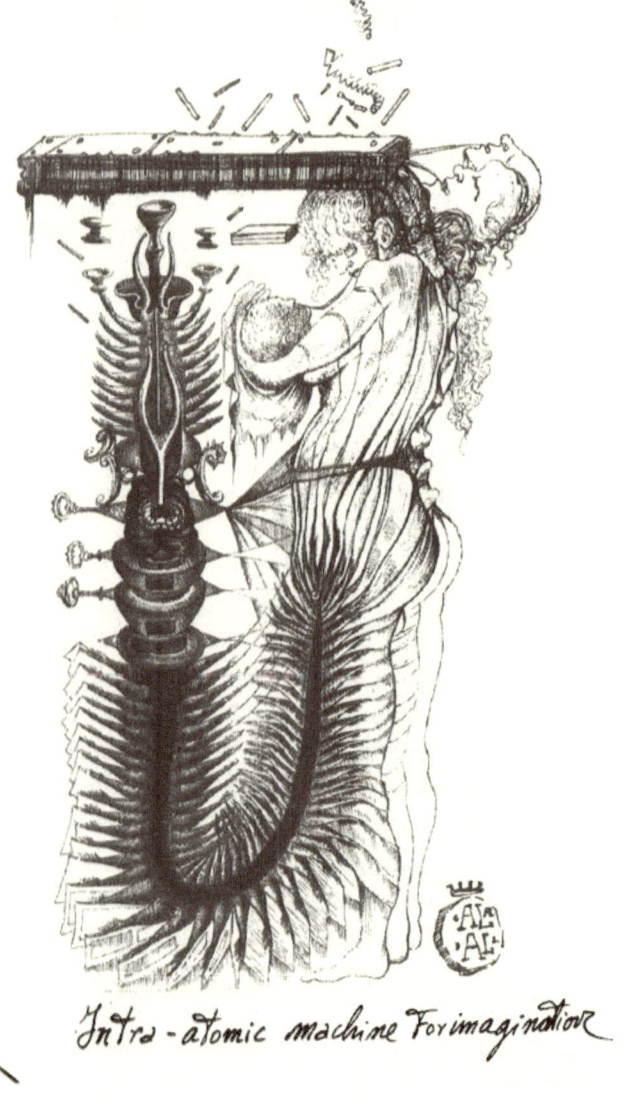

Intra-atomic machine for imagination

    Thus there is not the faintest shadow of madness in claiming, as I do, that if one places on one of the scales of a balance of pictorial justice a single drop of the medium with which Vermeer of Delft painted, one should not hesitate one second in throwing on the other scale of this same balance the left ear of Van Gogh, the left hand of Salvador Dali and an impressive quantity besides of viscera of all sorts, even the most intimate, snatched somewhat at random from the most disorganized anatomies of our modern painters. And if all this freshly cut raw flesh does not—as I strongly suspect—suffice to "make up the weight" one should not then hesitate to add for good measure the two ponderous hands of the touching Paul Cézanne. For the poor man, in spite of his wonderful and ultra-respectable ambition to "paint like Poussin from nature" and thereby to become the master and the greatest architect of nature, succeeded merely in becoming a kind of neo-Platonic master mason, so that instead of edifying eternal palaces for the princes of intelligence he was able only to build modest shacks capable, at best, of sheltering the indigent Bohemians of modern art who are used to sleeping under bridges or exposed to the elements of impressionism for a couple of aesthetic summers. Since this book is to be the book of the justice of painting, it will inevitably be cruel to modern painting, and if we owe an infinite respect to the dramatic obstinacy of Cézanne in aspiring to build, to the authenticity of his classicist torments, to the nobility of his ambitions, we do not regret having, at the very beginning of this book, cut off his two clumsy hands as we have just done, for in truth everything that he "realized" he could just as well have achieved with his feet!

Five thoughts on art

1. The work of art must impress you without touching you.

2. If the classics are cold, it is because their flame is eternal.

3. The eclat of the romantics is that of a fire in a strawpile.

4. If you understand your painting beforehand, you might as well not paint it.

5. Painting, as Leonardo da Vinci proved, is superior to all the other arts, because it is directed to the most noble and divine of all the organs, the eye. To compare the ear to the eye would be as absurd ae to compare the nose to the ear.

"Post-Cézannism" has erected into a system every one of the clumsinesses and the deficiencies of Cézanne and painted square mile after square mile of canvases with these defects. The defects of Cézanne, in his fundamentally honest character, were often consequences of his very virtues; but defects are never virtues! I can imagine the profound melancholy of the master of Aix-en-Provence, Paul Cézanne, when after having struggled so long to build a well-constructed apple on his canvas, possessed like a demon by the problem of relief, he had succeeded on the contrary only in painting it concave! Andinstead of keeping, as was his ambition, the "intact continuity" of the surface of his canvas, without making any concession to the illusory frivolities of verisimilitude, he finds himself in the end with a canvas frightfully lacking in consistency and filled with holes! With each new apple there is a new hole! Which, as the immortal Michel de Montaigne said in another connection, is *"chier dans le panier et se le mettre sur la tête."*

If I say that this book is actually to be the book of justice, I must add that the eternity of this book will be that of its inexorable truth; for I shall be faithful to truth to the very marrow of the bones of aesthetics, and let the reader not be frightened at hearing them often cracking between the vigorous hands of my brain. Thus, let this be said: Modern painters having almost totally lost the technical tradition of the ancients, we can no longer do what we want to do. We only do "whatever comes out of us." There is a Spanish proverb which defines the common people's reaction to a bad painter: "If it comes out with a beard, it will be Saint Anthony, and if it comes out without a beard it will be the Immaculate Conception." Picasso, whose case is even more dramatic than Cézanne's (more gifted to begin with, destructive and anarchistic rather than constructive and patriarchal), has often quoted this proverb to me, taking it for his own and applying it as a devise to his own manner of painting. In other words, he does this on purpose: he knows perfectly well that white "enamel" for painting doors, which you buy at the corner store and with which he covers his canvas, will turn yellow within a year, like the newspaper in his collages. Just as the anarchist who sets fire to a church is quite well aware that the effect of his act will be, not to preserve it, but rather to make it go up in flames.

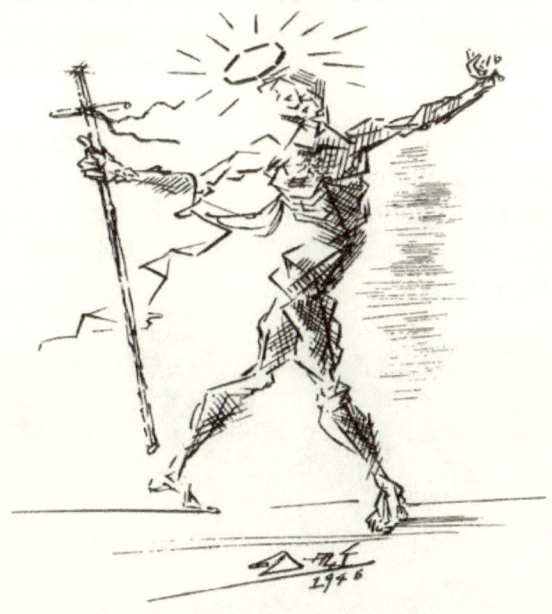

The Catalonian sculptor Manolo, looking with bitterness at a statuette which he had just completed and which his friends—"modern art critics"—were praising to the skies, exclaimed philosophically, "You like only the things of mine which turn out badly, for what I wanted to do was a Venus, and all that came out was a toad!" Today the love of the defective is such that genius is recognized only in defects, and especially in ugliness. The moment a Venus resembles a toad, the contemporary pseudo-aesthetes exclaim, "It's powerful, it's human!" Certain it is that Raphaelesque perfections would pass totally unperceived before their eyes. Ingres yearned to paint like

Raphael and only painted like Ingres; Raphael yearned to paint like the Ancients and exceeded them. There have been times when I silently admitted to myself, "I want to paint like Ingres," and it turned out to be like Bouguereau. Nevertheless I irresistibly paint like Dali, which is already enormous, for of all contemporary painters I am the one who is most able to do what he wants —and who knows if some day I shall not without intending it be considered the Raphael of my period? But what needs to be said, and what I wish to say here, and what people will soon tire of hearing repeated, is that the moment has finally come for calling bread bread and wine wine; the beautiful beautiful, and the ugly ugly; defects defects and virtues virtues; and that the so-called modern painting, if it remains in history, will remain as an iconographic document, or be incorporated in a degenerate branch of decorative art, but never, whatever anyone may wish, as "Pictorial Art."

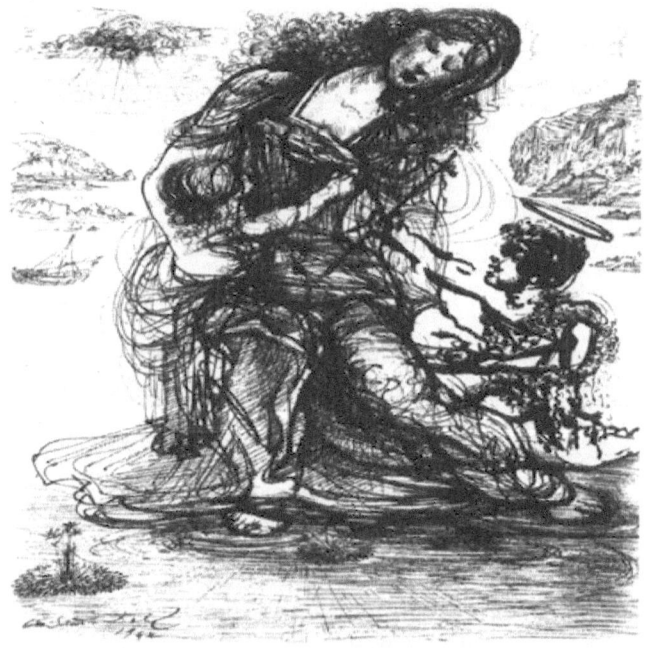

In 1936, in Paris, I visited an exhibition of so-called

abstract painting in the company of the late Maurice Heine, the erudite specialist on the Marquis de Sade, and he noticed that during the whole visit my eyes kept coming back to a corner of the exposition room in which no work was being exhibited. "You seem to be systematically avoiding looking at the paintings," Heine said to me, "It's as though you were obsessed by something invisible!" "It's nothing invisible," I replied to reassurehim, "I just can't help looking at that door—it is so well painted. It is by far the best painted thing in the whole exposition."

This was rigorously true. None of the painters who had hung their canvases in this room would have been capable of painting that door. And on the other hand, the house painter who had painted the latter would have been able very creditably to copy any one of the paintings exhibited! I myself was quite overcome by that door, and I wondered, with genuine curiosity, how many layers of paint there were, what proportion of oil and turpentine, to have produced a surface so homogeneous, smooth and even, so noble in its material solidity, which had demanded a minimum of honest workmanship which none of the exhibiting artists came anywhere near possessing. Let us beware, then, of that kind of would-be painting, whether abstract or non-abstract, surrealist or existentialist, whatever may be the pseudo-philosophic label it bears, but which a painter of doors would be capable of reproducing and copying satisfactorily in less than a half hour. And the perspicacious reader cannot but be very grateful to me for confirming him in the suspicion which his wise prudence, as I assume, had already aroused in his ever-alert mind, namely, that the value of paintings that can be so easily imitated runs the risk of dropping below that of the very doors in question, even though these were not painted at all.

Definition of painting

"Painting: representation upon a surface of visual quality through colors" — If intellectual elements intervene in this representation we have a sequel rate painting, called "decorative painting". If the elements that intervene are of the domain of ideas we have a second rate painting called "literary painting".

Conclusion: The only first rate painting is realistic painting. — Salvador Dalí

1948

On the other hand, quite the contrary holds true for pictures painted according to the tradition of the ancients. I venture to affirm that such works become each day not only more precious because of the fact that they cannot be imitated, but also more living, more existing—if to exist is to act; for in contrast to the modern works which barely last a season, leaving a more imperceptible spiritual trace even than the collections of dressmakers, the works of the ancient masters are even now giving life to the painting of the near future, for it is they and only they who possess all the arts and all the prescience of magic. And while around us modern painting ages spiritually and materially, becoming so quickly outmoded, turning yellow, darkening, breaking out in cracks and all the stigmata of decrepitude, a painting of Raphael, for example the Saint George slaying the dragon, grows younger day by day, not only spiritually, to the point of appearing today as philosophically the most up-to-date, but also materially: for a well painted picture is the very contrary of the most beautiful ruins—each passing year, instead of impairing a little of its beauty, only adds to it; instead of tarnishing it time seems to give it a new and more subtle light. Every true *connaisseur* possesses the precise, intellectual appreciation of that "visual savor" which is added to every beautiful painting by the phenomenon, imponderable among imponderables, which is called "patina," a phenomenon which I do not hesitate, this time, to call divine, since it is in the power of no man to reproduce it, being as it is the exclusive privilege of the god of time himself.

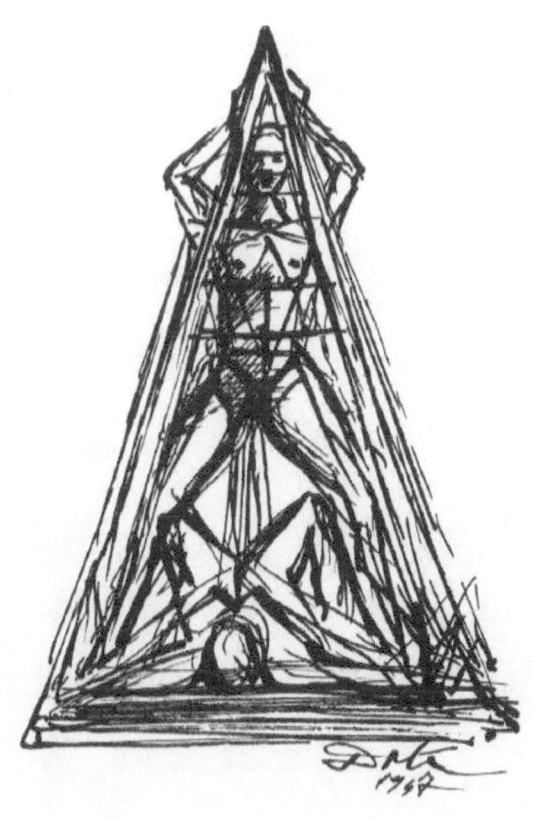

Where are the famous futurist paintings? It is curious to know that they died of old age twenty years ago. Raphael: *there* is a futurist painter, if by this one means that he will continue more and more to exert an active influence on the future! Yet history is tireless. Empires crumble, and Hitler, the great masochist, lays the foundations of a future Wagnerian opera, dying in the arms of Eva Braun beneath the burning sky of Berlin. Extravagant changes of power and of will shake the world, accompanied by calm atomic explosions resembling idyllic mossy and mushroomy trees of a terrestrial paradise after all the hells of the heaven of the war just ended. All this is nothing compared to the patina of a beautiful painting! That is strength: a painting by Raphael or Vermeer remains immutable in the midst of the most totalitarian

Capharnaums. Whatever the state, whether communist, monarchist or parachutist, all are alike in safeguarding the famous paintings as their most precious and their proudest heritage. What strength!

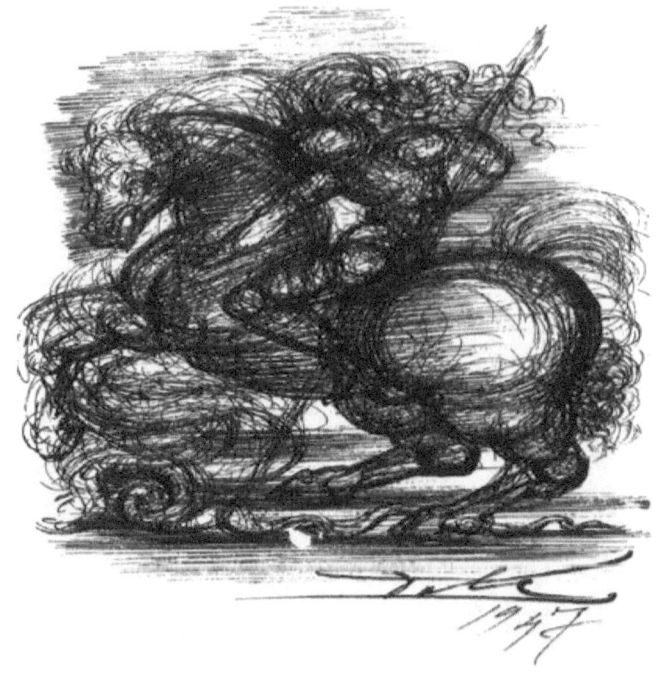

And what is a painting? It is a piece of canvas or of wood on which has been spread with art a little earth mixed with a little oil, by the aid of a few hairs attached to the end of a stick! Consider, by comparison, the means at the disposal of the motion picture industry, and the technical effort involved in the miles of celluloid that have been filmed up to the present day. How many screws, lenses, how much electricity, how much organization . . . And yet all these films perish and are condemned beforehand to the most anonymous oblivion after a few years and often after a few weeks.

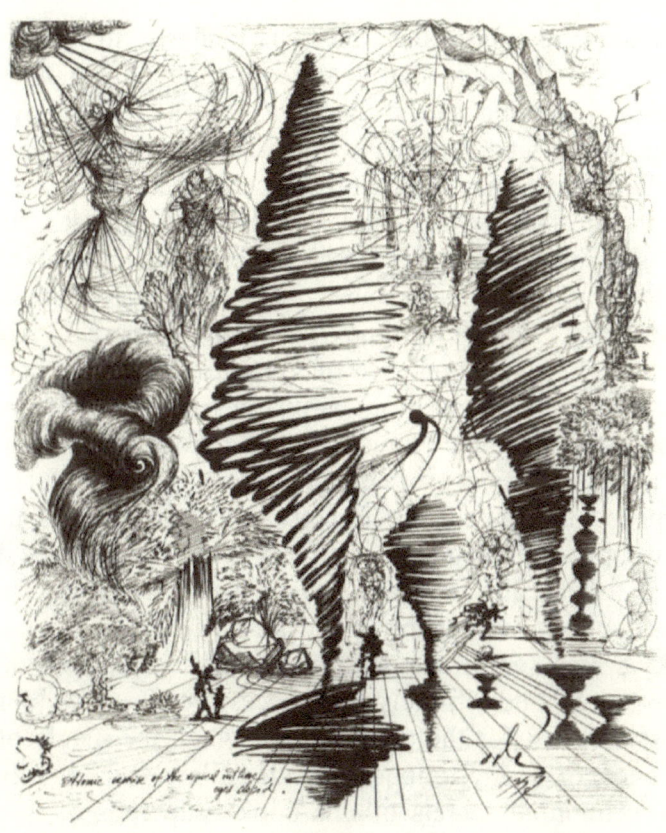

It would therefore be prudent to assume that in order, with such simple means, to spread paint on a piece of wood and to create a work appealing to the senses which will remain immortal, it must be necessary to proceed and to manipulate it with a kind of art close to magic, and that in any case the simple technique of house painters will not suffice. In point of fact, to limit ourselves for the moment to the medium, it must be clearly understood that the paint as it comes from the tube is nothing more than that which is used to paint doors; but that nevertheless, when knowingly used, it becomes, as it became for all the great ancient masters, a matter more precious and inimitable than all the enamels and all the gems of creation. And in order to make the reader sense, if not wholly understand this, I should like to recommend to him—and most particularly to every young apprentice in painting—that he gaze long and philosophically one afternoon in spring at the azure of the sky, on a day wholly without clouds and preferably in a Mediterranean country. Then he will observe that this azure is composed, as it were, of a precious substance which eludes his rational faculties, for at the same time that it will appear to him to be made up of an infinitely smooth and hard substance, like an agate sphere, this homogeneity, so opaque and materially corporeal, will seem luminous and as if composed of transparency and of spirituality itself. And in this the sensations just described will be in accord with physics, since the hardness and the violence, so to speak, of such an azure are constituted of nothing but infinite layers of superposed transparent air. Exactly the same thing is true of a beautiful pictorial matter. A color as it comes from a tube does not exist as a beautiful and transcendant pictorial matter. The latter, on the contrary, is constituted and formed, like the very azure of the sky which serves as our example, by a succession of subtle, quasi-spiritual and infinitely fine successive layers, as transparent as possible, and for the obtaining of which the magic of media intervenes; those mysteriously blended films—which will be one of the primordial secrets of this book—superposed, spread one over the other according to the harmony of their physical and chemical properties, attaining the maximum of brilliancy, more limpid than that of enamel and less fixed, since it is susceptible to all the future mysteries and aureolations of patina. And we shall have to be particularly attentive to this decisive subject of "matter," since it is by this specifically sensorial means that we shall be made aware of the most finely shaded ideas in the realm of the senses, and since nothing in the realm of visual sensuality is so capable of beauty, of nobility and of honor or, on the other hand, of ugliness, of ignominy and of degradation, depending on the manner in which this celestial or foul matter is used and manipulated.

Ten rules for him who wishes to be a painter

1. Painter, it is better to be rich than poor; so learn how to make gold and precious stones come out of your brush.

2. Don't be afraid of perfection: you'll never attain it!

3. Begin by learning to draw and paint like the old masters. After that, you can do as you like; everyone will respect you.

4. Don't throw to the dogs either your eye or your hand or your brain, for you will need them all if you are to be a painter.

5. If you are one of those who believe that modern art has surpassed Vermeer and Raphael, don't read this book, just go right on in your blissful idiocy.

6. Don't vomit on your picture, because it is the picture which can vomit on you after you are dead.

7. No lazy masterpieces!

8. Painter, paint!

9. Painter, don't drink alcohol, and chew hashish only five times in your life.

10. If painting doesn't love you, all your love for her will be unavailing.

Observe how, when oil color is improperly handled, it is smeared on the canvas, stigmatized by a crude, repulsive opacity, or by a "dull discontinuity" as of ejected matter, now soft and at the same time brittle, now lumpy, spasmodically leprous or running, dirty, turning green and yellow, with even the azures becoming muddy-colored and excremental. And observe how, on the other hand, when oil color is magically used in the manner of the ancient Flemish painters, this "matter" becomes actually translucid, with the hard consistency of a gem, opalescent, pellucid azure, in which the very browns of the most ammoniac earth seem to take on something of the glow of a silvery mist and the deep and rotting blacks assume a diamond sharpness. There is, in fact, so great a difference between a beautiful and noble "matter," in which the drops of liquid amber, the oils of polarized sunlight, the honey of patience and intelligence of the old masters harden and those other matters of the ignorant modern painters in which the colors pulverize, immediately disintegrated by the solvents of druggists, the poison of laziness, the detritus of impatience and the bile of rancor —so great a difference that it may well be said, without fear of falling into a Dalinian exaggeration, that whereas the matter of the old painters is so refined, so completely and continually modified by intelligence that it becomes spiritualized to the point of giving us the illusion that they painted their pictures with elements of heaven, one has the impression that modern painters paint their pictures with their stools, so directly does their matter flow from the tube of their biology without the slightest intervention of the heart.

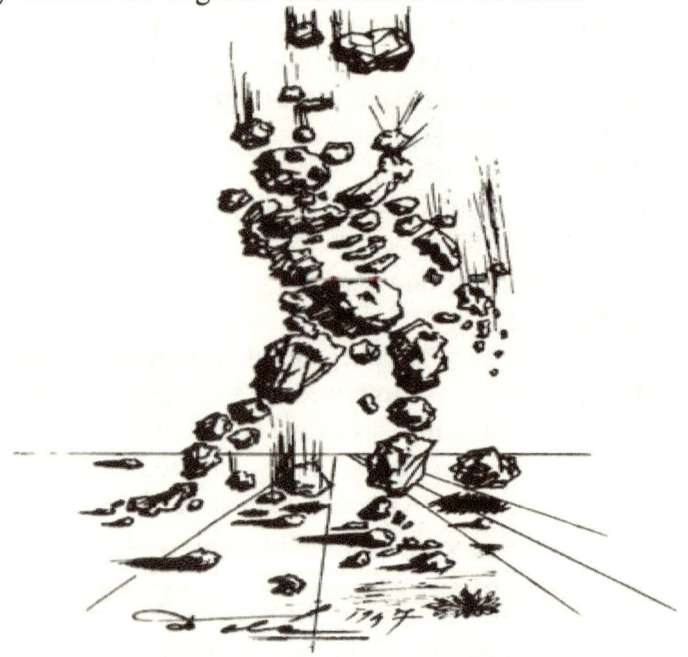

Matter is essentially so consubstantial with beautiful and true painting that I do not consider that "painting" was authentically and fully invented until the moment when the historic event of oil painting occurred. For in truth it must be obvious that before oil was mixed with the marvelous earth, mineral or vegetable elements painting creaks, jarring our teeth just as when one finds sand in one's vegetables, which one would like to imagine having come, rather, from the garden of the Hesperides of the spirit, from which every unpleasant material substance would be excluded, so that only the aesthetic enjoyment of the Eclogues might subsist. Tempera, fresco, egg-painting, etc.—how it creaks! Those painful brush-smears of a Giotto or of a Fra Angelico! In spite of the light of the whole Catholic faith, painting seemed on the point of becoming extinct when oil came to its rescue, just in time—to revivify it, lubricate it and preserve it. All painting before oil is dry, harsh and, as it were, against the grain. It was not possible, as it was later, to scumble with a fleeting badger-hair brush the pigments of gold, of air, the infinitesimal and suprasensitive shades with which reality itself appears to us to be "bathed," that is to say phenomenally solarized with the oils and the honeys of light itself. No atmospheric illusionism was possible. Nor could one paint the mystery of the flesh, the glory of painting, with that subsurface iridescence which characterizes it, nor the mystery of the azure of the sky, which is the very mystery of the transparencies of pictorial technique—for, even metaphysically, what painting can render with the greatest luminosity is precisely skies and flesh.

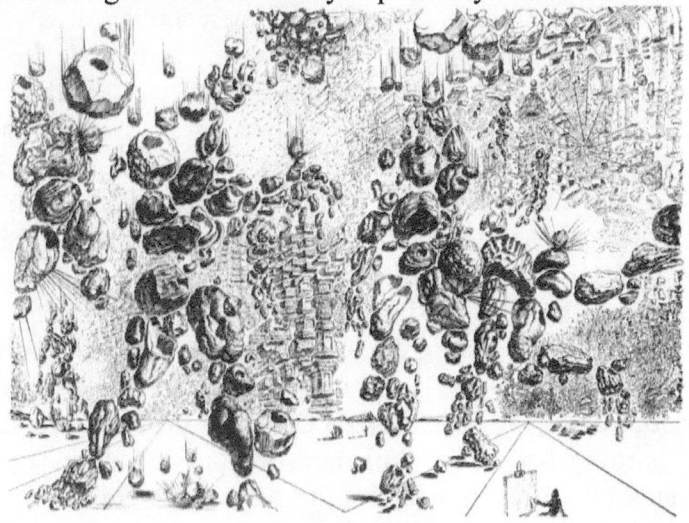

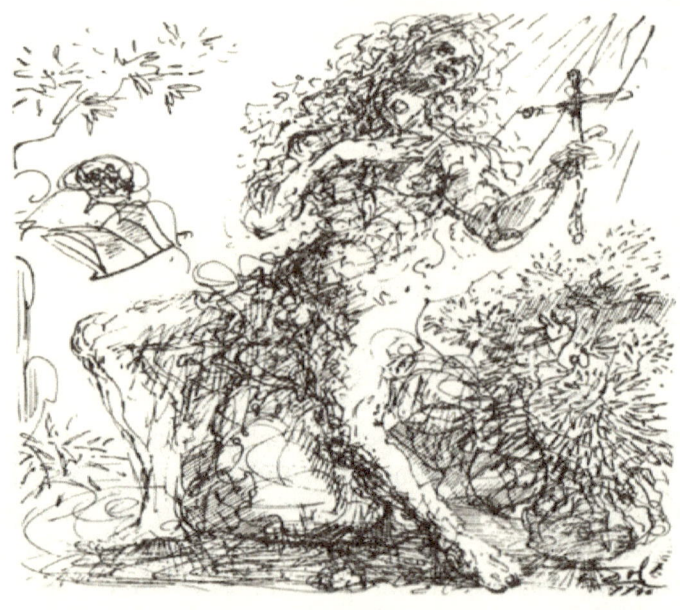

Before the memorable invention of oil painting by the glory of the Van Eyck brothers the images represented on paintings remained illustrations, iconographies, they remained images too physically separated from the phenomenal world of reality to be able to achieve the perceptible clarity of the hierarchy of our sensual knowledge. Between the image represented and this phenomenal world, between reality and the perception, there was still a too violent traumatism, composed of rasping, repelling and unyielding materials, too much hardness of outline, too many contours analytically separating each object. Isolated from the surrounding medium, cut off in a celibacy of conventional lighting which is at the opposite pole from the cognitive marriage of the senses and the synthesis of the perceptible and visual truth which is the most evolved of all philosophical activities—since to look is to think—there were therefore too many obstacles, too much earth, too much sand, too much aridity between the painter's vision and his idea, and the painter's eye often filled with the tears of despair at not being able, with his hand and his materials, to paint what he conceived, what he willed. For to "look" is also the highest and the most imperialist hierarchy of the *will*. His hand encounters materials that are just waiting to be combined and used together; but he lacks the "medium" capable of uniting them, of making them glide, of lubricating them in a synthesis which, like all syntheses based on the principle of lubrication, will result in a splendor of the intelligence.

The painter already saw clearly enough, but he could barely throw light on what he was painting, he could not be equal to his vision, and it was as though, unable to communicate the plain-chant of the iridescence of a pearl, he was reduced and condemned to a mere dry inventory, a wholly intellectual catalogue utterly unsatisfying to the senses. The hand could not execute what the brain had authorized, and it was as if the latter, like a wick twisted back upon itself a hundred times in philosophical circumvolutions, was on the point of drying out through its impotence and its inability to continue to give light.

Painting had, indeed, lighted the wick of the human brain, which for a moment burned intensely, but, we might almost say, burned dry. And for lack of an appropriate combustible liquid in which to keep alive, this little flickering and precious flame risked at every moment disappearing in the darkness of blind or abstract iconographies. It was at this precise moment that the uniquely memorable event occurred—the invention of oil painting. And it was in truth as if, in the painter's head, just as his intelligence was about to go out, oil had just been added to a lamp.

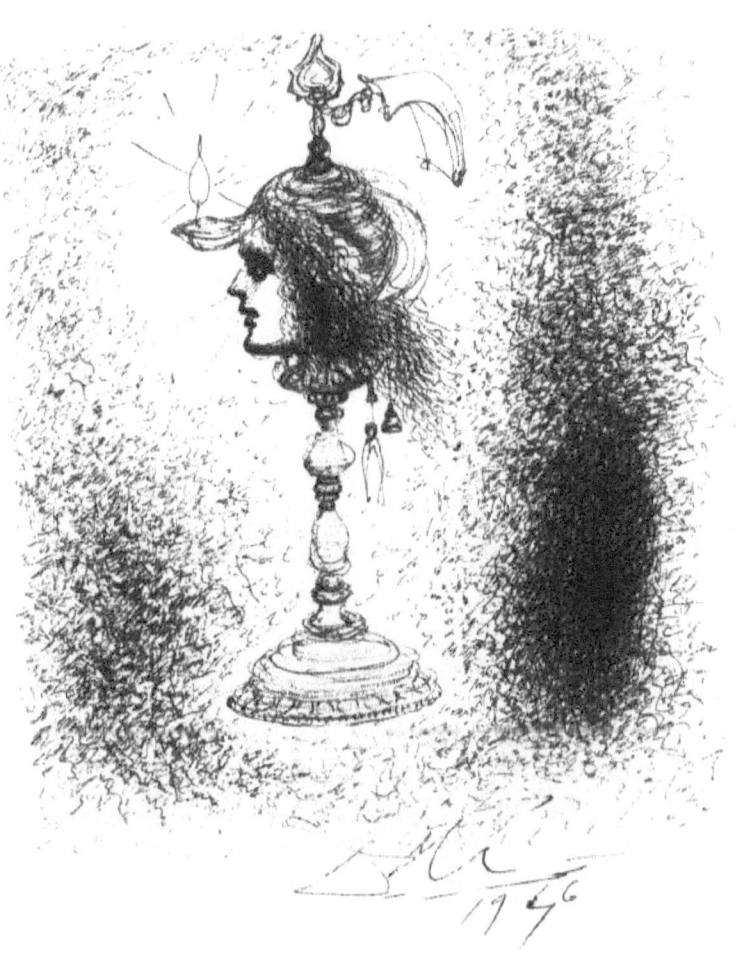

Comparative Table of the Values After Dalinian Analysis

Elaborated During Ten Years

	Crafts-manship	Inspiration	Color	Design	Genius	Composition	Originality	Mystery	Authenticity
Leonardo da Vinci	17	18	15	19	20	18	19	20	20
Meissonier	5	0	1	3	0	1	2	17	18
Ingres	15	12	11	15	0	6	6	10	20
Velasquez	20	19	20	19	20	20	20	15	20
Bugnereau	11	1	1	1	0	0	0	0	15
Dali	12	17	10	17	19	18	17	19	19
Picasso	9	19	9	18	20	16	7	2	7
Raphael	19	19	18	20	20	20	20	20	20
Manet	3	1	6	4	0	4	5	0	14
Wermeer de Delft	20	20	20	20	20	20	19	20	20
Mondrian	0	0	0	0	0	1	½	0	3½

CHAPTER TWO

Description of each of the five different movements corresponding to each of the five different types of brushes–Of the position and the springboard necessary to effect blending with the fan-shaped brush–Treatise on the painter's slumbers–Of the sleep called the "slumber with a key"–The slumber obtained from sea urchins and the slumber with three cooked sea perch eyes–Of the sympathy and antipathy of things in nature and in the painter's eye–Of how and with what the painter's eye must be nourished–Of the diverse reasons why painters are produced only in certain countries–Of what kind of vegetation the painter must plant around his studio.

YOU WILL NEED five different types of brushes and each type is to be used for quite distinct and complementary ends.

The flat, square brush you will use exclusively in "under-painting" to cover, spread and build your foundations. With it you will proceed almost as a mason does with cement, and it is the only one which may be hard and need not be of sable hairs, for your paint must be as dry and compact as possible. It is also the only one of your brushes which may touch a small amount of rectified turpentine, and your movements will inevitably be slow, monotonous and parsimonious. After the under-painting, turpentine must never be added to your media except on extremely rare occasions.

The round, short brush you will use for your "over-painting" Here you will need a fine sable brush, for the matter in which you work, which must grow more fluid as it becomes richer, requires more suppleness of your brush. Thus the finer the transparencies you wish to produce, the more supple must be your brushes, and these can acquire suppleness only by becoming longer and more slender.

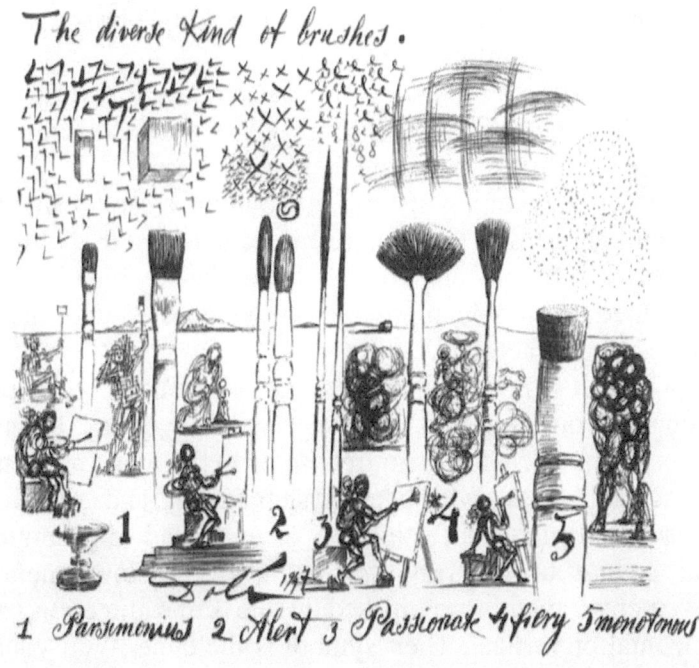

1 Parsimonious 2 Alert 3 Passionate 4 fiery 5 monotonous

You will have a third brush, which is the long, thin brush, the best of which are an inch and a half long, with which you will be able to use only mixtures of an extremely liquid consistency, and this in direct proportion to their richness. Remember this, for it is already almost a secret: it is only toward the end of the painting that such brushes are to be used, and they are the only ones that may be dipped in opulent media and that can be used to apply the ultimate shadings of those final touches, which must be made with "Venetian turpentine." The movement of this brush is rapid, rhythmical and, as I like to call it, "wing-like."

Now I have only to tell you of the fan-shaped badger brush and the stipple brush, which are not, properly speaking, intended to be used for painting, for their function is a complementary one. The former must be in the shape of an open fan, or of a half-open fan. The badger brush is very similar to the wing of a bird, and you should use it to blend, with a dreamlike lightness of touch, what you have tried to smooth out with your brush or what, more mechanically, your stipple brush has ground down and made uniform.

The stipple brush you should use only for surfaces which you wish to be pitilessly uniform—skies or architectures which are to be lengthily and repeatedly smoothed out.

For the painting of flesh, it would be a capital sin to utilize the stipple brush, for this texture can be obtained in the final overpainting only by the long thin brush and then by blending with the fan-shaped brush, which process can be repeated until the desired artistic effect is achieved.

Let us now summarize the movements that properly belong to your five brushes, and herewith you are learning my Secret Number 1—for in no treatise have the movements peculiar to each of these ever been systematized, and yet this is a fundamental matter affecting the good or bad of painting. With your square brush, very dry paint, even, slow, monotonous movements, always superposed in the same direction, whether horizontal or vertical. Their symbol is the cube. With your round brushes, using a somewhat more fluid paint, your rhythm becomes accelerated, subdivided and interlaced. Their symbol is the "X," and their use also corresponds exactly to the moment when, in the technical problem of your painting, you set down, without being conscious of it, the "X," the unknown, of your future solution.

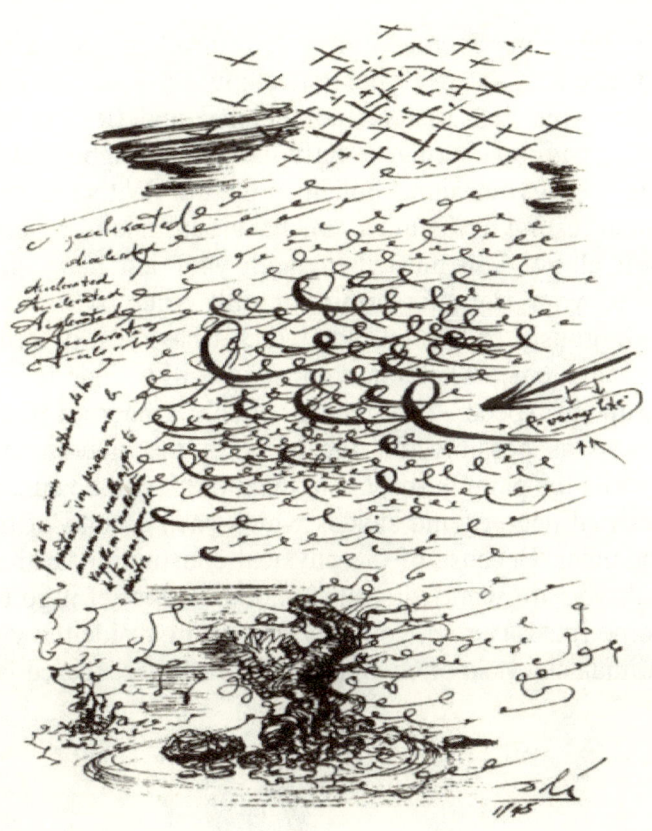

The rhythm of your "tapered" brush will be that which I call "wing-like," and its symbol will be the loop. The rhythm of this brush attains the lightness and the speed of flight, for its tapered point will barely touch the canvas and its movement must appear to you each time, accustomed though you are to it, a thing of wonder, a miracle.

The movement of your stipple brushes must be as mechanical and indifferent as your human organism will allow. And, finally, the movement of the fan-shaped badger brush is the most rapid of all—so rapid that it cannot even be seen, exactly like the wings of the hummingbird.

To execute this exceptionally rapid movement of wing-like blending with the badger brush you must proceed as follows, and here I give my Secret Number 2. You roll up your shirtsleeves to your elbows, you rest your left elbow on your left knee, and you place your left foot on an inclined and flexible tabouret, preferably having a spring, exactly like the springboards used for jumping in a gymnasium, but in miniature. With the weight of your torso resting in the most nonchalant attitude of relaxation on your left elbow, you must then, with your left hand, grasp the middle of your right forearm—for only your right wrist must move vigorously. In this attitude which I have just described, the rhythmic movements of your right wrist will be able to attain the maximum of speed. This speed should, theoretically, be as vertiginous as possible, for the more of the blending you can effect while the paint is still fresh, the more it will be enhanced by infinitesimal degrees and shades which each second of time lost will endanger. Because of the physical constitution of the matter in which you are working, you cannot afford to let it go to sleep, to become fixed. Herein, you may be certain, reside the virtues of the Dalinian skies, so often and so inexplicably rendered famous.

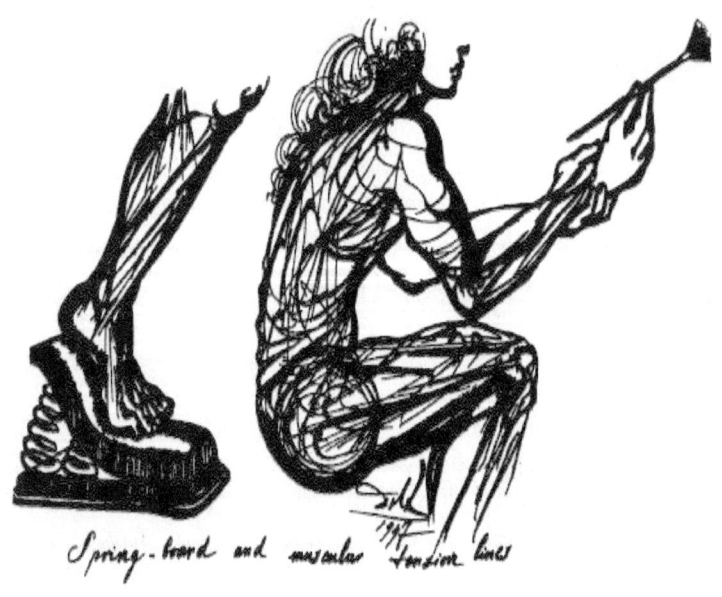

Spring-board and muscular tension lines

But for Heaven's sake, don't be so impatient! Leave your brushes reposing on the table! For before I will allow you to use them I must enlighten you on other astonishing matters.

Know, then, that Secret Number 3 is that in undertaking an important pictorial work which you are anxious to bring to a successful completion and on which your heart is particularly set, you must before anything else begin it by sleeping as deeply, as soundly as it is possible for you to do. This is absolutely necessary, for without this inaugural sleep you almost surely run the risk that your work will be undertaken prematurely, so that the impatience and the nervous strain involved in the project will make you, so to speak, start on the wrong foot—which is almost the worst thing that could happen to you at the outset. For a pictorial work badly begun, badly launched, even with the most meritorious efforts of which your will is capable, cannot be completed successfully and with honor. Therefore be assured that in this realm of brush strokes the first shall be last—that is to say, that on the timid beginning depend not only the final and categorical touches but, I make bold to say, even the very matter of the picture and the adequacy with which it is varnished.

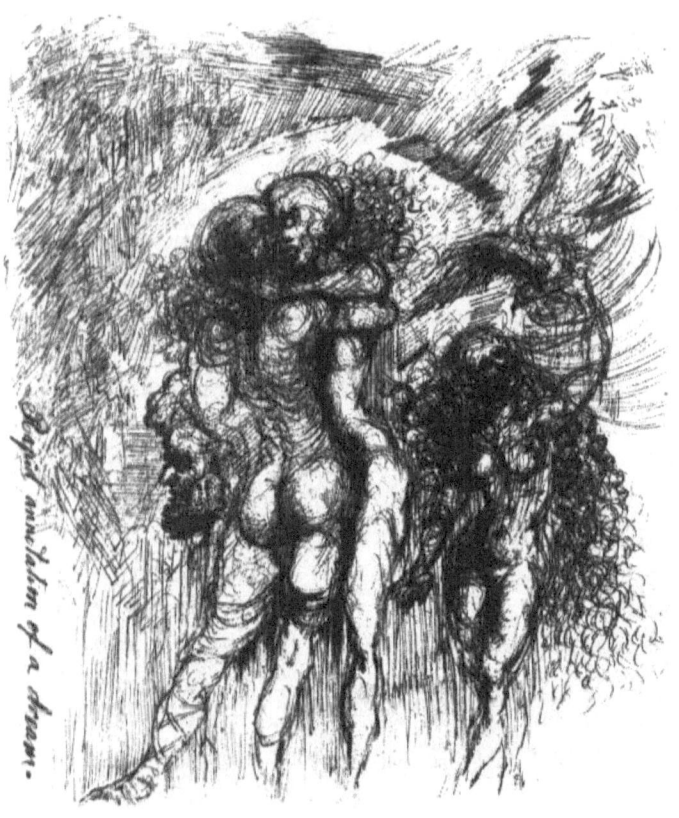

Rapid annihilation of a dream.

A heavy, long and peaceful sleep will therefore be most propitious, not only to create the physical and psychic calm to be desired in order to attain the coolness necessary to face the white and menacing bull of your virgin canvas which, at the end of your *faena,* is to fall immortalized by the death stroke of your last touch, but also and especially, you must know that it is precisely during this sleep, which you wrongly regard as reducing you to a state of paradoxical inactivity and indifference before the imminence of the work which you are preparing to execute, that you will secretly, in the very depths of your spirit, solve most of its subtle and complicated technical problems, which in your state of waking consciousness you would never be humanly capable of solving. So that, at the moment of awakening from this precious preliminary sleep, as you are stretching and yawning voluptuously before the Immaculate Conception of your virgin and intact painting, you will be able to say to yourself, without fear of falling into exaggeration, that the principal part—that is to say the sleep—of the work is already done.

It is Montaigne, here again, who enlightens us with a long list of anecdotes in which appear the names of the most illustrious emperors, philosophers and men of arms in history who had recourse to deep slumber before—and very often during—the most decisive moments of their lives. It would be possible and easy to add other illustrious names to this anthology of sleepers—Napoleon (a spectacular example); Joffre sleeping while the battle of the Marne was at its height; Hitler, habitually a prey to intractable insomnia, sleeping during crucial moments; Dali, ordinarily so active, shutting himself up, irresistibly seized by sleep amid the excitement on the eve of the opening of his ballets at the Metropolitan Opera, etc., etc. The sign *"Poet at Work"* which Saint Paul Roux used to put on the door of his room during his slumbers seems to me to express a much more tangible reality when applied to painters. For it is precisely in the case of the painter that before beginning his picture the stamping impatience of his conception seems materially to transform each of the bones of the phalanges of his hands into brush handles, and he seems to feel budding at their extremities the sable hairs which, as they grow, make the pink tips of his fingers prickle with anxiety, producing irresistible itches, in which it seems as if torrents of dormant deliria of exteriorization, confined since the beginnings of his atavisms, have suddenly awakened, and can no longer do otherwise than at last to break through this chrysalis-skin in order to people with their wings of color the inevitable picture, whose coming into being nothing now, whether good or evil, can hinder.

Wherefore, young painter, when you feel such itches at the tips of your tender and still inexperiencd fingers, I should like you to tell yourself, as I tell you, that itches of this kind are not likely to predispose you to that calm, deep sleep which I have just recommended to you. You must agree, then, that my advice to sleep well is not so easy to act upon, in the state of creative fever in which you find yourself, and that in consequence it will be wise to continue to instruct yourself by continuing to read this book, in order to learn in what manner it will be possible for you to restore to your spirit the beneficent sleep which is to permit you to begin your work "with the right foot."

Three rules for controlling your dreams

Only the last dream, the one closest to waking, can be influenced and directed. This is what you must do:
1. Choose carefully the fragrances and perfumes which evoke concrete periods of your adolescence. Have your valet pour one of these fragrances or perfumes on your pillow one hour before you awake, and the time, the situation or the persons associated with that fragrance will appear in your dream.
2. What I have said about perfumes also applies to music. A melody associated with a memory or a being will evoke that memory or being in your dream if the melody is played quietly while you sleep.
3. A very intense light on our pupils, or a gradual pressure upon them by an appropriate pneumatic apparatus, will make you dream in colors.
To achieve a painter's slumbers will, in fact, require a long period of training. And the most characteristic slumber, the one most appropriate to the exercise of the art of painting, among all the kinds of slumbers that exist and that have existed since antiquity is the slumber which I call "the slumber with a key,"—and this is Secret Number 3—which ought to be called the slumber with a brush, if one were to replace the key by a very heavy metallic brush. This one would do if one had a little more time to devote to the ceremonial of painting.

But in this world if one aspires to do something very well, or even merely well, the problem immediately becomes one not merely of sleeping but also and especially one of working very hard. You will therefore have to get up each morning very early in order to take advantage of the maximum of daylight, and for this reason you must at the outset plan the afternoon nap that will be indispensable to your efficient labors at the end of the day.

But this "siesta" (as we shall call it for the moment) will have to be of very short duration. So don't be astonished if I tell you now that a half hour's sleep would even be much too much and that ten minutes would still be a good deal, and this for the simple reason that one minute would also appear to me excessive. Know, therefore, that your afternoon sleep must last less than a minute, less than a quarter of a minute, since, as you will immediately realize, a mere second is infinitely too long.

This whole preamble is merely to prepare you to realize that your afternoon slumber must last less than a quarter of a second and that perhaps even this exceeds the limit, and that you must resolve the problem of "sleeping without sleeping," which is the essence of the dialectics of the dream, since it is a repose which walks in equilibrium on the taut and invisible wire which separates sleeping from waking. And this kind of slumber, which is conscious of the fact that it does not even achieve the state of slumber, is called the "slumber with a key." And I shall give you now one of the most naive and simple ways of practicing it.

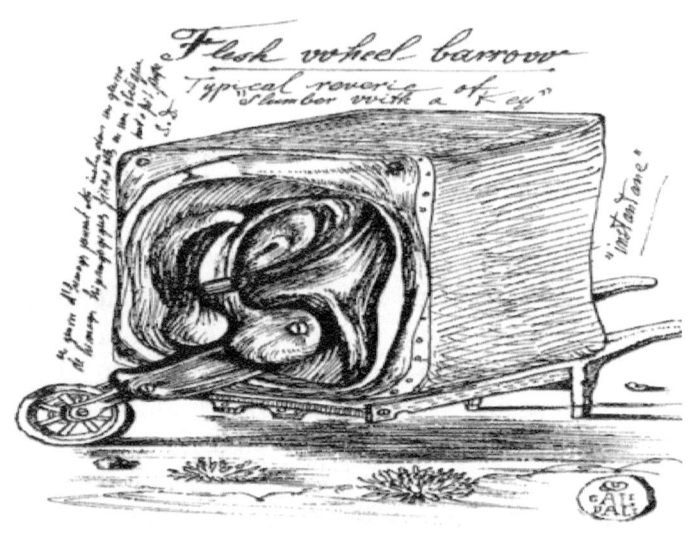

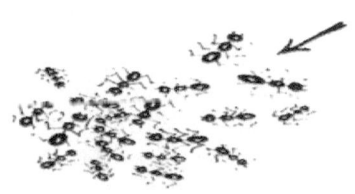

In order to make use of the slumber with a key* you must seat yourself in a bony armchair, preferably of Spanish style, with your head tilted back and resting on the stretched leather back. Your two hands must hang beyond the arms of the chair, to which your own must be soldered in a supineness of complete relaxation. Your wrists must be held out in space and must have been previously lubricated with oil of aspic. This is intended to facilitate the benumbing of your hands at the moment when slumber approaches, inducing the tingling that is produced when one of your members goes to sleep—a tingling which is in reality a counterpitch, the physical ants, antidotes of the psychic ones of your redoubtable impatience to paint.

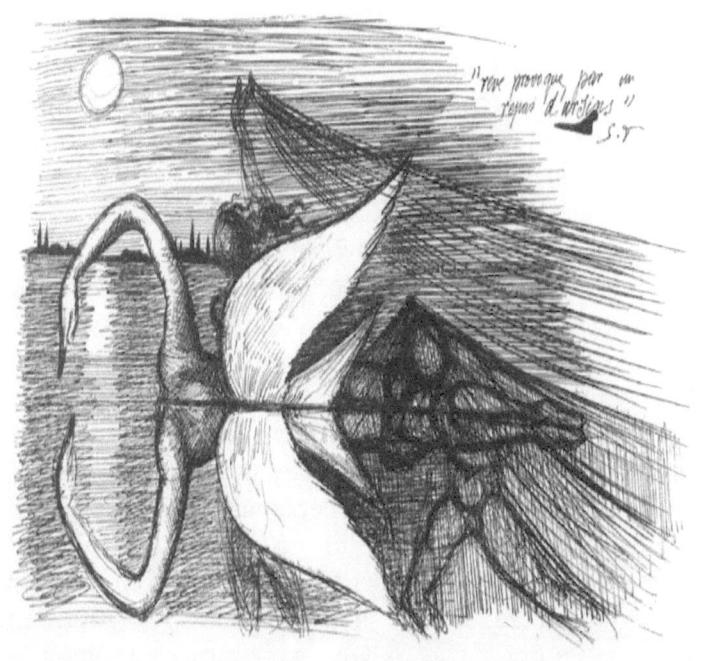

In this posture, you must hold a heavy key which you will keep suspended, delicately pressed between the extremities of the thumb and forefinger of your left hand. Under the key you will previously have placed a plate upside down on the floor. Having made these preparations, you will have merely to let yourself be progressively invaded by a serene afternoon sleep, like the spiritual drop of anisette of your soul rising in the cube of sugar of your body. The moment the key drops from your fingers, you may be sure that the noise of its fall on the upside down plate will awaken you, and you may be equally sure that this fugitive moment when you had barely lost consciousness and during which you cannot be assured of having really slept is totally sufficient, inasmuch as not a second more is needed for your whole physical and psychic being to be revivified by just the necessary amount of repose. For it is exactly, and neither more nor less, what you needed before undertaking your virtuous afternoon labors.* If, on the contrary, paying a deaf ear to the call of your key, you should persist a quarter of an hour more, or even just a few minutes, this would be harmful to your work, for these few minutes of laziness would have sufficed, by themselves alone, to "enslave" you by their heaviness for the whole rest of the afternoon. For it is well known that in order to shake off the sleep of a siesta, no matter how short it may be, it is necessary to have recourse to violent physical exertions. Thus it is that only those who do heavy labor can indulge in long siestas. Those whose work is of the mind, on the other hand must only practice the slumber with a key, especially painters, extremely delicate workers, who must take care of their hands as though they were creatures apart, seeing to it that they too get their required sleep. This is so true that I have personally carried the matter to extremes, as when 1 used to go for walks over the paths surrounding my house at Port Lligat, wearing my arm in a sling as though it were broken in order to rest it. And sometimes, meeting some noisy friends who were curious to know what had happened to my hand, I would whisper to them, with my forefinger to my lips, "Shh! It's asleep!"

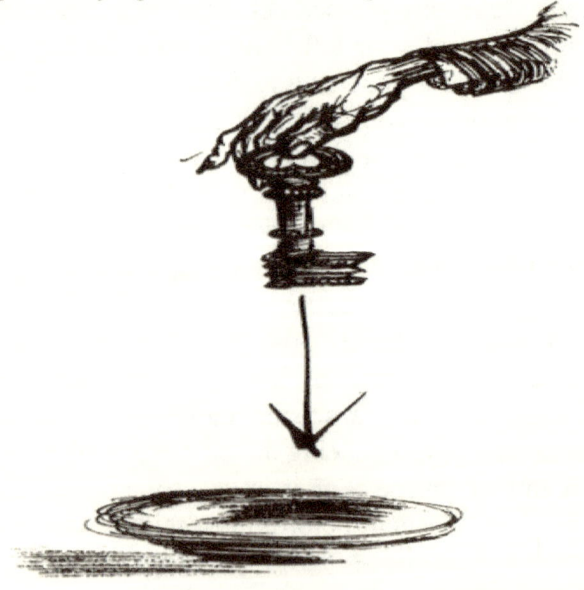

If, then, you have for a long time had the habit of the slumber with a key, it will be extremely easy for you to decide to undertake the very important work, which you tell me you are particularly anxious to have turn out successfully, on your customary weekly day of rest. On this afternoon you will choose a softer armchair than usual without, however, too greatly relaxing your accustomed posture, for a too radical change from your routine might jeopardize your sleep. And on this afternoon you will eliminate both key and dish, for you are now about to learn my Secret Number 4. But beforehand it is very desirable that you should have eaten a meal composed as follows:

To begin with, you will eat three dozen sea urchins, gathered on one of the last two days that precede the full moon, choosing only those whose star is coral red and discarding the yellow ones. The collaboration of the moon in such cases is necessary, for otherwise not only do you risk that the sea urchins will be more empty but above all that they do not possess to the same degree the sedative and narcotic virtues so special and so propitious to your approaching slumber.[*] For the same reason these sea urchins should be eaten preferably in the spring—May is a good month. But in choosing the time you must make the gathering of the sea urchins coincide with the precise moment when the first tender new beans are picked, and this varies according to the years.[1] These tender beans, prepared in the manner called *àla Catalane,* are to be the second course of your meal, and I guarantee you that this is a dish worthy of the ancient gods and quite Homeric, for I am convinced that the Greeks of antiquity were acquainted with it and therefore that they were also familiar with chocolate—for, strange as this may seem, the tender beans *à la Catalane* are in fact prepared with chocolate as a base.

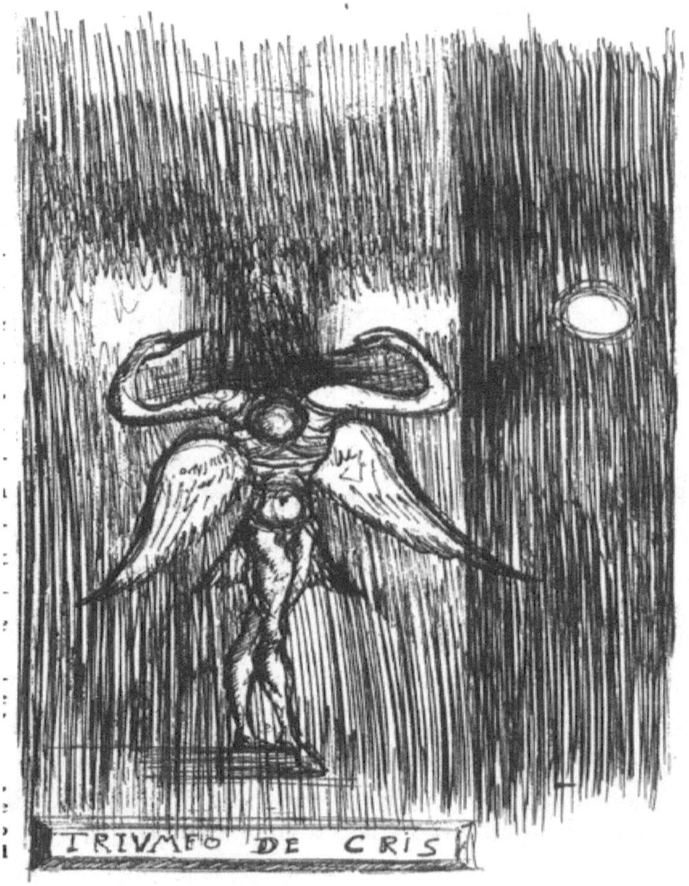

TRIVMFO DE CRIS

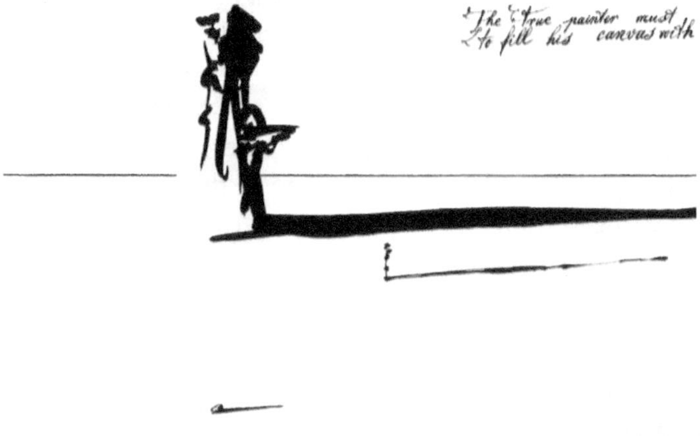

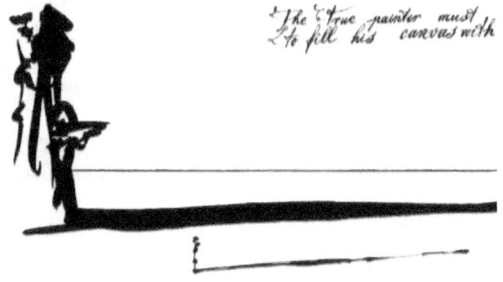

The true painter must
to fill his canvas with

42

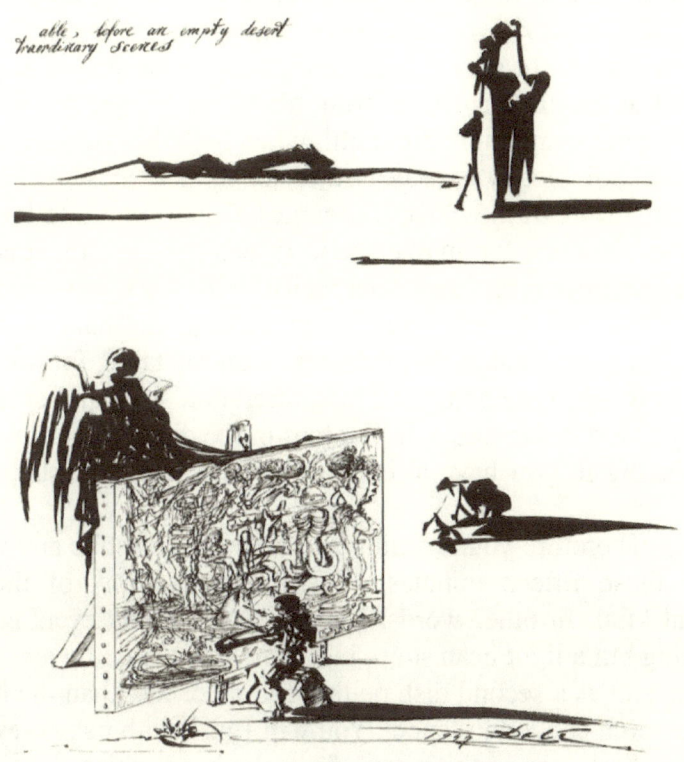

Once you have finished your repast, which you will wash down with a light, very young wine—the kind that will prick your palate ever so gently—you may calculate that if you begin your "slumber without a key" and without a dish on that day at about half past one, when the sun is still beating down hard, you will not awaken before six o'clock, when the sun is already setting and you no longer have enough light to work, and so much the better. For this is exactly what you need—that is to say, that you should find yourself at the crucial moment, at the most propitious moment for beginning your painting in all security, but that you still should not touch it.

For you will execute no other act than that of going and seating yourself before it and considering at length the whiteness of its intact and ultra-white surface, so that it will be as though you were looking into the very whites of its eyes. You will contemplate it for a long, long time, without turning on any light, so that at length you will in truth almost no longer see it. It will become more and more dim until, when night has submerged you, you will completely have ceased to see it, or at most will only be vaguely aware of the space it occupies. Continue still to look at it, without remorse, for another good fifteen minutes, for it is under these circumstances that your spirit will work best and most decisively, and do not worry about making the maid wait when she calls you and says that the soup is on the table, for after what you have eaten at noon, your long afternoon sleep and everything that you are in the midst of painting in the dark, without yet even suspecting it, you have already in a sense had your supper, and more.

Therefore your evening meal may be, must be and will be, after these fifteen minutes of delightful waiting, of the most frugal kind. In other words, I advise you on this evening to eat nothing but a light bean soup, into which you may dip a couple of crabs, and as a second dish neither more nor less than the head of a sea perch cooked in fennel. You will finish with its two eyes and you will take, in addition, one from the head which your wife is eating, and which she will relinquish with a loving and understanding smile.

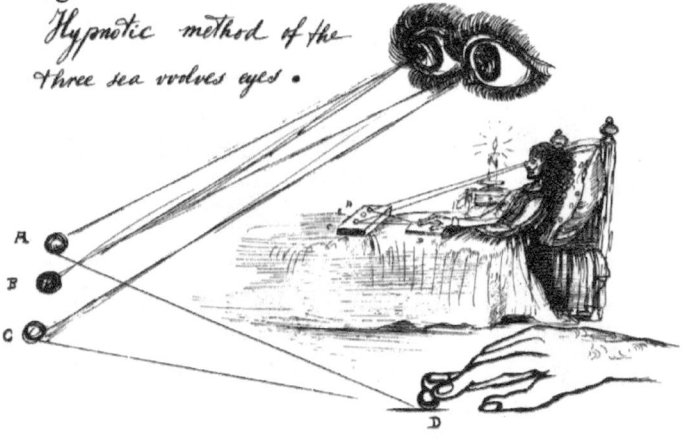

Once you have regaled yourself by sucking the superfine gelatines of these three eyes you will keep their three ultra-hard kernels in your mouth. Listen carefully, now, for I am about to initiate you to Secret Number 5. As soon as you are lying peacefully in your bed you will take these eyes out again. Keep one in your hand, and put the other two on a small book or on a black box which you will rest on your knees, placing them at a certain distance from each other in such a way that, when you hold your forefinger in front of the two super-white balls and focus on your forefinger, the eyes of the sea perch will join, thanks to the precious distance between your own eyes, the grace and the mystery of your binocular vision, and the two eyes of the sea perch will become one single ball. This ball will seem to exert a hypnotic effect on you, and it is very desirable that on that night you should go to sleep while looking at it.

But at the same time that you are staring at these two balls which have become one, it is furthermore necessary that, holding the third sea perch eye—the one which your wife has smilingly yielded to you—between the crossed forefinger and middle-finger of your right hand, you should gently caress it. You will then have the striking and unbelievable sensation of having contact with two sea perch eyes, and not merely with the one which is really between your fingers. Let me repeat, then, so that you do not fall into error: before you the two sea perch eyes placed on the black box have become visually joined into a single one, while simultaneously you are touching with your crossed fingers a single ball which seems to you, by your sense of touch, to have doubled and to be quite distinctly two, so that you see exactly the contrary of what you touch and touch exactly the contrary of what you see, and are sure that the two sensations are both completely false and in no way correspond to reality. Nothing, I assure you, could be better calculated to make your night's sleep start off on the right, good and wise path!

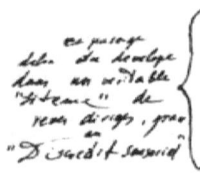

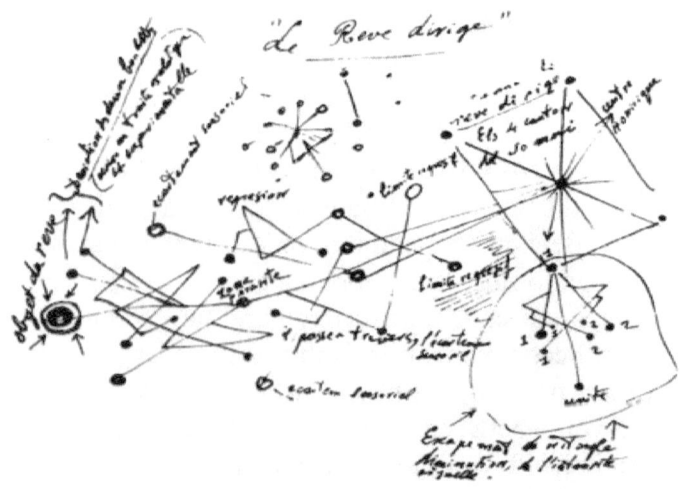

Sleep peacefully, then! For your day has been well filled. And while you were grating chocolate to flavor your beans, or cutting open your sea urchins, while you were doing things which seemed to bear no relation to the picture which is so dear to your heart, in reality of truth, secretly, silently, without anyone in the world being able to suspect it and without suspecting it yourself, in the course of this day and this night which is to follow, during which time you have not even grazed with your fingertips the intact canvas—which is often, indeed always, too quickly and irreparably soiled—the labor of your love which for nine months you have borne in the belly of your brain and without yet having experienced the slightest pain will already have been conceived!

But, apprentice painter, who have just awakened from that last sleep of dawn which Plato lohg ago called the "sleep of truth," and, guided and led by the three sea-perch eyes, you would be wrong in assuming that at this matutinal hour when you are materially to begin your work your attitude, which until now has been evasive, dilatory and slumberful, must suddenly change altogether. Quite the contrary. And in spite of the fact that as a result of all the rest and sleep of the day before you will feel exceptionally wide-awake it will be absolutely necessary for you to go on sleeping some more, but this time in a more difficult manner, since you will have to sleep while waking, while being as wide-awake as possible. And this is Secret Number 6. For the moment to paint has at last sounded!

It was in order to put painters to sleep while keeping them awake that at the height of the Renaissance it was usual to surround them with diversions and to play Aeolian music, so that during their long and patient hours of manual labor they might keep their minds elsewhere as much as possible. For it is well known and recognized that the painter who reflects is always a bad painter, and I dare say also that the same is true for the philosopher who reflects too much—of whom the prototype is that lamentable "Thinker" by Rodin. For inside the head of such beings one may be almost certain beforehand that absolutely nothing happens. "When you paint, always be thinking of something else," said Raphael. This truth is like a temple.

I am told that Manuel de Falla, shortly before his death, made an astonishing political declaration, one of the few to cross his lips: "I come back to the conviction that the best regime for the people is a monarchy." Taken aback, the Republican refugees who were listening to him asked, "But why do you think this, Don Manuel?" "Because Saint Jerome said so," Don Manuel de Falla answered laconically.

And to me it appears quite sufficient to answer, "Because Raphael said so!" But not only did he say this, he also practiced it—he practiced "thinking of something else." If to this we add that other Raphaelesque principle, "I paint according to a certain idea," we see that they form a kind of monarchy which governs the progress of each of his paintings from the height of the cupola of his angelic spirit. These two precepts of Raphael—to paint while thinking of something else and at the same time to paint according to a certain idea—precepts which give the impression of having been uttered casually, on the contrary establish the exact dosage of distraction and of automatism which must go into the execution of a successful pictorial work. Two precepts, divergent because they radiate imperialism, but which follow a single path, ample and royal, on the firm ground of which all the pictorial cavalcades of the future can sweep without constraint in the august space of triumphs.

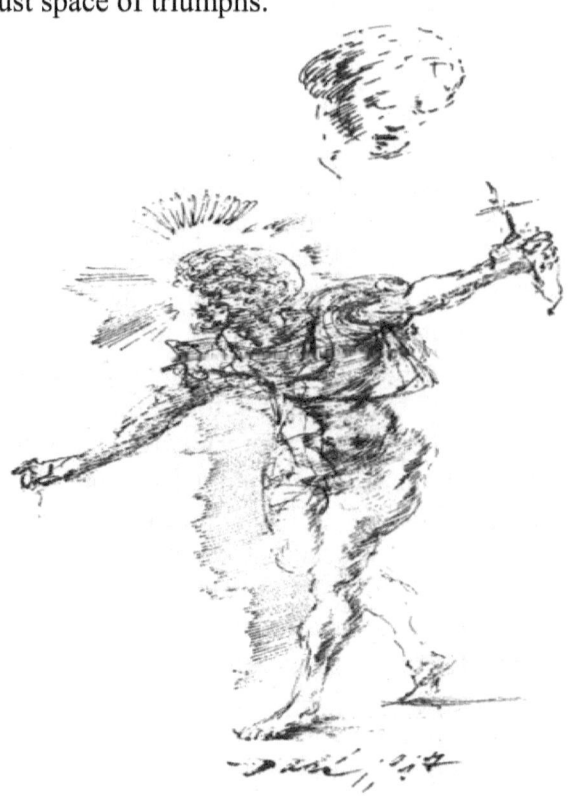

For months the painting, integrated subconsciously into the daily life of the painter, takes shape in his spirit. The day arrives when he feels an itching to begin his work, when it is already stirring within him. This is the propitious moment for the intervention of Dalinian magic. Every enforced inactivity, before the impatience to act, becomes accumulated into creative force which, so to speak, is purified, directed. The essences separate into their hierarchies, and sleep, oriented in the direction of the realization of desire, ferments, sparkles, miraculously resolves itself and selects. What you prevent yourself from doing and force yourself not to do, the dream will do with all the lucidity of desire and without any of the blindnesses consubstantial with your champing gluttony and the grating hyperchloridities of your still-green fruit. But in order to enable your dream to work in peace you must cretinize yourself by the "hypnotic doubt" of your sensations, and the infantile game of discrediting the evidence of your senses by means of the three sea-perch eyes suffices, even for the most adult spirits, to encourage it to seek the most natural paths to an effective oniric solution. This choice of the sea-perch eyes is all the more happy as their superlatively white surface is the most sensorially evocative of that of your own canvas, having moreover the virtue of roundness which, symbolically means unequivocally the perfection of your future painting which you must, given its real plurality, make one and indivisible. That is to say, you guide yourself hypnotically toward the concentrated objective of synthesis by which no dream, however awkward and sluggish it may be, given the creative state in which you find yourself, can fail to profit.

But you still have in your right hand the contrary of that very painting which you saw as one, but which you feel as two, being one. This symbolizes in your spirit the constant plurality of your technical and manual problems, but you will not be disturbed because you will at all times be conscious of the fact that this is illusory and that your canvas is one and indivisible and round, hence complete, enclosed within itself and perfect as a circle. I know that this is the first time in the history of humanity that artistic creation has been dealt with in this fashion, but this is not a reason that can prevent me from writing this treatise which, no matter what I do, is condemned beforehand to be the most original in the twentieth century.

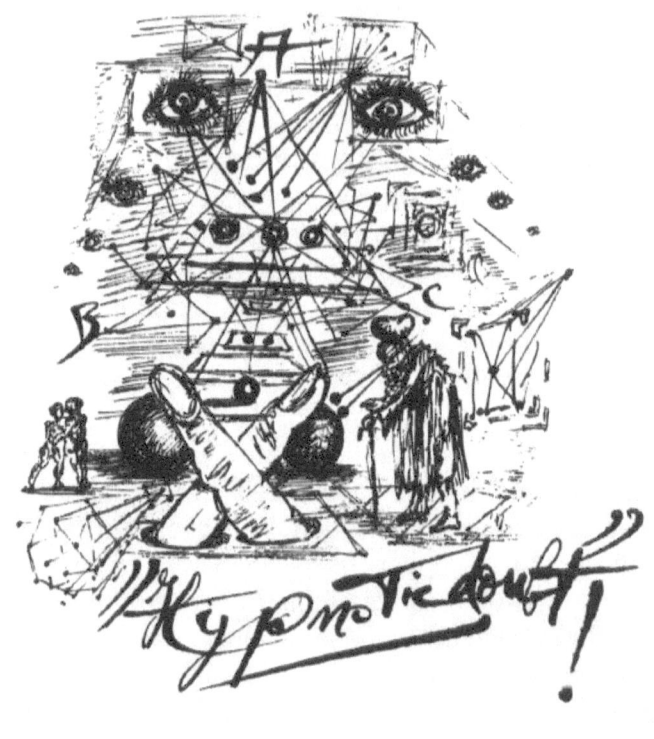

Nevertheless, in former times magic has often dealt with concrete recipes. But mine is incomparably superior, thanks to Sigmund Freud and to the advances that have been made in the young morphological sciences, and especially thanks to Dali who, besides being unique, knows things which no one knows today, which were not known in the Middle Ages either, though that was an age when men felt their way in the dark amid dazzling treasures of intuition and superstition.

Men have attempted to interpret dreams, and even to guide them, but never yet have men attempted to use sleep to guide and to control artistic creation which is to be executed in a waking state. Rather than discuss my recipes, which are not to be found written in any book in the world, it would be wiser to test them, and this is what I do. For these recipes are not the product of surrealist fantasies. They are very elementary and simple recipes at the disposal of any apprentice painter. It is easy also to smile at the apparent childishness of my "finds." But consider Newton's apple or Columbus's egg. As for me, let me tell you that I sleep very soundly on the fact that posterity will some day accord much more importance to my three white, round sea perch eyes than to the egg of Columbus himself. And not only because each one of the former is worth three of the latter. Just consider this: Columbus's egg is a myth, whereas my three little balls are a discovery. He who laughs last laughs best!

The painter is above all one who likes this and who does not like that. His eye lives only by sympathies and antipathies, by continual affinities, relations and choices. This is known as "having taste." The painter is one who, among all the "paint-able" things which exist in the world, chooses as a subject a piece of bread on the corner of a table, a woman pouring milk into a crock, a certain man holding a red carnation between his fingers, or the betrothal of the virgin. The painter is one who, among the limitlessness of colorations, limits himself to only a few of them with fanatical constancy.

Painter, you will therefore surely be obliged at the very beginning of your work to decide: for on your white canvas it will not be given to you to paint the entire universe. You must choose a small part of it and nevertheless, in this small part, you will have to make felt all the antipathies of the entire universe.

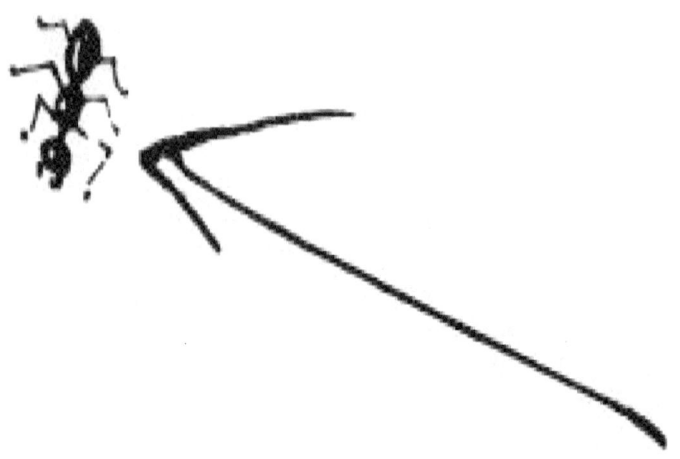

    Begin, then, by knowing that according to the Dalinian aesthetic, the tulip is a horrid thing next to celluloid, that sardines, if they go beyond a certain size, become a banality, that the crayfish is the most admirable architecture that exists, and that the form which best goes with it is that of the onion, and that if this form is done in silver and placed next to the crayfish the effect will be excellent, for nothing is more sympathetic than silver and crayfish. Know also that the orange combined with lettuce is a moral monstrosity and that this monstrosity becomes even greater at the approach of a storm. I tell you all this in order to help you to discover for yourself and in order that you may begin to find your own way and to choose amid the cosmic complexity of the world which surrounds you.

    But in this connection listen for a moment to J.-B. de Porta, who had great knowledge of these matters:

    "Thus there are in animals, in plants and generally in all species having occult properties a same passion which the Greeks call sympathy and antipathy and which we more commonly call attraction and aversion. For certain ones of these join and embrace one another sympathetically, while others on the contrary have an aversion and an antipathy to one another without our being able to assign the true reason for this sympathy or this antipathy.

"And yet this reason exists, for nature has formed no thing without giving it its creator, and there is nothing in the hidden things of nature which does not have a secret and special property. Empedocles, struck by the marvels which he saw before his eyes, affirms that all things were brought into being through struggle and concord, and were dissipated in the same manner. He adds that these two contraries were the seed or the source of all things, that they were to be found in the elements by means of discordant and concordant qualities, as we have expounded above. He continues by saying that the same is true of the bodies of the heavens, alleging as an example that Jupiter and Venus have an attraction to all the other planets, except Mars and Saturn …

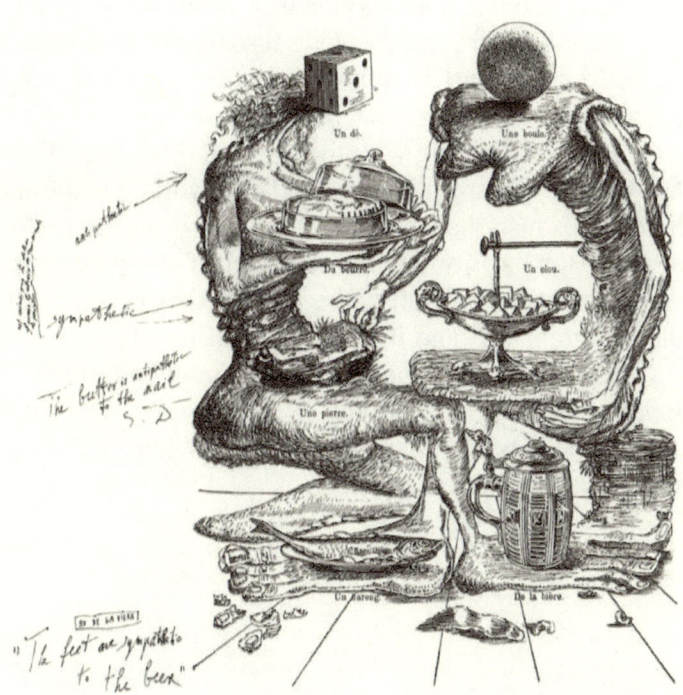

"These things may be seen still more clearly in the books of the astrologers, but they appear even yet more indisputably in the animal kingdom. For example, I will mention man and the serpent, who hate each other with an irreconcilable hatred: so that man, having seen the serpent, suddenly takes fright, and this pernicious creature, presenting himself before a pregnant woman, induces in her a miscarriage and causes her to lose the fruit of her womb. The saliva of a young man likewise has great power, for it will kill scorpions. The crocodile of the Nile and the panther are most cruel animals and most dangerous to man, for the former, attracting him by feigned tears, devours him on the spot, and the other causes him a mortal fright. The Indian rat is pernicious to the crocodile, for nature has given it to the latter as its enemy, so that when this violent animal relaxes in the sun it creates a trap for itself by which it dies. For, perceiving that the crocodile sleeps with its mouth open, thus exposing a monstrous chasm, the rat enters it and slips through the wide throat into the beast's belly. It gnaws its entrails and finally emerges through the belly of the dead creature. However, this animal has no fondness for the spider, and often fighting with the aspic, it dies. The glance of the wolf is also very harmful to man. If the wolf sees the man first, the latter loses his voice, so that even if he wishes to cry out he no longer can, for he is suddenly deprived of the power of speech. But if the wolf feels itself to be observed it becomes silent, its cruelty is diminished and it loses much of its strength. If the wolf bites a horse it is a fact that it will become wonderfully light and fit for running. But if by its fall it comes up against the trace of the wolf it will be all terrorstruck and its legs will become all numb, so Pamphilius assures us.

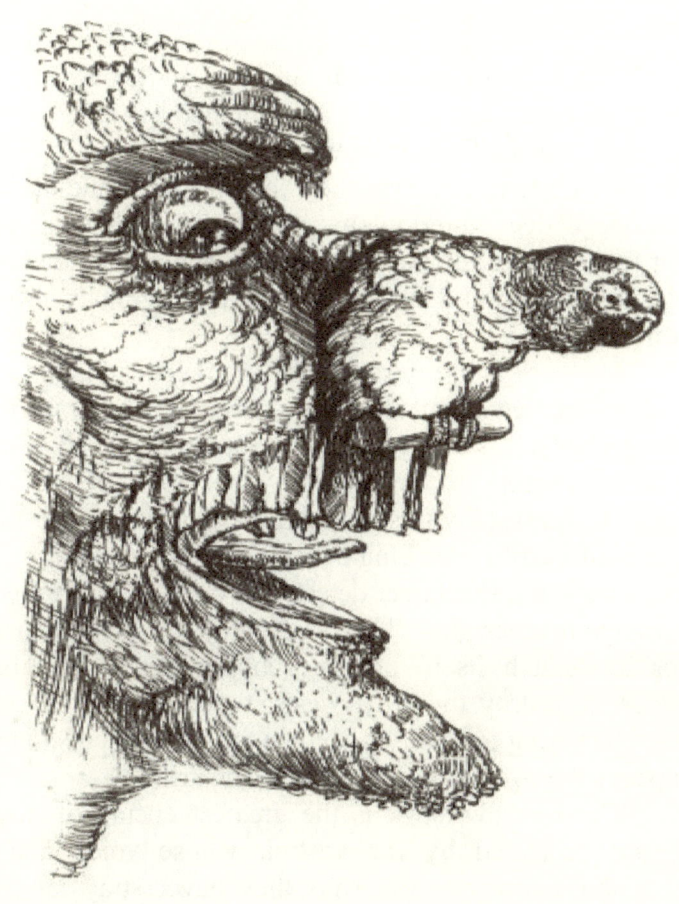

"The wolf has a mortal hatred of the lamb, in which it inspires such fear and terror that if garments are made of the skin or of the spun fleece of a sheep killed by a wolf, they will engender more lice than those of another. But also the flesh of sheep that have felt the teeth of a wolf becomes more tender and tasty. The tail and the head of a wolf hung in a sheepfold will cause the creatures to be consumed with regret and melancholy, so that they will leave off grazing in their pasture and implore aid and succor by their pitiful bleating. The dog is the enemy of the wolf and the friend of man. And the latter is also held in affection by the horse. But the horse has as enemies the griffon and the bear.

"The lion surpasses all animals in generosity, and it frightens all other beasts. But it is frightened by the mere crowing of the cock, especially if it be white, and the rooster's comb also inspires it with terror. The monkey has a horror of the turtle; when it sees one it flees, uttering savage cries. The elephant which is the largest of land animals experiences acute fear upon hearing the grunts of a sow. It is also in continual struggle against the dragon.

"The cock is indifferent to the elephant and is not afraid of it. It despises that great and heavy mass, but it fears the kite. When an elephant is carried away by fury and cruelty, if it should perceive a sheep it immediately becomes gentle and its impetuosity ceases. By this ruse did the Romans put to flight the elephants of Pyrrhus, the king of the Epirotes, and won a dazzling victory over him. The linnet detests the donkey and fights with it in a strange manner. For when the donkey draws near bushes and shrubs to scratch itself, and in rubbing against the branches threatens to destroy the birds' nests, the linnet, lest it cause the eggs or the young ones to drop, comes to their rescue and with its beak pecks the soft part of the animal's nostrils.

"The sparrow-hawk is the greatest enemy of doves, but these are protected by the kestrel, whose voice and glance frighten the sparrow-hawk. Thus they never stray far from the kestrel, in whom they have full confidence. The rook and the owl are perpetually at war; they spy on each other's nests and eat the little ones which they find in them. The owl operates at night, but the rook works by day and has more strength than its enemy. The weasel is the enemy of the crow, and the kite cannot endure the presence of the crow. The strength of the kite resides above all in its claws, which are very hard.

"The red woodpecker likes neither the heron nor the yellow hammer, the crow hates the buzzard, the wasp is the relentless enemy of the horse and of the donkey. When the donkey sleeps in its stable the wasp enters its nostrils and, when it awakens, prevents it from eating. The heron makes war on the eagle, the lark on the fox. Against the eagle a night-flying hawk named *cibidus* wages furious warfare; bent upon extermination, they kill one another.

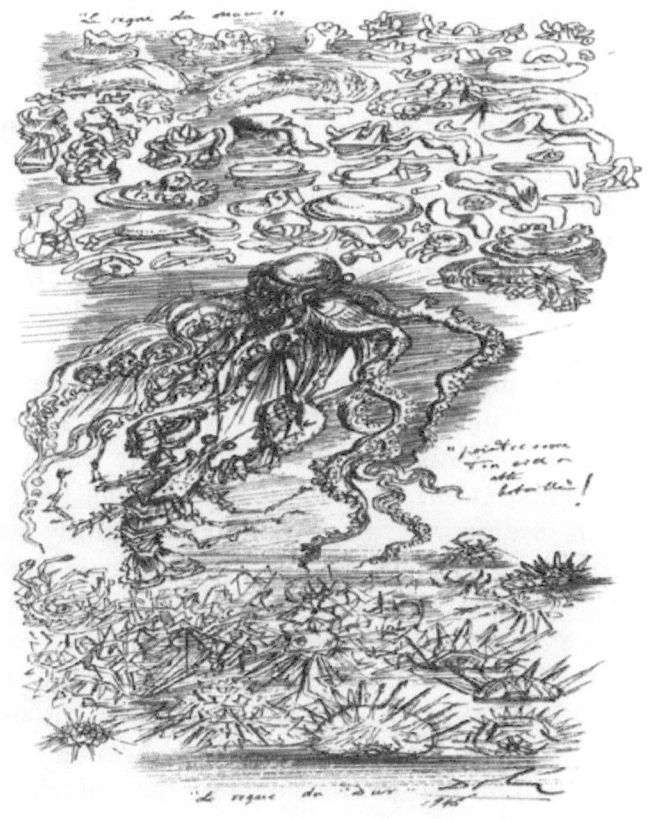

"The aquatic animals also war on one another continually The conger and the lamprey, for example, eat each other's tails Spiny lobsters have a horror of octopi, which envelop them with their powerful tentacles and choke them. There is also in the ocean a small worm, similar to the scorpion, large as a spider, which with its stinger penetrates under the fins of a fish named *thinnis* and presses them in such a fashion that, overcome with pain and rage, it jumps on board the ships which sail in its vicinity.

"The cabbage and the vine are pernicious to each other, for although the vine, by its curling tendrils, will usually wind itself around all objects, nevertheless it eschews the cabbage and the repugnance which it feels for this vegetable is such that, sensing the cabbage near it, it turns in the other direction, as though someone had warned it that its enemy is in its neighborhood. And this is also worthy of note: while cabbage is cooking, if you put a little wine in the vessel in which it is cooking, the cabbage will not cook properly and will not keep its color. Nor can the vine endure the laurel, because by its order it affects its quality adversely. The hellebore and the hemlock are, as is known, dangerous to man. Yet it is to be noted that quail eat the one and starlings the other.

"**The ferula is a most agreeable fodder for the donkey, but it is a cruel poison for other beasts, which it promptly kills. Which is why this animal is dedicated to Bacchus, even as is the ferula. If the scorpion crawls at the base of the aconite it is overcome with terror and promptly becomes numb. There is an herb named** *cerastis*, **the virtue of which is such that if you rub its grain between your hands the scorpion will do you no harm, but you may on the contrary crush it at your leisure. Cats will not touch birds which have grains of wild rue under their wings. The weasel which wishes to do battle with a serpent also fortifies itself by arming itself with this plant. The lion if it brushes against the branches or the leaves of the holly oak at once becomes very fearful. If the wolf touches an onion it loses its strength, which is the reason why foxes habitually cover and line their holes with them. The leaves of the plane tree repel bats, hence storks fill their nests with them, in order to preserve themselves from their attacks.**

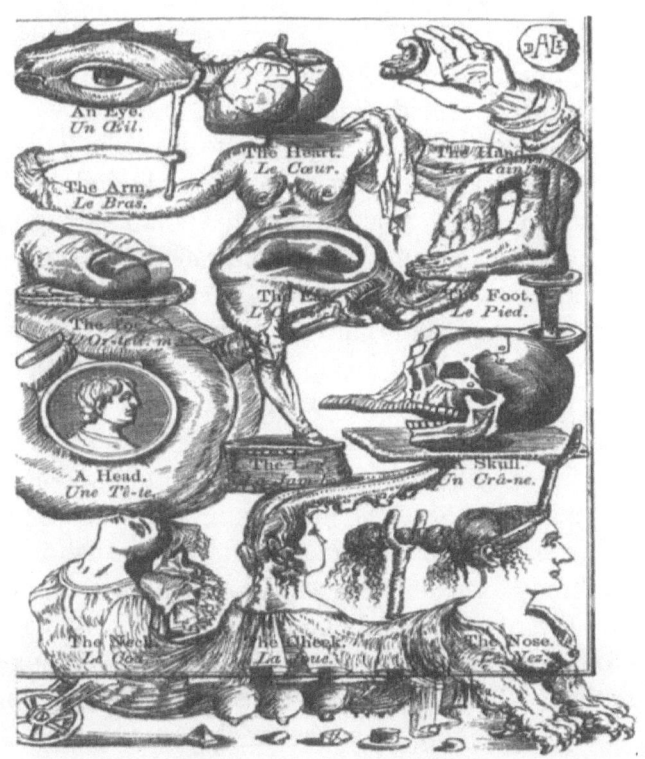

"The birds which are called *harpae* seek out ivy, rooks verbena, the thrush myrtle, the partridge reed, the heron carline, the lark dog's teeth, which has given rise to these verses:

In the gracious lustre of the dog's teeth herb
The lark builds its home and its repose assures.

"**Swans wishing their young to come forth bring vitex, or** *agnus castus,* into their nests.

"But if we have told of things contrary or harmful, how much more marvelous shall we find those which are agreeable and beneficent! If I have said that the serpent is the enemy of man, I shall note on the contrary that the lizard loves and cherishes him and that it rejoices in his sight. And indeed what animal is more friendly to man than the dog, who caresses him even to licking his saliva? And among aquatic animals, what is more friendly than the dolphin: so much so that it has appropriately been named *philanthropos,* and it is well known, according to Appion, that it is subject to love. As Theophrastus relates, dolphins have been known to fall madly in love, so much so that on seeing pretty little children navigating along the shore in boats they have suddenly become entranced by them. The fox lives on good terms with the serpent. Peacocks are fond of doves. Blackbirds, thrushes and parrots quickly fall enamoured of turtledoves. Ovid speaks of this in the following verses:

And the green bird sighs with love
For the night-black turtledove.

"Rooks are fond of herons and come to one another's aid against the insolence of foxes, their common enemy. There is the same familiarity and the same mutual aid among fish who live in schools. There is for example a real friendship between the whale and a small fish of the size of a gudgeon, which it freely allows to swim before it to serve as its guide, and this little creature it will follow as the one to which it owes the safety of its life. And when the one rests, the other rests, and when the one resumes its course the other does likewise and is entirely subservient to it.

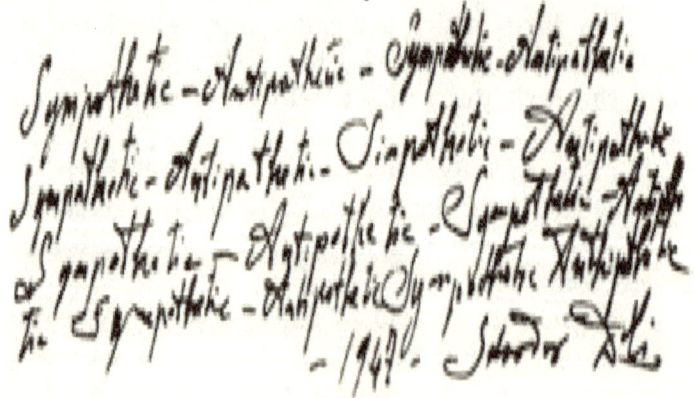

"Thus also, in the vegetable kingdom, vines are fond of elms and poplars, so much so that they grow magnificently in their proximity. For, married in wedlock, as it were, the vines send out their tendrils, climb daintily and embrace the branches of these trees, to the point where they can no longer detach themselves, which is not the case for other trees. Palm trees cherish one another with a vehement love. They languish for one another and are so titillated by amorous desire that they bow their tufted heads toward one another and interlace their fronds in a sweet and loving attachment. And if, being planted next to one another, they are joined by a cord, they will embrace with mutual caresses and revel in the sweet gifts of Venus, and joyously will lift the foliage of their graceful crowns. The planters have a remedy for this amorous madness, which we shall relate further on, a remedy by the aid of which this extravagant love is extinguished, and the tree henceforth is rendered fruitful. Leontius also speaks of the ardent desire which these trees exhibit and bases himself on what the ancients had said on the subject. Carnal desire, he says, is so great and so lively in the palm tree that the female will relinquish her amorous desire only when the beloved male has consoled her. If her love-yearning is not assuaged, she dies—a fact well known to the agricultural expert. Accordingly, having provided himself with the remedy which is required in order that he may know and recognize the one to which she desires to be joined in marriage, he goes and seeks out all the male palms which surround the languishing female palm, and having touched one, he puts his hand to the passionate loving palm, and so he does with one after another. And when he feels that his hands are grazed as by a kiss, he thereby recognizes that the palm announces that her desire is assuaged, and she waves her sweet and gracious crown. Then the prudent husbandman goes and plucks flowers from the trunk of the male and therewith crowns the head of the lady-love who, thus laden with her lover's gift, bears fruit and, rejoicing in this pledge of love, becomes fecund. The fruit will not ripen on the female palm if the husband's pollen is not sprinkled on her.

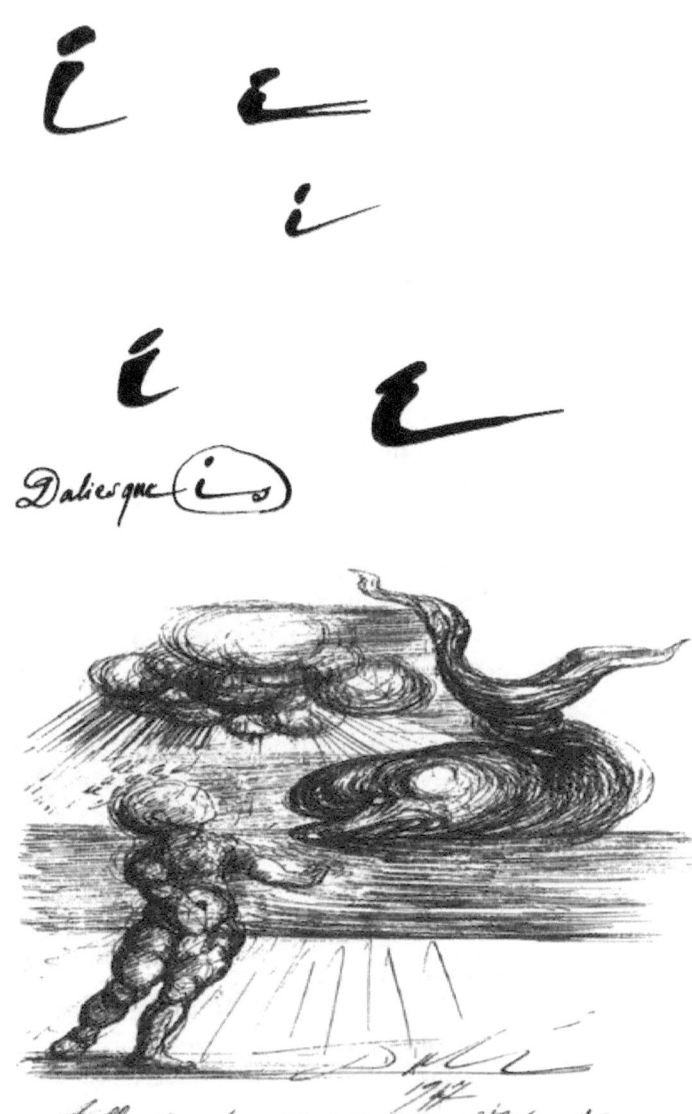

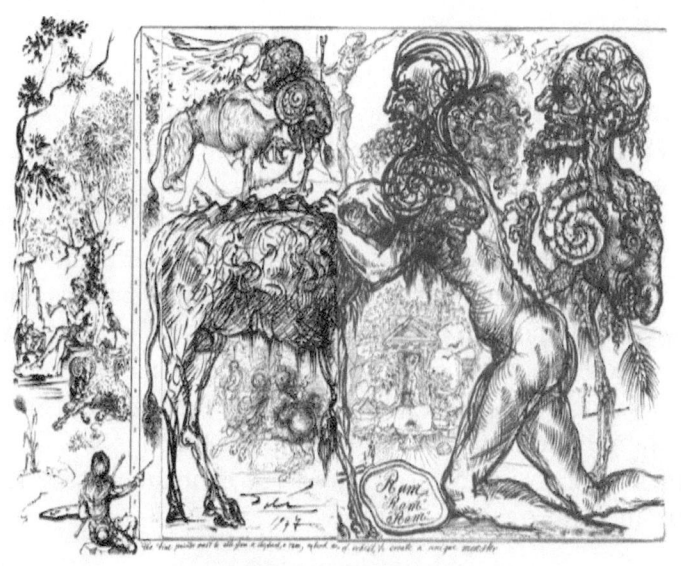

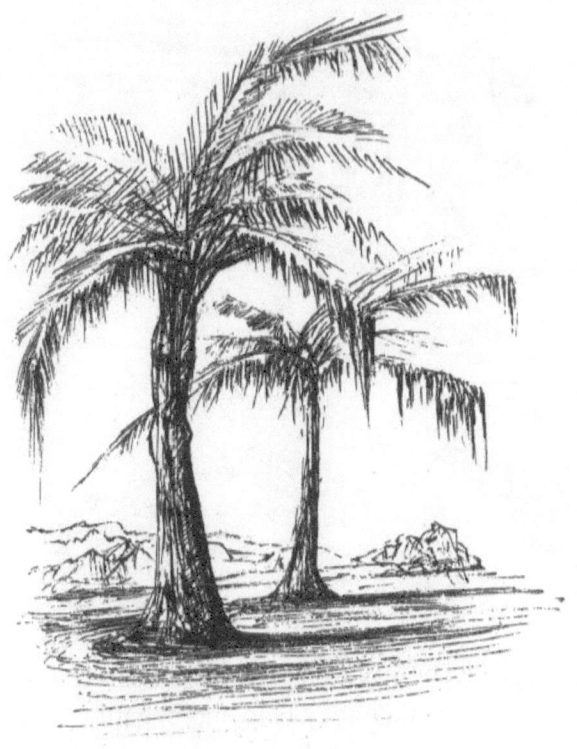

"The olive tree and the myrtle also have a great affection for each other, as Androcius relates, the branches of the latter interlacing with the olive tree's, and their roots wrapping around one another. Hence no other tree is planted near the olive tree, except the myrtle. It is, in fact, the enemy of the fig tree and even of all other trees. The myrtle also likes to be near the pomegranate tree, for if they are planted next to each other they become more fertile and abundant. If the pomegranate is grafted on the myrtle it bears more heavily. So Didymus assures us. There are also several other trees which become sterile if a post is not driven into the ground near them or if the male tree is not right close to them. The shoot of the wild olive tree counteracts sterility in the domestic olive tree.

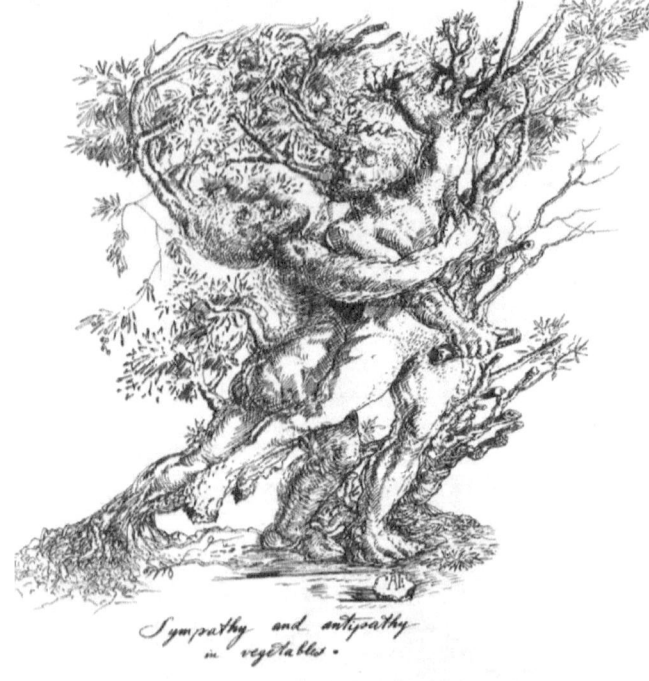

Sympathy and antipathy in vegetables.

"Between roses and lilies there is a secret sympathy, so that in growing side by side they help and benefit one another and produce more delicate and fragrant blooms. Where the squill is planted all other plants do exceptionally well, just as all kinds of vegetable herbs are favored in their growth if rocket is planted close to them. Cucumbers have as great an attraction for water as they have an aversion for oil. The rue is never so handsome as under the shade of the fig tree, or even grafted into the latter's bark.

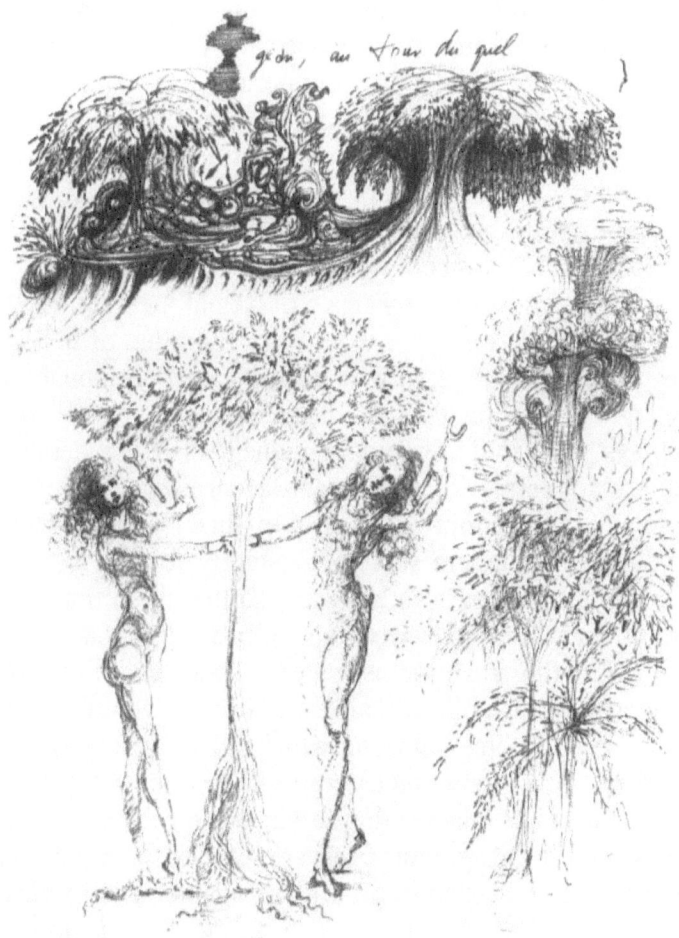

"The cat rejoices in the presence of verbena, because this plant strengthens its eyes.

"I think that I may well close this chapter here, for I believe we have amused you, friend reader, more than was mete."

Now that you have had a glimpse into certain mysteries of sympathy and of antipathy in the world closest to natural magic, you must begin daily to apply these principles to the sensitive impressions of your own eye. For the eye of the painter is a battle field, and at the same time an idyllic prairie. Certain images, in fact, shock the eye while others caress it, some nourish it and others denutrify it, and so on. Consequently, if you wish to make your eye vibrate happily, remembering that your eye will be ceaselessly engaged in choosing, in struggling for holy unity, which is *your* holy unity, you must creat it with very special care. Since a singer must take care of his throat, how should you not take care of your eye! And there is this difference, that while the vocal chords are viscera which are blind, deaf and without memory, the eye is the persistence of retinal memory in person!

Indeed there is no grosser error than that of believing that when you cease to look at a chair, this chair disappears. No, and again, no! Know, on the contrary, that at least until the end of your days there will remain permanently in the depth of your retina a place to sit down! You can accordingly without any fear of going wrong, adopt as your own this Dalinian maxim: that everything that the eye sees is constantly formed by everything that this eye has seen before—and also that the retina and history resemble each other like two drops of historic retina.

After the two months which I spent in prison during my adolescence I was able to realize the truth of the phenomenon of the so-called "flying bars" of which all prisoners speak. For a long time after their incarceration, in the most unexpected circumstances and places, they often see the bars of their prison window appear before their eyes, sometimes fixed but more often as if in flight, now standing out dark against a light background and again—more frequently—appearing as negatives, even against very light backgrounds, like the sky, for instance, on which I often observed the bars of my prison in Gerona, appearing in a blue tonality even more luminous than the sky itself. These apparitions, which lasted about three months after my liberation, made me give a good deal of thought to the persistence of retinal impressions, leading me almost immediately to a practical conclusion which my intuition had already, since my earliest childhood, unconsciously put into practice.

You must therefore know, young painter, that the Seventh Secret of your art resides in the sympathies and antipathies of your retina, in the manner in which you daily nourish it. For this you must surround it, as habitually as possible,* with a propitious environment, with a favorable retinal company, capable of serving as, of performing the office of, a kind of continual mosaic, persisting invisibly in the depth of your retina against which you will see real, full figures stand out more sharply. As a result, as in the case of all mosaics, your fancy, choosing paranoically, will be able to make the lighted images of your fancy appear and disappear, especially when you shut your eyes, and it is at this moment that the retinal mosaic which I advise you to form in your eye will appear exactly like the prison bars, but more lastingly.

Thus you realize that what I am advising, good inquisitor that I am, is that you should surround yourself with a prison for your eye. For nothing is more harmful to it than the freedom to see everything, to attempt to embrace everything, to want to admire everything all at once. But the prison which I advise for your eye must be mobile, transparent, and its flying bars aerial an tiny.

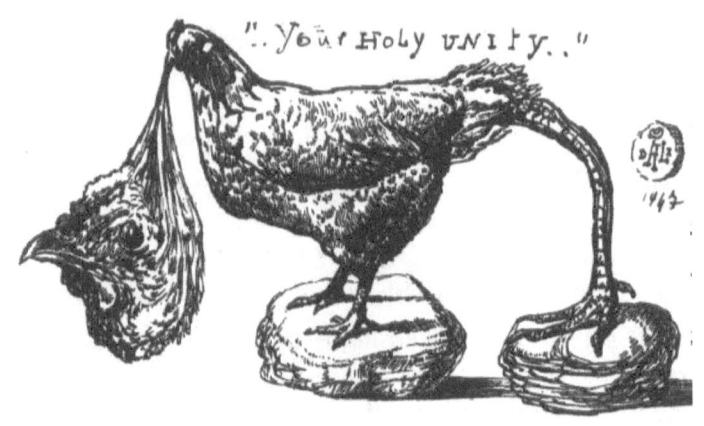

The ideal prison for the delicate eye of the painter is therefore vegetation, and the best of all vegetations is that of olive trees, and consequently also that of myrtles, since at the moment of planting the former around your house you have already learned that olives and myrtles sigh for one another and grow best together, in one another's arms. It is the olive tree, with the counterpoint of the myrtle, which by the constant, subdivided and tiny glittering and quivering of their leaves will surround your eye with that silvery mosaic so nourishing in trembling reminiscences for your retina that, whether your eyes are open or closed, all that you see will appear to you more silvered, minute, ample, gracious, smiling and euphoric—just as though, on the Mediterranean and brilliant lake of your retina, there were blowing at every moment that same light air which overturns, in silvery gusts, the leaves of the olive trees, of those olive trees which you will have become so accustomed to seeing that you already carry them planted in your retina and which, no matter where you go or what you paint, will never leave you for the whole rest of your life. You must understand now that since the light of the olive trees has the equivalent of certain screened lights of the Ile de France *⁎* or of Flanders it is exceptionally conducive to educating and refining your retina. On the other hand, nothing in the world can be more harmful to the education of your young eye of sixteen—this is the moment when you must already have decided your vocation as a painter—than the frequent sight of colors that are too vivid or too absolute. Your eye must become educated in nuances. This is why you must avoid planting flowers around your painter's house and shun, as you would the pest, the confused juxtaposition of their strident and brutal colors, molesting not only your eye but, it seems to me, capable even of piercing the tympanum of your very ear. Live, therefore, amid silvery graynesses, in order that the true colors of your soul may never descend to being some day compared to those—ephemeral and untranscendental—of flowers and eliminate these from your surroundings, or at least those of loud coloration, like the geranium, for example, which you must especially avoid and for a thousand other reasons.*— You may be certain that excessively strident colors mixing constantly in your retina will end by soiling and darkening it, just as when you stir together, without order or method, all the vivid colors on your own palette the latter turns dark like a venomous and threatening storm sky. Furthermore you must also avoid green lawns and all vegetation in which the green of the chlorophyll utters its desperate biological shrieks for oxygen! For there is nothing worse for the painter's retina than the loud and grinding Veronese of the parrot of the exotic and orgiastic dogdays of vegetation.²

→ *impossible + Vermeer in Sweden!*

Hence, nothing of the green of chlorophyllic exaltations in the painter's proximity. They are the veritable and treacherous enemy of his eye. There is nothing more tyrannical than those greens, nothing more disturbing and more insistent, for they will be shouting to you every second, "I want oranges! I want oranges! I want oranges!" weeping until, in one way or another, they somehow manage to get them even against your own will. Avoid, therefore, radically, even in the vicinity of your house, the presence of those snotty brats which are the violent greens. Once they have entered your retina you will no longer be able to silence them, they will not leave you alone for one second while you are at your work, for which it is very necessary to have that august calm which alone an eye exclusively nourished on olive-hued tapestries with threads of silver silk of airy light can procure you. And this is the Eighth Secret, from which you have just learned a little of why and how to give your retina a little of its daily bread—may it be blessed.

All this will help you to begin to understand also that the phenomenon of painting is consubstantially linked to geography, to geology, to botany, etc., which will form the subject of another volume entitled *The Geomorphology of Painting*.

GEOMORPHOPSYCHOLOGY ←{
Transcendent?

Here redolent truffles grow—there not. In a given piece of land a certain rare wine or a certain unique sea urchin, while half a mile away the wine has no exceptional quality and the sea urchins are hardly edible. This Mediterranean slope swarms with tempting subjects for the painter, while on the other coast, facing the Atlantic, not even a half of one has ever been able to grow. This is a law so rigorously inevitable that never, alas! will a single exception offer itself to prove the rule. That England, which has had sublime writers, has never given birth to a single great painter is known and recognized by all the world—in this world in which one cannot have everything. I am speaking of painters of the first order, that is to say, a Velasquez, a Raphael or a Vermeer.

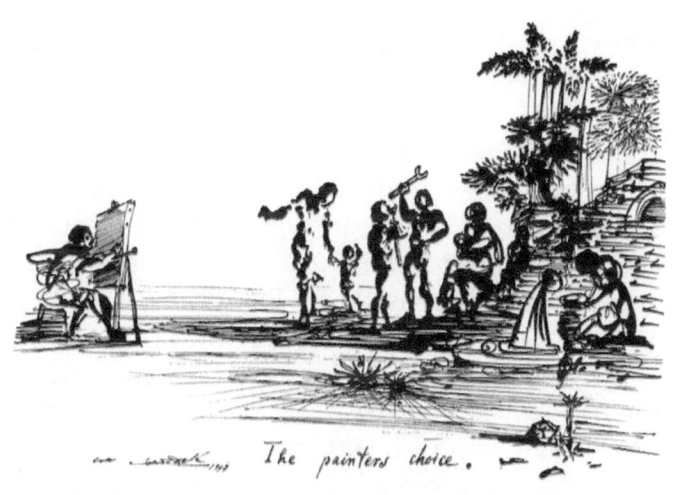
The painter's choice.

But other much more impenetrable mysteries make the work of painters even more exceptionally precious. For the works of these painters are never equally successful. All painters know this by bitter experience, but you will never be able to explain it. At a given moment you achieve, without hardly being aware of it, a miraculous masterpiece; at another moment, to all appearances similar, another painting executed with a thousand times more effort and knowledge brings you only greater shame at each fresh sitting and you can barely muster the courage to finish it. Such contradictions give rise to vague words like "inspiration," or "stroke of luck" or you may be quite ready to believe yourself the victim of an evil eye, as though your worst enemy among the other painters had managed to cast a spell over you.

Why did that turn out so well, and today, with the same procedure and with a thousand times more experience, I bungle it? Why, with this same medium and this same brush and this same subject, does the same thing which yesterday turned out divine today turn out unspeakable? This enigma is not an altogether hopeless one. Once you have read this book, you will be in possession of certain rules of the natural magic of craftsmanship. For in certain happy cases you have followed these rules very closely, or even gone beyond them, and in other circumstances on the contrary, and also without knowing it, you have violated them, stubbornly contradicted them and trampled them underfoot.

I beg you, therefore, to consider the most extrapictorial events of your secret and ultraintimate life, and especially those most secretly linked to your love-life—and there we are! It is precisely those imponderables of your libido which are the greatest hypocrites, responsible for the good and the bad fortune of your work. You tell me now that you had already vaguely suspected this. And how right you are! All the more reason why I should hurry—quick, quick!—and pass on to a new chapter, for its subject is well worth while. I assure you that even though the present one is very, very good, the one which is to follow is even better, not to say most astonishing.

*I owe my knowledge of the "slumber with a key" to the fact that it was practiced by the Capuchin monks of Toledo. But many years after I learned of it, on traveling out of Geneva by automobile, my great friend, the painter Jose Maria Sert, explained to me in a memorable conversation on the different kinds of slumbers according to the arts that the slumber with a key was traditionally practiced by the *aviso* painters of architectonic drawings who needed for their craft an exceptionally calm and steady hand.

* I have discussed this matter at great length with scientists. Can the interval between the moment when the fingers let the key drop and the noise which it makes on the dish be considered "sleep?" Most of them are of the opinion that true sleep occurs only five or six seconds later. Others, on the contrary, believe that this varies according to the individual. The fall of the key may occur after one second of sleep, and all the images that precede the fall might have to be considered as hypnagogic, rather than oniric images. I personally believe that this will remain a mystery for centuries of years.

* The fishermen of the Cape of Creus, where the best sea urchins in the world are to be found, proverbially say, instead of "sleeping like a log," "sleeping as though you had eaten three dozen sea urchins."

[1] The ancient painters all agree that the drawings, composition studies, tracings, etc. should be prepared during the winter months and that the artist should not begin to paint before the season when the days begin to lengthen, thus assuring himself, through the coming months of spring and summer, the maximum of sunlight.

* If your retina is extremely sensitive, and consequently a painter's retina, you can immediately test it for yourself: The pale blue of the verbena creates a desire for ashen colorations; a fig tree surrounded by olive trees awakens in the mind the absurd and anti-pictorial urge to paint flames, just as the prolonged contemplation of a view of the Atlantic Ocean robs you irresistibly of all desire to paint.

* The chromatic substance is as important for stuffing the eye of the young painter as grain for the goose's liver—the *pate de foie gras* which corresponds to the sybaritic and succulent *pate* which it is the object of every painter to produce.

* The worst enemy, for your eye of a painter who respects himself, is exotic and tropical flora, which besides is absolutely and radically antipictorial. The chromatic hyperchloridity of a Gauguin should suffice to cure the acidity of any young painter for the rest of his life. For that matter, the idea of a good painter coming from the tropics would be as absurd and ludicrous as that of a good Swedish painter.

[2] The Russians, with the whole vast expanse of their territory and their eminently artistic temperament (consider their writers and their musicians) have in spite of this never had a single great painter. They don't have one today and they can never have one, and the explanation of this astonishing phenomenon is, besides many other more subtle ones, the snow. No snow country has ever produced good painters, for snow is the greatest and the most harmful enemy of the retina. It is the hyperaesthetic

negation of all visual culture. The white of snow is simply blinding, and it is for this reason that the colors of their painters are violet-hued, congested by anilin acids, and poisonous to the eye as well as to the spirit. This is why the Russian painter is the worst colorist of all.

CHAPTER THREE

Of whether or not and when the painter must make love–Of how a masterpiece must be realized in six days and no more –In which is described the manner, very complicated but essential to the painter, of constructing a telescope with the skeleton of a sea urchin, by means of which he will be able to know the moment when he must cease to work on his picture, considering it as finished–Of why the painter must be a happy man–Of the painter's *ménage à trois,* of his mistress and of his love life in general–Of how Gala loves painting and of how painting loves Gala–Of the very simple manner of constructing an aranearium and of the ineffable emotions which the painter may derive from its retrospective use–Of the comparison, most bizarre but full of truth, between the head of a painter and a ruminating camel, of which the hump is occupied by the monstrous brain of the former, and of which the mouth is his digestive eye which, like a lamp, gives light–Of the surest manner of painting a masterly landscape.

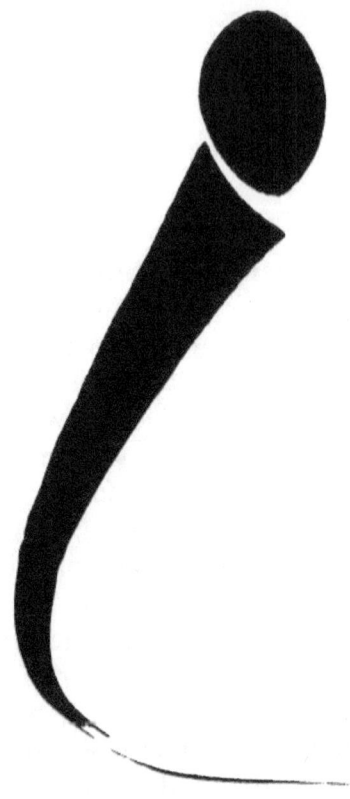

KNOW that you were greatly struck, in reading Cenino Cenini's treatise on painting, by the fact that he recommends to the painter the greatest possible chastity—even as he forbids him to carry heavy weights—lest his hand tremble. I was personally even more struck as a schoolboy when the Marist brothers, in order to moderate our solitary vices (if to prevent them was impossible), often told us that this did us as much harm as though we were to manipulate with our own hand the delicate substance of our very brain.

"Man and the Angel
will never cease
being right"

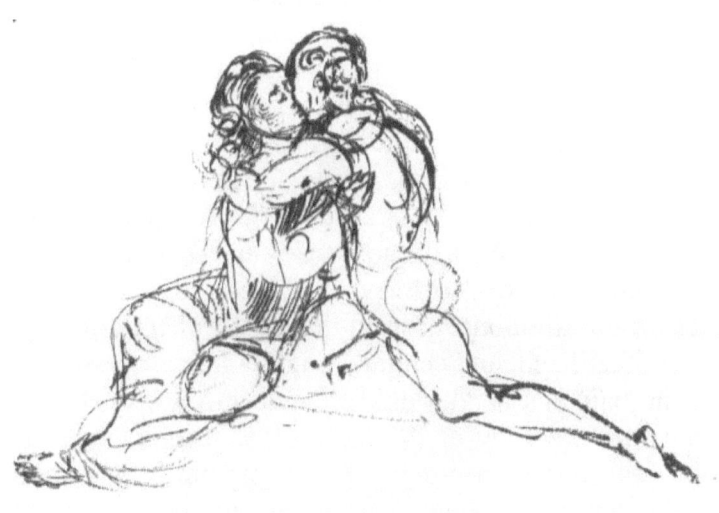

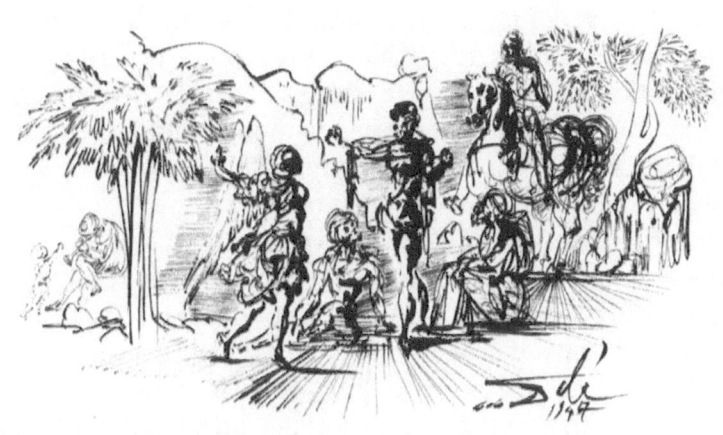

But all such vague and metaphoric observations serve only to disturb the emotions and give rise to a host of lugubrious superstitions and feelings of guilt. One must say everything or nothing. Here, then, in all frankness are exact details, and these constitute Secret Number 9.

Be as chaste as possible, and practice carnal abstinence during the periods when you are not materially launched on your work—that is to say, during the inspiration and the conception of your painting. For during this spiritual process it is most desirable that the accumulation of your libidinal impulses, unable to find outlet in an actual realization of desires, should nourish the process of your dreams and reveries, especially in the state of gestation which is, as Paracelsus said, above all a state of digestion, of transformation—of transubstantiation—and today that we know Freud we may add also and above all, of sublimation which, as we also know today, is the state which characterizes the constitutional basis of the artistic phenomenon.

On the other hand, and contradicting the fear expressed by Cenini that the painter's hand would tremble in consequence, I shall tell you that precisely at the moment of placing yourself really before your canvas in order to begin to paint it, it will be very desirable that you should establish the regular habit of making love once a day at the least. And note also this, that you must never do it in the morning, but immediately after the "slumber with a key" and once more according to your disposition before going to sleep. Remember, then: abstinence during the period of conception, and love during your periods of realization. For you know already that while you are working all anxiety must be absent from your spirit, since I have already explained that you must execute your work in a half-waking state, lulled by zephyrs of memories, mingled with readings that are sufficiently monotonous so that you will barely hear them. This state is exactly the one which the regular gratification of your carnal desires will procure you, whereas during your period of conception these must appear to your imagination by turns, as if torn from the fiery and drooling parchments of the annals of demonology and caressed by the downy scores of the solfeggio of cherubs. On the contrary, when you are actually painting, when you are *realizing,* these same carnal images must appear real to you, in their full reality, and instead of tearing pages of chimerical love from deceptive time it will seem to you that you are simply tearing out leaves of the calendar.

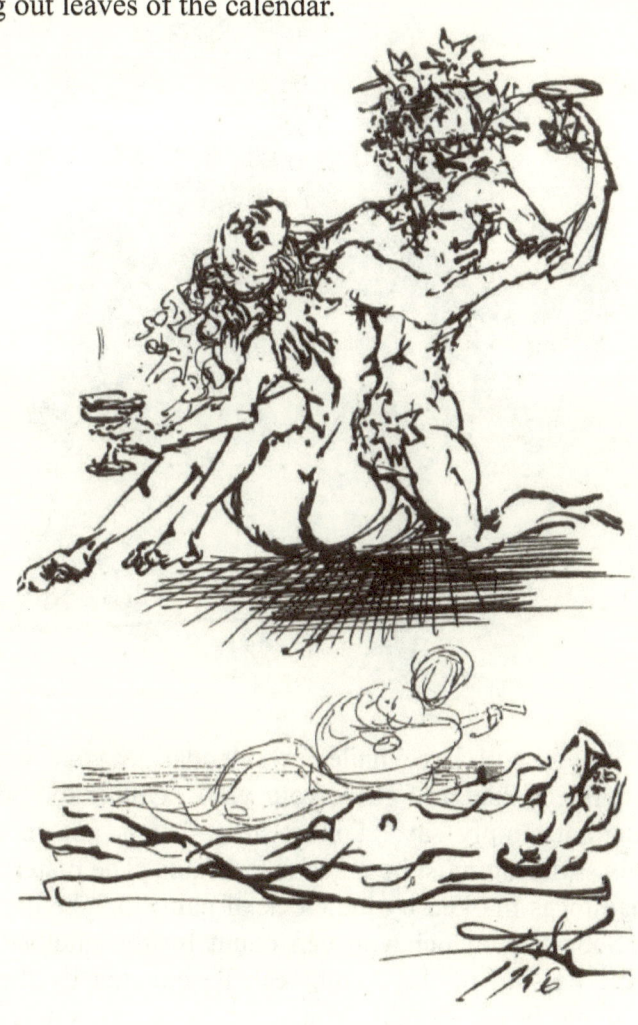

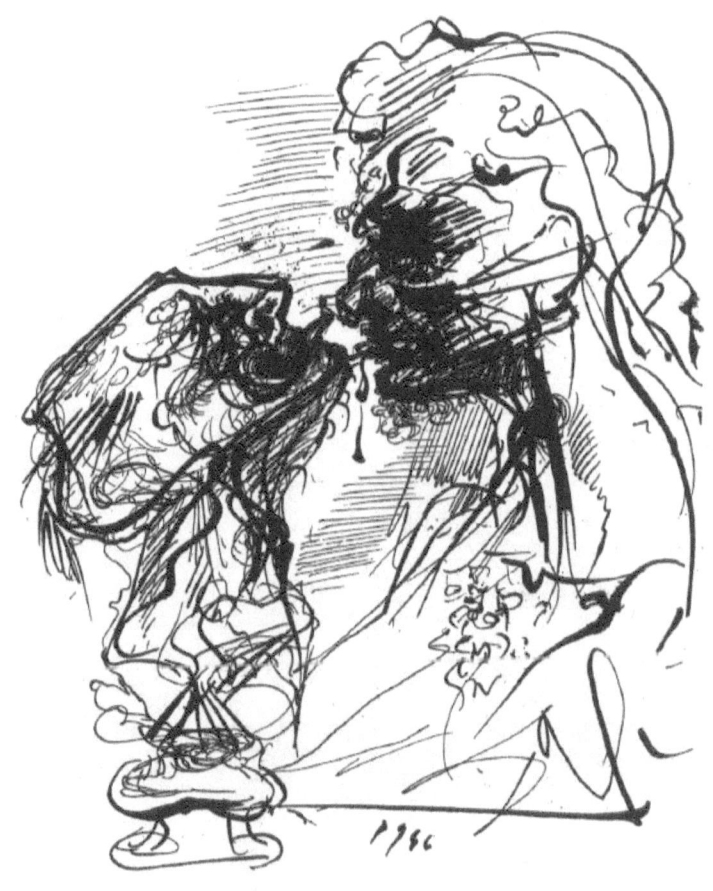

    For you will have nailed a calendar to your wall: the calendar will regulate and guide your work. Unlike the poet, the painter cannot simply say, "I must do it." It is not enough to suffer: this suffering must be made measurable. The material time for the painter is marked by the clock of pain: for like the agony of Saint Sebastian, which you can count by the number of his arrows, the passion of the painter can be counted by the exact number of his brush strokes. You must mark on your calendar beforehand the course your work is to follow, and afterwards mark each point in the progress of its execution. Thus the painter's calendar will be riddled with notations: "Thursday afternoon completed the expression of her smile!" "Tuesday from eight to ten filled in the sky!" "From ten to noon began the sea!"

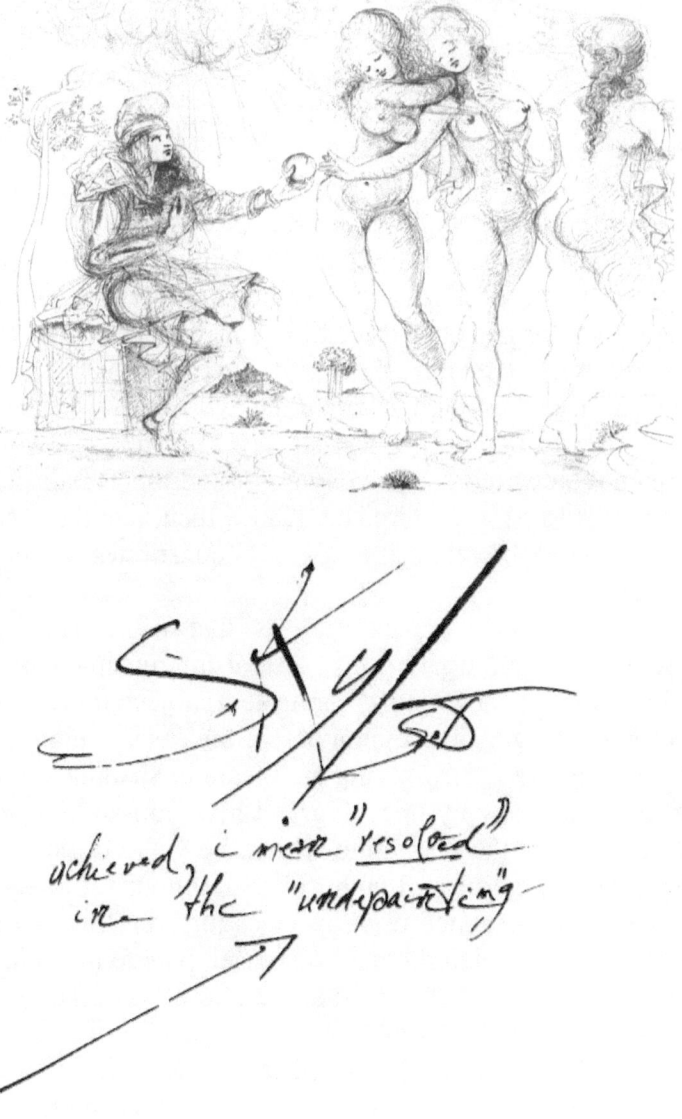

The painter Jose Maria Sert once informed me that he had counted the interruptions in the fresco *The Burning of the Borgo,* deducing from them that this gigantic work was finished in exactly six days. I am unable to verify this for myself, but it is in any case possible, since severe calculations, based on pictorial technique, have convinced me that the most important work can and must be resolved in exactly six days. One may go on "finishing" it endlessly, but at the end of six days the picture will have been executed to the point where it can be *seen,* all filled in and such as its destiny has willed it to be. One day more is not only unnecessary, but is a dangerous symptom that the masterpiece is already foredoomed to failure.

I should despise you if you were to regard as trivial the mention of the calendar in conjunction with the word love. You must know that the entire passion of the painter is inscribed in the calendar. Even as God created the world in six days, so the painter must "realize" (I do not say "finish") *his* work in six days—not a day more, not a day less—and this is indispensable if the work is to be a masterpiece. Know, then, that the requirement that your work be realized in six days constitutes Secret Number 10 of this book.

The most complex case is that of a painting which represents human figures in a natural, architectural or fantastic setting (there is no more complicated subject in painting). The painter who begins his session before the easel at eight o'clock in the morning can easily, giving great care to shading and brushing out, finish any sky by one o'clock. I give you an hour for lunch, half an hour as the maximum which the wake of your "slumber with a key" should last, I authorize a half hour for love—you see that I am making generous allowances for everything—but I want you to be seated again before your easel, palette in hand, at three. I guarantee you that if with the five and a half hours that I give you to fill in the landscape or the sea you do not have enough, and if consequently at the moment of sitting down to dinner at half past eight you have not yet finished, you are not the great painter of genius that you claim to be and your work will not be the masterpiece which we expected from your brush.

But since you reassure me by telling me that your background is completed and ask me how and at what point you are to continue your work tomorrow morning at eight o'clock, I shall ask you to mark down the following on your calendar (I shall assume that your painting features two figures in the foreground): from eight to ten you will paint one torso, and from ten to twelve the other torso; this leaves you an hour, which you will use to fill in the mountain distances, if there are any; if not, the hair of your two figures. From three to six will be the propitious time for the face. You will always choose the masculine one to begin with, if your figures are a man and a woman. If not, your choice will be determined by the difficulty, and must always go to the easier one. The face must be begun with the lighted parts of the chin; after that the cheeks and the forehead, then the nose, the mouth, the ears and finally the eyes. The longest and most difficult always are the nose and the forehead. From six to half past eight you will begin the architecture or the fantastic elements.

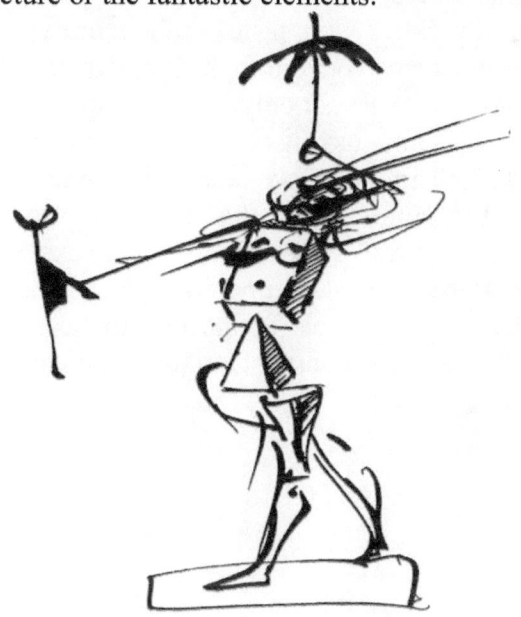

This brings you to the following morning. From eight to ten you will complete one body, from ten to twelve the other body, except for the hands and the feet which I give you the whole rest of the afternoon to complete, for since these terminate the extremities you will be able to execute them more effectively at this hour than, for instance, the architectural elements, which fatigue might render awkward and arduous.

You may now spend the whole morning of your third day working exclusively over your figures, without any other order than that of lingering over the details that appeal to you. You see that we have already reached the third day, and already your canvas is satisfyingly covered with paint, except for the feminine face. Be easy in your mind and work without haste, for I give you the three remaining days to realize it!

You see how comprehensive I am. I have not wanted to encumber you with the architectural elements, for these need only be well traced out. You will find that you have executed them in your spare moments without quite knowing how. If you happen to be one of those droll painters who, instead of sky or earth, prefer to introduce elements borrowed from their fantasies, the painting will go even faster, since you will only have to make skies "of a sort" or earth "of a sort" and, having no objective model to which you are bound you will immediately be satisfied with whatever comes out of you. But you won't do this if you are projecting a masterpiece, inasmuch as you know from the whole experience of the history of art that the greatest enemy of a pictorial masterpiece is fantasy. And that even the most divine imagination exacts of you only that you become consubstantially, biologically and inquisitorially a slave of reality.

"Fantasy" (NOTHING IS WORSE)

After the realization of your painting, it is necessary to finish it, and sometimes even to patch it up. And here is the mystery. If six days have been more than sufficient for you to realize your painting, it may sometimes take you several years to finish it, since it has never yet been known exactly when a painting is finished, or even if a single painting exists which *is*. My own opinion is that no painting is ever finished, and that it is to this that paintings owe the force of their existence, the perpetual influence which they exert over the years.

If it is humanly impossible to know whether your picture is finished, it will be almost as difficult for you to know when you must stop working on it. There comes a point where you run the risk of overlaboring and overrefining it instead of finishing it, and thus of ruining your work in the most disastrous fashion. Hence you must know exactly at what precise moment you must definitively remove your picture from your easel and stop painting on it. For this your own feeling does not suffice and may often deceive you. Remember how many times you have bitterly regretted having continued to overpolish your work and thereby having spoiled it irremediably.

Heed, then, Secret Number 11, by which you may infallibly know with all sureness that the hour of giving your last brush stroke to your masterpiece has struck—you will not be sorry to learn it!

Before initiating you into this secret, however, there are several expedients that you may have recourse to as you reach the stage at which you consider your picture to be nearing its final form. At the end of these sessions you should make a habit of observing the reflection of your picture in a mirror with a scrutinizing eye. This will help you considerably—seeing what is on the left on the right, and vice versa—to determine its defects with more accuracy, especially to discover things which are out of balance or out of proportion. The asymmetries and irregularities which are not called for will immediately strike you. Your eyes, too much accustomed to seeing the picture constantly in the same way, tend to allow your vision to be contaminated by your conception and to correct disproportions in an artificial manner.

Another useful expedient is to have your wife trick you into coming upon your picture in the most unexpected settings and at the most unexpected moments—in an odd room, in a corner of your garden—so that you find yourself suddenly and irreparably confronting your picture. Such brutal surprises are very effective in tearing from your eyes the bandage which your affection for your work often contrives to weave in the course of the long sessions which you have spent at your work, even though you have strived conscientiously to render the beautiful rather than to try to persuade yourself charitably that this is what you were really doing. But I shall assume that your picture has resisted all these tests, and still others, like the fascinating one of representing it to yourself in imagination, in the course of a prolonged revery, hanging in a museum next to one of your preferred Raphaels. And I shall assume that in spite of all this, convinced though you are of its beauty, you cannot make up your mind, you cannot muster the courage to stop working on it definitively, and finally to inscribe your signature on a certain spot which is often so difficult and anguishing to choose.

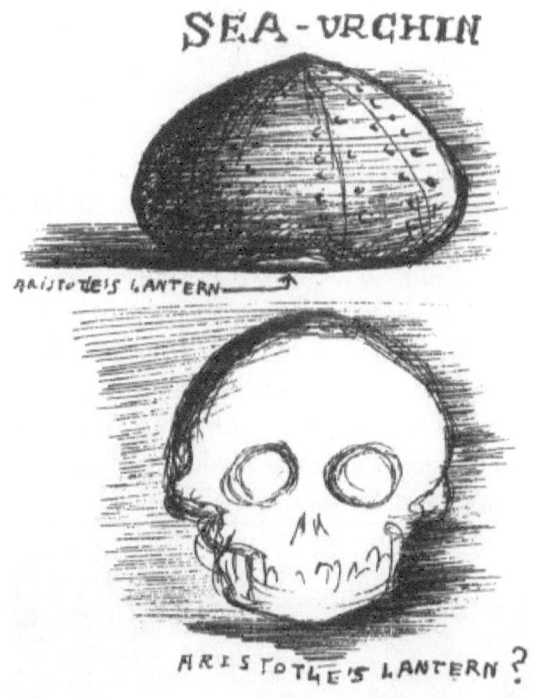

It is precisely at this moment of doubt that you should have recourse to my secret. Pay careful attention now to what is to follow, for it is thus that you must proceed. Take the skeleton of a sea urchin of an unusually large size. Against the pentagonal aperture formed by what is known as Aristotle's lantern, place the concave face of a crystal lens which may be secured in place with a little wax. Then take the web of a spider and with it form lines across the lens, connecting the five points of the pentagon so as to form a star. At the opposite point of the sea urchin's shell make a hole with a drill, large enough to accommodate a small magnifying glass. You will then see for the first time in your life—since before me no one had ever had the idea of looking through a new, artificially drilled hole, into the interior of a sea urchin—you will see, I repeat, the interior of one of the most beautiful natural cupolas which it is given to a human, creature to contemplate, and the center of this cupola— which I might compare to the Pantheon in Rome—would correspond to the hole which looks out on the sky, round in the one, pentagonal in the other. I shall ask that you hold this up to your picture, so that its reduced image will appear in it. This test is something which you must experience for yourself. For if the picture, observed under such conditions, through such a telescope, appears finished to you it is because it is truly finished, and if it does not appear finished, then it is because it is not. For you see it really surrounded and pressed, as it were, between the teeth of the perfection of a closed and finite world, in the center of the veritable monarchy which governs the painter, as will become transparent to you in the last chapter, in which I shall deal at the length which it deserves with themorphology and the aesthetic transcendency of the skeleton of the sea urchin, and with Aristotle's lantern in particular.

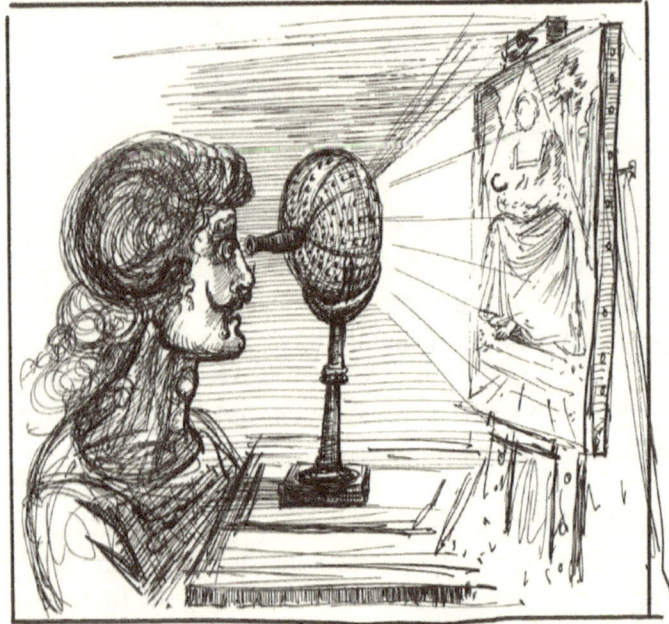

The eye glass of the painter.

You may now already begin to suspect that in order to have the humor to contemplate the mysteries of creation by introducing holes in the most secret receptacles of nature, so that you may see revealed through them universes of the ocean depths even when they bristle with spines, you have obviously to be not only curious, but also and especially you have to be a happy man. Even to be simply "happy" would not suffice, since in addition to your happiness you must not only have, but be filled with, authentic good humor. And as I have already made you anticipate that the secret of your happiness and your good humor resides in your love-life I shall ask you once more in this connection to follow my experiences in this realm of the flesh, which is filled with such sweet thorns.

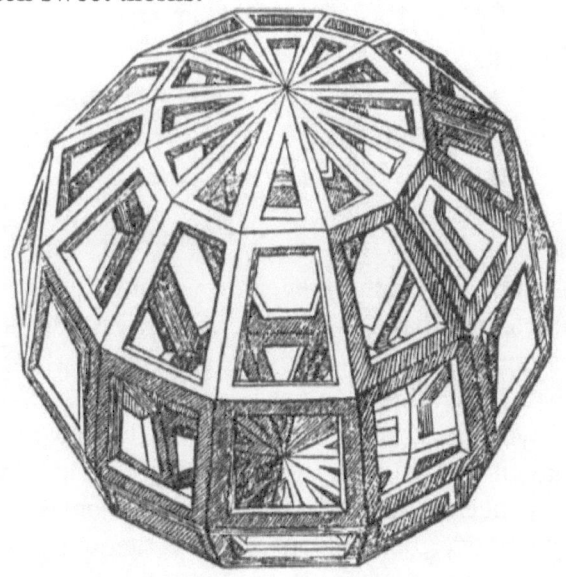

Septuaginta duarum basium vacuum

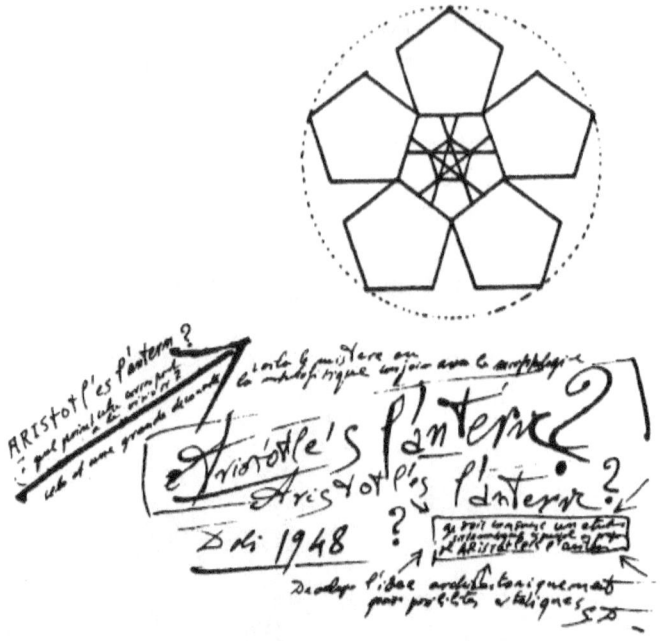

The moment has come to reveal to you my Secret Number 12: Every painter must have a wife and a mistress. But all three must live together, and live in the most perfect harmony. You realize immediately that this involves a *ménage à trois*. With your legitimate wife you must begin to cohabit at the age of twelve, and at this moment she will be exactly 1300 years old. Her name is Painting, her cheeks are fresh as a rose, her breasts are the roundest that it has ever been given you to contemplate, and you would take her, at the most, for thirty-six. And you must know that she will never age.

In order that your marriage with Painting shall be a happy marriage your love must not, as you might think, be absolutely reciprocal, though it is quite necessary that it be shared. Remember the unhappy love of Cezanne with *his* Painting—he worshipping her so completely, and she, ungrateful that she was, remaining utterly indifferent. On the other hand, remember the uninterrupted honeymoon of Raphael with *his* Painting. In my own case I must avow frankly that Painting loves me more than I love her. And she is often put out with me, for each time that I neglect her a little in order to write, I feel her languish—even when, as I am doing now, I write only about her. I know that she will overwhelm me with bitter reproaches. For Painting cannot be satisfied with words, which the wind sweeps away. She wants you, my dear friend, to possess her at least three times a day, and not a single night will she fail to slip into your bed.

This is why it will be so difficult for you to find a mistress, and at the same time why she will become for you the rarest and most precious thing in the world, if you succeed in finding her. Rare and difficult, because at all costs she must not be jealous of your Painting, but on the contrary she must love her not only as much as you yourself do, but even more! And precious, because in spite of the fact that with Painting you will experience ecstasies, you have already understood that they are of a platonic nature. She cannot therefore gratify your libido, painter though you be. See, then, how lucky you are, since the one you will really marry when you are in your middle twenties and who, in the eyes of all the world will pass as your legitimate wife, or at least as your morganatic wife, will in reality of truth be only your mistress, with all the perpetual romance which this implies, while your marriage, without secrets or veils, your marriage of all the most everyday moments of your life will be that into which you entered through the sacrament which you contracted in your early teens before the muses of Olympus, with your dear and well-beloved Painting. See, therefore, once more how happy you may consider yourself among men! To be able to live with your very wife as though she were a mistress into whose arms you were escaping from the soft, but too habitual conjugal bed!

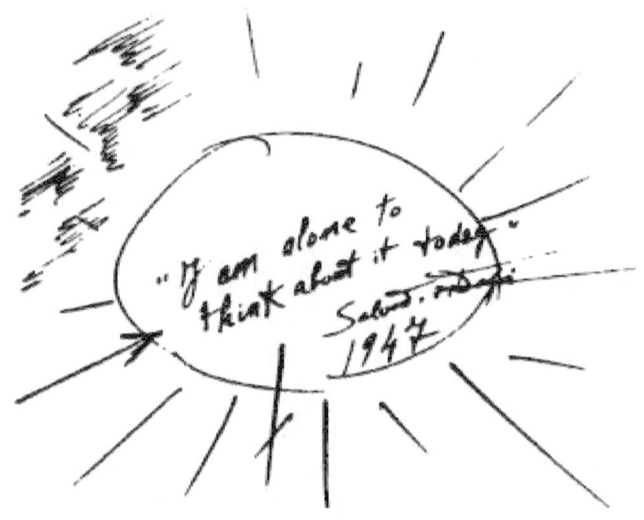

I must tell you now, by way of introduction to Secret Number 13, that every good painter who aspires to create authentic masterpieces must before anything else marry my wife. Thus you are advised: the painter's wife is called Gala. For Gala is she, creature of grandeur, who advances and who operates cures for the perverse aberrations of your spirit, Gala is she with whom you may, in marrying her, live continually as with a mistress and who will adore your painting more than you do yourself— warning you without pride, when the occasion arises, "This may distress your Painting . . ." "Let's not do that: it would grieve your Painting!" "You're neglecting your Painting . . ." "Look how beautiful your Painting is—some day you'll be sorry that you did not love her enough!" And Gala is also the one who reads to you, with the sweetness of an Aeolian harp, for hours on end, from her favorite Russian texts—all Pushkin—of which, since neither you nor your Painting knows Russian, you do not understand a single word but whose musical monotony half puts you to sleep while you are in each other's arms. And Gala is also the one who brings you, like a bee, all those honeys with which you and your Painting feed your perverse gluttony and she says, as she comes home and puts before you these flasks of rare media, "I'm bringing this for your Painting, I think she will like it." But the hard kiss of Gala's mouth is for me, for Painting herself can be kissed only with one's eyes.

But if I have just given you a sketchy idea of how Gala loves painting, I must now complete for you the description of the setting of our *ménage à trois* by telling you how and to what degree painting loves my Gala.

You must know, then, that oil painting fell in love with Gala at first sight, and that she became from that moment her constant and exclusive model and was thenceforth called her olive, because of the color and the volume of the oval of her face, which resembles that of a Mediterranean olive as two drops of oil resemble each other, and although olive oil is not appropriate for painting, because it would dry too slowly, the olive itself remains nevertheless the symbol of oils—for it will no doubt be admitted that the best symbols are those which never dry. You must now clearly understand this, that the ideal of the perfection of the feminine oval, during the period of "egg painting," and at the very beginning of oil painting, remains that of the volume with a hard, rough, brittle surface, that of an egg, which is exactly that of the "ovoid" heads of the madonnas of Raphael, whereas a little later, when full oil painting develops, the ovals of beautiful women become humanized and lubricated, approaching that of Gala, that is to say, resembling that of an olive, those olive faces which were best painted by Vermeer of Delft and by the divine Giorgione. As in an olive, the imponderable hollows of the dimples and facial irregularities become suffused with those olive tints which—remember this—can be obtained only by the skilful mixture of Italian earth, emerald green and blue black magically applied *à la volée* with the finest of all your brushes.

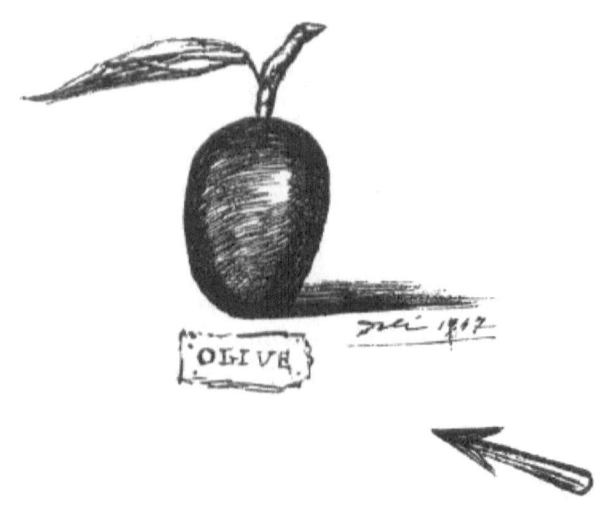

Painter, I counsel you therefore to balance an olive on your easel, and let your eye not cease to question it often, for he who has understood the form of an olive will have penetrated the most subtle suprasensible secret of all painting! Thus—and this is Secret Number 14—accustomed to recognizing at a glance the morphological virtues of an olive, you will be able to choose amid the abundantly antipictorial multitudes of feminine ovals those of the authentic Galas which painting loves, assuring yourself thus, by this unanticipated procedure, nothing less than the certain choice of your own happy marriage.

Let me now tell you other advantages that you will find in being married to a Gala. And since I feel that this is what you have been waiting for, wondering what in the world this Gala does to make her so precious to every painter, what she does to be so useful, my answer shall be simple: she does nothing, she lets potentialities, processes and affinities take their course—that is to say, she poses. And to pose means to architecturalize space. But also, with her pose she "silences," she dematerializes, she quenches your thirst, she banishes anguish. And in the course of your walk, when your spirit roams a thousand miles away, losing itself on the misty confines of obsessive conjectures, she points out to you a flower in the path where you are walking like a somnambulist, bringing your distracted spirit back to the savory reality of your walk. "Look at that flower!" she says. And it is the same flower which, that evening, on rereading Michel de Montaigne, he in turn counsels you to observe, in order to prevent your spirit from becoming the prey of your chimeras.

But I say that Gala does nothing. I wish to say now, in order to have the pleasure of contradicting myself immediately, that she does everything, strictly everything. And yet I am right in saying again that she does everything while doing nothing, that is to say without touching anything, while flying about like a bee, which is also one of the names which I have given her, for like a bee she brings me all the oils, all the media, and it is thus that I find the pentagonal hive of my studio filled with all the pollens which the painter, at every moment of the day, needs to be able to spin the integral honey of his work. And when she lets her eyes rest on an object, Gala the olive becomes an observer, and her glance is inestimable. Its extreme acuteness, capable of seizing the difference of a hair in the mounting of a jewel, caused the Duke de Verdura to exclaim that Gala had the eyes of a lynx. Now if it is true that a painter's two eyes do not suffice him, and that he must often have recourse to other eyes, even though they may be less good than his, you can tell yourself that the greatest good fortune that can befall you, in this regard, is to live with a woman who possesses the eyes of a lynx!

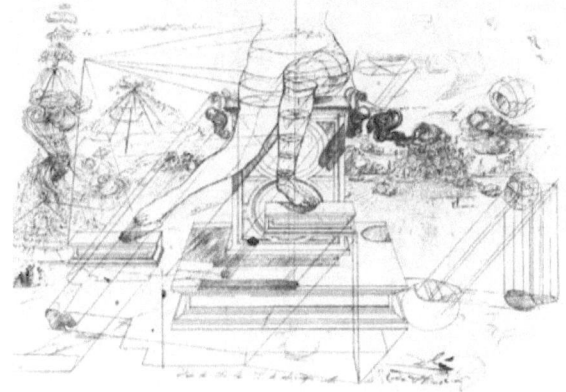

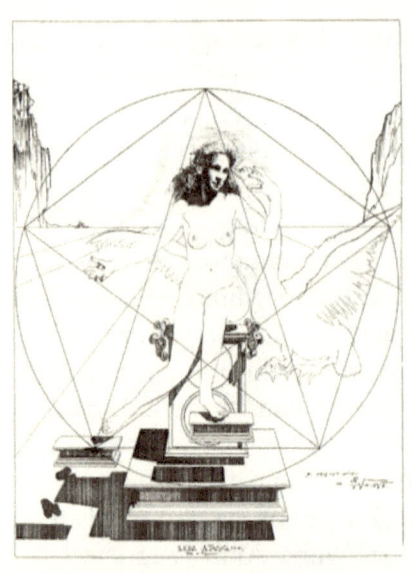

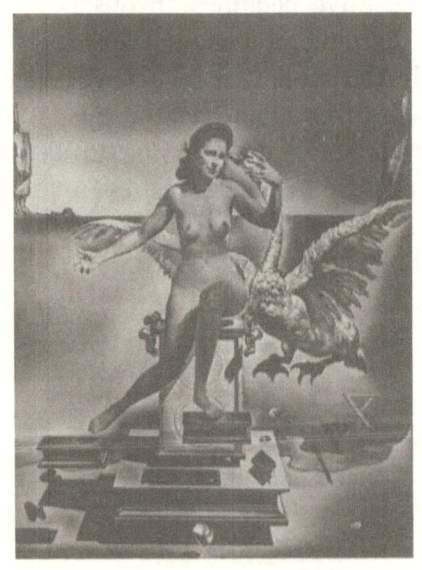

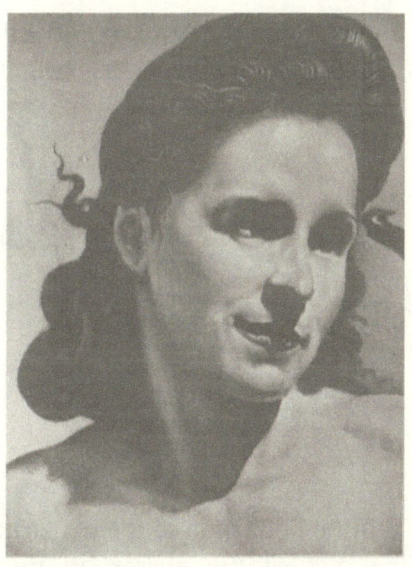

And finally, this is the place where I wish this to be written: It was Gala who reinspired the Renaissance of classicism which slumbered within me since my adolescence, who has surrounded me progressively, almost without my being aware of it, with all the rare architectural documents of the Renaissance.

One morning, toward the end of October in 1941, I was seated in my studio and I was looking at a pomegranate divided in two halves which I was holding in my hands while with my tongue I was trying to work loose one of the little seeds which had become obstinately wedged between two teeth. It was at this moment that I understood the supreme beauty of the architecture of antiquity, based on the biology of numbers. And I remember very well that at that moment my tongue was pleasurably caressing my gums with the maximum of force, registering the relief of each of my upper teeth, as if this pressure could help me better to understand and to remember my thought, more and more clear, which seemed to spring from the very depth of my blood. This idea may be expressed thus: "Numbers are not bones, numbers are flesh." And with clenched teeth I uttered silent "vivas!"

With clenched teeth I cry again today, "Long live the roses of geometry, long live Vitruvius, long live Gala, long live the pomegranate of my life!"

Secret Number 15 will be dedicated to the construction of "araneariums." Here is the gist of the matter, in the fewest possible words, to give you solely a slight but sufficient glimpse of a new compendium of original methods of inspiration, for this book would become interminable if it were to explain and develop everything.

Believe me, when I advise you to guard your studio with the utmost rigor against the intrusion of any living creature besides your wife, that is to say your Gala—with the exclusive exception of the spider which, on the contrary, you must consider the true geometrist, the minute Luca Pacioli, the intimate friend of the painter's hours of labor, and from whom you will derive much instruction and a continual feast, for your eyes as well as for your mind. Banish, then, to begin with, monkeys, parrots, dogs and cats, for these can but involve you in innumerable and unnamable disorders and miseries and filth, from the constant menace of finding irreparably smeared by a rapid and disagreeable tail-swish of their dirty hairs the archangelic smile which you had patiently achieved with three thousand conscientious and airy tail-swishes of the minute badger hairs of your careful brushes, to the flying about of their animal dust, and crowning the whole by their overwhelmingly depressing propinquity, even when, assuming the most favorable circumstances, these beasts are well-behaved and unobtrusive. For when you feel yourself possessed, or when you possess the holy retinal furies of your inspiration, the stupid presence of a dog, with its lachrymose sentimentality, cannot but strike you as lamentably out of harmony with the cruel tension of your lucid spirit, which is one of the principal vital and fecund characteristics of every authentic creator.

The company of the spider, on the contrary, will appear to you sympathetic, lucid and cruel like yourself, and it will spin the mathematics which you, leaning over your easel, bear inscribed in the lines of tension of your own bones. Thus, no dog for you, but spiders, yes! And know that there do not exist in all creation two more contradictory secretions than the foul and supremely anti-geometric drooling of a dog and the quintessential and mathematical saliva of the spider. The spider is one of the painter's good fairies, and its Ariadne thread will guide you at every moment in the menace-filled labyrinth of your studio. Begin, then, by learning the most simple and rudimentary manner of constructing your aranearium, and wait a few moments before I tell you not only all the excellent and useful things which can be derived from these instruments but also the unsuspected resources of pleasure which they contain: I promise you that the retrospective utilization of such araneariums not only will make you drool but will, I swear to you, even make you weep.

The best aranearium is constructed with a slender olive branch, which you shape as nearly as possible into a perfectly round hoop, leaving four or five olive leaves clinging to the outer part of the circle, on which the spider will enjoy placing himself on various occasions. This hoop of olivewood you will secure on a four-foot pine pole provided with a solid base. At the bottom of the hoop place a small box in the shape of a perfect cube, of very green pine, provided with two holes, one in the top, and the other in one of the sides. This empty cube will serve as the spider's nest. Within the previously moistened box, introduce a little earth and allow it to dry well in the sun. Since amber is very sympathetic to the spider—and how much more to the painter!—you must always keep a little ball of it on the cube, which you will use to magnetize the tip of your wand, with which you will manipulate and train your spider, so to speak, and with which you will reach to it its feasts of flies, of which you must always have several in reserve, which you may keep in a little bowl beside the ball of amber—for between amber and dead flies there also exist numerous affinities.

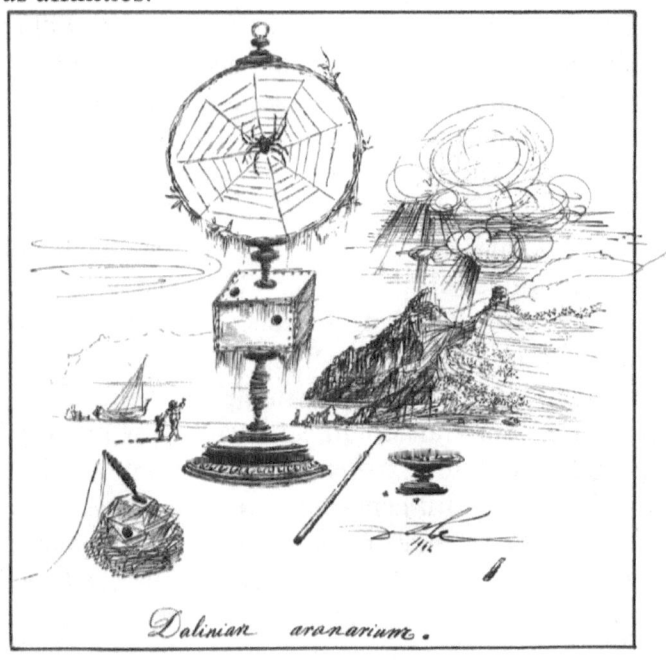

Dalinian aranarium.

For your aranearium to be successful, you must achieve its principal object, which is to oblige the spider you have chosen to construct its web exactly within the circle of your aranearium. You will not manage this without some difficulty, and you will have to bring the spider back to the hoop of olivewood as many times as necessary until your spider finally decides to weave his web there. Once his work is accomplished a few tidbits of flies will make him feel at home and he will stay there, and even if he should abandon his web for a time he will suddenly reappear at the moment when you least expect him, even if you should move your aranearium to a different place.

Now that you have learned the manner of constructing an aranearium, you are ready to learn how to make use of it, but do not on this account rest content with the building of just one, since you will have to build five: that is the minimum which every artist's studio should contain. I am assuming, then, that you are in proud possession of your five aranariums with their five perfect spiderwebs. Now hear how and why they are to be utilized and presently you will understand that this Secret Number 16 involves nothing less than a typical magic ceremony of witchcraft, whereby you will voluntarily fall in love, madly in love, for the rest of your life, with the bit of landscape which you have already wisely decided, by your understanding, to be the one among all those that you love to be most worthy of all kinds of sacrifices.

As your studio must be situated close to the spot where you were born, and as, if you are to be a good painter, this spot must have an admirable natural setting, the choice of the landscape with which you decide to fall in love will be relatively easy for you. Having determined on the view to be used for the ceremony in which you are to put yourself under a spell, this is how you must proceed.

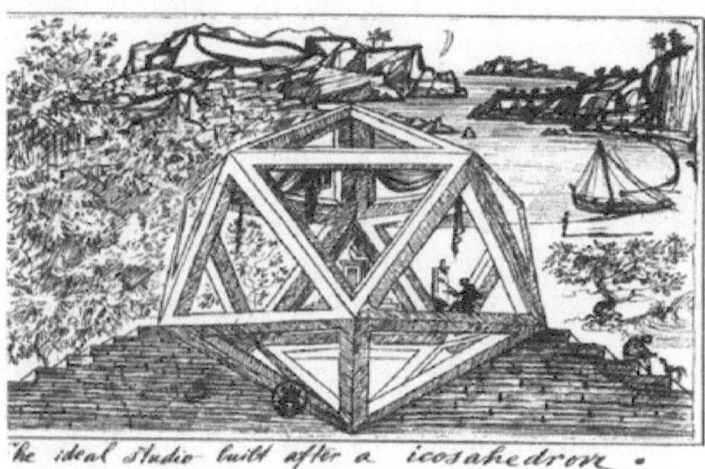

The ideal studio built after a icosahedron.

First, the ceremony is to be performed when you are about twenty years old, when your love affairs follow one another in unbroken succession, but at a moment when you feel yourself particularly in love, to the point where your love-anguish makes all the operations which I am about to describe, simple though they be, appear onerous and almost unfeasible. These operations will seem to you—and this is highly desirable from a psychological point of view—to be an unwelcome interruption of your continual dream of love. But this is all to the good, since what you are about to do is in fact to disturb that dream, to displace it and change its object, to provide the round, vague treasure of tenderness which you bear within you with a new, transparent receptacle in a special place, so that by means of your araneariums you will at last be able to see it. You will see it, without seeing it, for what you will see will be something quite different from the image of the girl you are so much in love with. Instead, you will see the landscape which, you tell me, your acute and refined painter's taste has definitively selected among the admirable spots which surround your studio.

Begin, then, by placing opposite this favored spot a flawless crystal bowl filled with the purest water, so that you can see the landscape of your love reflected in the bowl and your eye can possess it isolated, reduced and perfectly contained in its crystalline sphere, as though you were seeing, separated from your person, the congealed mystery of your very retina. The most propitious moment for your sentimental exaltations being that of the last oblique rays of the sun, you will choose precisely that moment to place your five araneariums in a straight line before the crystal bowl. Looking through the five cobwebs you will be wonder-struck as you see the bowl, by virtue of the rays of the setting sun, become irradiated by the most subtle and golden mother-of-pearl tints of thousands of rainbows. Remain where you are, marvel at the vision, which will appear to you one of the most ineffable sights you have ever seen, though you are as yet unable to explain your ecstasy. Look, and look again, but at the same time move your araneariums, now closer together, now farther apart, so that the rainbows which they produce will intersect one another in a variety of intricate geometric patterns, weaving aeolian strophes of exquisite iridescence cadenced with the regularity of the crystal sphere in which the image of the landscape of your love begins to turn ruby-red, then darker, like the blood of a ripe cherry—for the sun is about to disappear behind the horizon, and you already feel the warm hand of the shadows of the spring twilight touch you just behind your head in the nape of your neck with the tip of its ring-finger which might very well, if you wish, be adorned with a clear garnet.

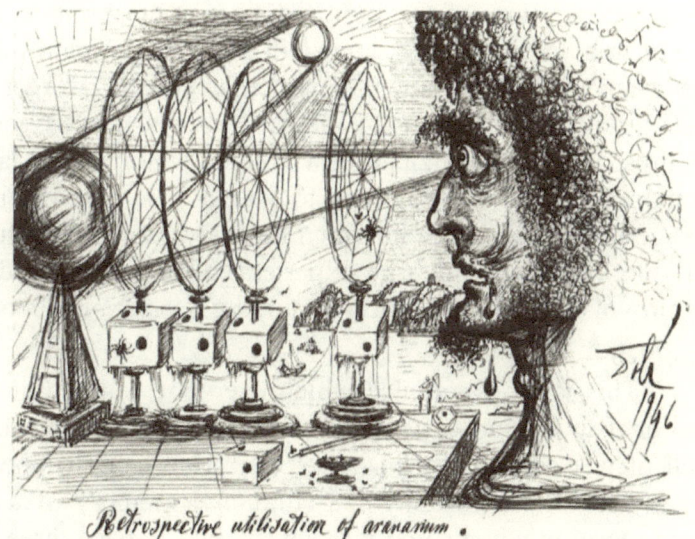

Retrospective utilisation of aranarium.

Remain, I say—and even if I did not tell you, do so nevertheless—for now that the sun has gone, and with it the glorious rainbow aureole produced by the irisation of your araneariums, you feel so overwhelmed by the spectacle which your eyes have just contemplated that it seems to you that the potency of the charm which you have undergone keeps you there, glued to the spot, incapable of making the slightest movement, even that of wiping off the drop of saliva which has begun to flow from the corner of your lips. For admit that you are drooling,*— and you must not stop drooling until you have heard the song of the nightingale at least once, and until the bowl which contains your landscape and the night make but one single round.

After this evening on which you have been so carried away by the spectacle of your favorite landscape which the araneariums and the crystal bowl have procured you I order you to avoid seeing it again on any pretext. This you must do systematically, orienting your walks in other directions and even suppressing the landscape from your thoughts as much as possible, thus depriving yourself for a long time, that is to say for twenty-seven years, of the sight, whether at close range or from afar, of this spot which, as you shall see, must remain buried in your memory. For the more completely you can forget it, the better it will be for what is to follow. Perspicacious as you are, I can already see you anticipating what I am coming to, at last!—to the moment when I shall recall to you, as I am now doing, the passage in Marcel Proust in which he analyses so masterfully the ineffable emotions which he experienced toward the end of his life, provoked by the sensation of dipping a *madeleine* cookie in a cup of tea.*—

This is an experience which everyone has had at various emotional levels, an experience which can be so intense that a smell of wet cement, for instance, can bring tears to one's eyes, reviving in all its intensity the childhood memory of a certain spring morning when some masons came to replace three broken tiles in the dining-room floor. But painters experience the phenomenon with greater acuteness in the form of images. On seeing, at the age of thirty-six, a completely insignificant post card of the Tibidave of Barcelona, which I had not seen since I was a child, I was so moved that for over a month everything that came into my mind constantly reverted to this inexplicable emotion. Since then I have eagerly been searching for the books of illustrations of my childhood in order to study their images, which have become a treasure to me. How barbarous it is, therefore, not to set traps when we are young for our future adult emotions! For to do this would be nothing less, once it was systematized, than the realization of Faust's dream, without having to have recourse to Mephistopheles and without having to rebel against old age. Proust's *Remembrance of Things Past* is not the hyper-individualistic lucubration of a blasé. It is the very healthy basis of a whole Dalinian system by virtue of which the physical span of our life could be at least doubled. For you could then tell yourself that what you are now living you could live again better, at the same time that you were living something different. I especially. Everything which I miss living at every instant, everything that I am wasting at present, all the ineffable congealed cascades of sensation and emotion which escape me at this moment without my even being aware of it, this whole treasure of life, of time which I am losing, one day I shall find again, with a fresh wonder, in a new and real terrestrial paradise.

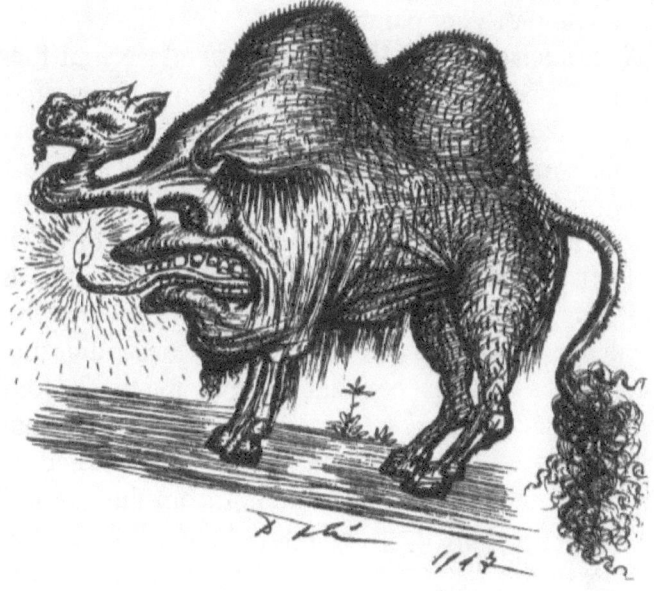

Compare yourself, therefore—to come back to you, painter —to a kind of dromedary masticating visions which constantly make you drool with satisfaction. These do but repair to the monstrous hump of your brain and go to sleep—a brain which I have already once happily described as being filled with a wick folded and refolded in infinite circumvolutions inside an oil lamp. Now that I am comparing you to a dromedary, listen carefully to the rest of the comparison, for it is no less apt and resplendent with truth than that which likened you to a lamp luminous among all others, for the search for Proust's "vanished time" is for you the search for vanished images, but which are no longer lost since, as you know now, they are merely asleep in your hump, or in your humps, if you are a camel of images, as I have the great good fortune of being. Imagine then that all the wonderful images of your vanished time, those which you looked at without seeing them, have nevertheless remained intact, kept like a blind rosary strung along that combustible wick which you keep folded in intricate convolutions like an intestine inside the monstrous hump of your painter's head.

And precisely when you begin to exercise your function of a ruminant, which is that of transubstantiating and quintessentializing all the visions which "since the vanished times" your eye had simply stored up, and when the end of these visions is brought up again, passing through your mouth which, acting now in the role of a veritable stomach, with its digestive saliva of images which is that of your own retina, this digestive mouth of images of the camel of your head becomes the eye of your head, for with the heat which all these digestions will produce, all the images contained along the wick folded and refolded in the circumvolutions of the hump of your head, successively digested, will be consumed, will burn and will shed light, one after the other, as if springing from the magic lamp of your life and you will then see appear the whole ineffable and lucid rosary of this life of yours before you, in your painting. In addition to all this you will recognize the miracle by another sign which, however untouched you may be by great world-shaking events, will in this instance not fail to manifest itself, so that you will no longer have the slightest doubt, in that other unequivocal and physiological sensation of feeling the burning of your own tears.

And you may be certain and convinced that experience will corroborate what is to follow. Let us go back to the landscape which you contemplated with such ecstasy in your crystal bowl at the age of twenty, surrounded by the memorable circumstances of the araneariums, and which you assure me you have not seen again since that distant time. If now you bring with you those twenty-seven years during which you have traveled and lived in the Americas, in the course of which very dear friends have died, and the tender notions of geometry of your childhood have grown to the necessary vigor and the rigor to command your sentiments; and if you have now become accustomed to separating the chaff from the wheat of your emotions, to the point where you no longer confuse the envelope, which the wind carries away, with the germ, heavy as lead, which bears fruit—inasmuch as those things which have not grown within you since the araneariums of your adolescence were but chaff to be carried away by the winds of vain illusions, like the spider-webs, once they are broken and without geometry; and if, after all these things and many others which are already beginning to wrinkle your face you return at last to your birthplace with the desire to settle down there, and after a few months' delay you decide to see again exactly the landscape which you saw at the age of twenty reflected in your crystal sphere and which you have not ceased to carry within you, slumbering, and you feel a stirring anguish at the mere thought that the hour is approaching when you are about to see it again; and if, having decided this in the afternoon, as you have just done, you finally repair to the spot, bearing with you your old araneariums with their new and at the same time perennial spiderwebs and if, awkward, with a beating heart, or even filled with indifference, you sceptically and meticulously get everything in readiness, following my orders to the letter, in order to look perfunctorily through the fine-spun iridescent meshes which gave you such great delight twenty-seven years ago at that same landscape which at that time you cherished as being the most beautiful of all; if you at last see again that landscape superposing itself on the landscape of your memory, so that they become like two identical crystal spheres which contain them, I warn you beforehand that if this vision made you drool the first time, today, twenty-seven years later, this same vision will not only make you drool again but it will also make you weep.

But wipe your tears, do not weep, do not weep overmuch, for it is now the spiderweb's turn to weep, to weep all its geometries for you. That evening you will depart, leaving all your araneariums out there in the open, facing the sphere of your beloved reflections. Very early the next morning, that is to say just a little before sunrise, you will go back to that same spot. Walk there worshipfully, for it is now that the most marvelous sight of all awaits you—that of your five cobwebs evenly and harmoniously bedecked with limpid dewdrops! And this I do not want to tell you about, because you must simply see it—for how could I describe to you the innumerable reflections which your adored landscape will produce in each of the droplets of dew balanced on the fine-spun threads or, what is worse and better than all, the reflections of the crystal sphere itself containing the entire landscape entirely reflected in turn in each of the dewdrops on every web of your araneariums? This sudden and auroreal Lilliputian multiplication, so round and crystalline that it is as though the whole retina of your eyes were expended and poured out, sprinkling the landscape of your love in order to fecundate it with the very marrow of your vision, will bring this time to your face, become serene again in the new dawn, neither the drooling of the delectation you experienced at the age of twenty, nor the recent tears which you shed over your adolescence recaptured at the age of forty-seven, since instead of this your mouth will simply distend in an expression of pride, brushed by a smile of melancholy superiority which you will never be able to banish from your face for the rest of your life —the pride and the superiority given to you by the consciousness that Salvador Dali has existed.

Comme cette réflexion est ossie!

And now remove from your presence, but with all the gratitude which you owe to them, your sphere and your araneariums, and paint from nature as honestly as you can, that is to say, effacing yourself as much as you can before your model, and thus trying to copy it as anti-artistically as is humanly possible for you. Do not doubt that this picture will be one of the surest and most convincing masterpieces of your maturity.

Let us suppose that, instead of the apprentice that you are, you have become a great painter, that in your adolescence (at the moment when, because of the fresh and new ebullition of your biology, you saw all things through rose-colored glasses, according to the vulgar expression, and this without needing to resort to any kind of araneariums) you produced some masterpiece as complete as Raphael's *Betrothal of the Virgin*. This is not only possible but even frequent and in the natural course of things. But on the other hand, it is also frequent and in the natural course of things that, toward the period of your maturity and precisely when you might make the best use of the advantages given you by your experience and your wealth of technical means, you should find yourself a little dried out, having lost that freshness of almost childlike inspiration which so moves your admirers, who now are inclined to consider you more master of yourself, incomparably more learned, but no longer possessing that indefinable and elusive thing which was the very bloom of your soul and which, as by a miracle of heaven, you were able, without knowing how, to project in your work, crystalline like the crystal of your own soul and invisible like your own retina, distributed in regular round and perfect drops on the entire surface of your first masterpieces. You now know how, by virtue of the magic of the retrospective use of your araneariums at the moment of your maturity, to achieve these ineffable states of grace, as precious and exceptional as that described by Proust, provoked in his case by the sensation of dipping a madeleine in a cup of tea, a thousand times more intense than those of your clover days, for this emotive and receptive state will be multiplied for you by at least as many times as your crystal sphere containing the landscape will be in turn by the number of dewdrops of all your five araneariums. You can therefore judge how precious such devices can be to you.

"Le deuxième plus beau Tableau du monde"
— S. D.

You will find in many books recipes for making essence of turpentine, but where has anyone before this ever described a method like mine which can serve as a galvanic key that will open the sluicegates of the emotions slumbering in the depths of your spirit and make your eyes, before a particular landscape, more virgin and avid than at the age of twenty, with all the visual culture and the manual dexterity of your forty-seven years? Thank me, therefore, once more, with the respect which you owe to a great master who, so generously, gives you such secrets. And rejoice now to learn still further uses—these by way of amusement and without importance—to which you can put your araneariums.

Know, then, that your five araneariums, perfectly adorned with dewdrops, will serve to make a very original decoration for your long festive table on the day when you wish to celebrate the successful completion of one of your pictures. In honor of this occasion you will also construct combs formed of miniature araneariums, for which you will use tiny spiders, also adorned with dewdrops, to be worn by your wife, your Gala, on this evening. And if, by chance, the waiter as he is serving should inadvertently brush against one of the webs that adorn the combs and break it, the spider will immediately and on the spot proceed to repair it with its habitual rapidity and diligence.

I have counted as many as fifty-five ways, equally lacking in transcendency but of an equally amusing fantasy, in which I have found diversion with my araneariums, but to enumerate them here would be too frivolous for the tone of this book. I wish, however, before concluding the subject of araneariums, to mention one more adaptation which is extremely useful for the painter's studio. For this you must use heavy webs of barn spiders, which you must have them weave on hollow parallelepipeds two feet long, suspended at both ends. These parallelepipeds will very effectively attract and absorb the dust[*] and all kinds of matter floating in the air which cause so much annoyance and inconvenience to the painter while he is working, when tiny particles of all kinds come and stick to the wet paint. When the picture is very small and detailed these may cause serious damage, for often in trying to remove such particles one may destroy some imponderable detail, always the longest and hardest to dO, and especially to redo. To avoid this, I shall give you my Secret Number 17, a tiny secret, but important, and of a suggestive ingenuity. You construct a very light little paper roof to protect the wet part that you are working on. To attach it to your canvas you should never use thumb tacks, which would puncture your canvas irreparably, nor sticky paper, which would soil it, even if you were afterwards to wash it with ammonia and then rinse it with soapy water, and finally with clear water. What you do, avoiding all necessity of having to wash the canvas afterwards, is simply to attach this little paper roof by means of spiderwebs which will suffice, without any soiling, to maintain it solidly in place, and all the little particles that fall vertically will settle on it.

Also every painter while he is working should wear a necklace of large amber balls which should be rubbed at length before he begins painting, so that it too will attract flying hairs. I have even noticed that long mustaches like those which I wear are also useful to the painter to attract small particles, preventing them not only from attaching themselves to the canvas but also from entering your mouth or your nose. Regard this as Secret Number 18. Mustaches must be frequently washed, as is done so instinctively by the animals who wear them. It may also be suspected that for man, too, mustaches serve as antennae. This is all somewhat mysterious, but I no longer have any doubt that with my mustaches I feel more alert, that I am more acutely conscious of everything that goes on and especially of everything that moves around me. Because of their very length, with the tips pointed and curled up, the least change of light registers on the ends, immediately communicating itself to my eyes. Thus one day I became aware of the sun that was setting behind me, for I saw something like two tiny red cherries gleaming at the tips of my mustaches.

Now that I see you wearing your necklace of large amber balls, dressed preferably in black velvet, raising long mustaches, your studio adorned with araneariums, and assuming that you are now ready to paint your work, knowing even in what manner it is necessary for you to sleep before beginning to paint, and as I have explained to you what you must do in order really to paint well, it is necessary, going back once more, for me to deal first with the kind of knowledge that you will need before beginning to manipulate your oil colors. For if all you had to do was to follow Rembrandt's advice, "take a brush and paint," it would be unnecessary to write this book. And never fear, the moment is bound to come, sooner or later, when you will have to take this brush in your hand if, as you fear, painter, while listening to me, you do not wish your canvas to be condemned to remain virgin, immaculate and irreparably white. But as I understand your natural impatience, and in order to satisfy it, I promise you that I shall forthwith begin the next chapter, which by itself alone, as you will presently see, is capable of making you immortal, if you are predestined to it. For it contains within its pages all the basic secrets of the first disciplines of your art.

"Jo pinto i Ford"!

(NONELL)

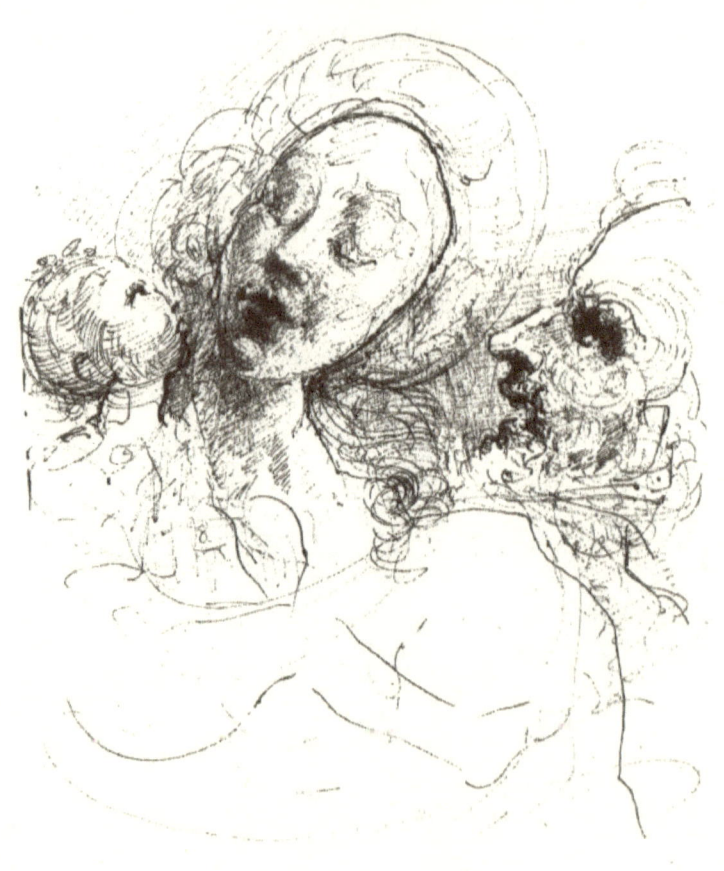

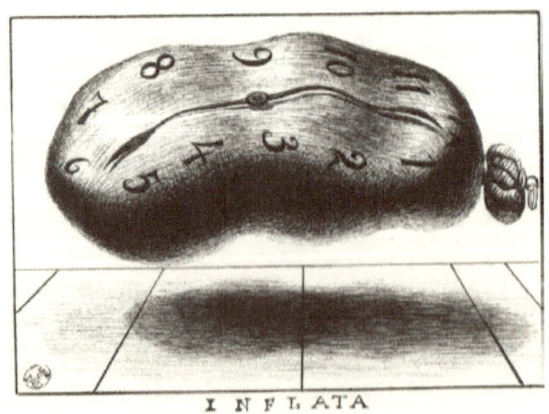

INFLATA

** It is undeniable that every good painter drools. This results from the concentration of his attention and the satisfaction which the visions appearing before his eyes procure him, visions which while they often, or perhaps only rarely, leave other mortals completely indifferent, nevertheless do not make them drool. When the painter paints, his two hands are busy, and his attention is wholly absorbed by his dream. It is quite useless to tell him to wipe the corners of his lips every few minutes, and even if his loving Gala, in her maternal solicitude, were to try to wipe them for him, she would run the risk of being pushed away, if not bitten, so much is the painter with his picture like a dog with his bone. The continual deposit of saliva on the corners of the lips produces unpleasant sores, which can be very painful, especially while eating, thus casting a shadow over this pleasure which is also so characteristic of painters. To cure these sores the painter should apply an unguent to the corners of his lips. Doctors have spoken to me about the possibility of eliminating drooling, just as perspiration can be eliminated, but this strikes me as monstrous and in contradiction to catholic theology. One must drool, but eliminate its major drawbacks, for it would be a sin to suppress entirely the pain of these mouth-sores, hence the satisfaction which produces them.

* ". . . One winter evening, as I came home, my mother, noticing that I was cold, suggested that against my habit I take a little tea. I refused at first and, I don't know why, changed my mind. She sent for one of those short, plump cakes called Little Madeleines which seem to have been molded in a grooved scallop shell. And presently, mechanically, overcome by the dreary day and the prospect of a melancholy morrow, I brought to my lips a spoonful of the tea in which I had soaked a piece of madeleine. But at the very moment when the mouthful mingled with crumbs of the cake touched my palate, I trembled, attentive to the extraordinary thing that was happening within me. A delightful pleasure had invaded me, isolated, without the notion of its cause. It had immediately made the vicissitudes of life indifferent to me, its disasters inoffensive, its briefness illusory, in the same fashion that love operates, filling me with a precious essence: or rather this essence was not within me, it *was* me. I had ceased to feel myself mediocre, contingent, mortal. . ."

(Marcel Proust: *Swann's Way.*)

*The peasants of the Emporda, my native region, have discovered from experience that the barns which are most filled and bedecked with heavy spiderwebs are those which are best for the health of their cattle. This belief is so deeply rooted that they are convinced that in a barn without spiderwebs the cattle would die.

CHAPTER FOUR

Of the painter's passion for his disciplines–Of the basic art of making a wash–Of learning to draw–Of the use of crutches to immobilize the most astonishing and airy poses of your nude models–Of the devise for obtaining the geodesic lines of a turgescent nude–Of the transfer of the sketch to the painting surface–How to become a colorist by the exclusive use of black and white–How to hold palette, brushes and maul stick–The great secret of the vulnerability called the Achilles callosity of the painter–Of the virtues and the perils of viscosity–Of experimentation and the avoidance of new agents–Of colors to be used and of those to be banned from the palette–Of the head of the painter compared to a miller–Of the technique of the imprimatura–Of the sponge of Protogenes–Of the under-painting and the wasp medium–The tale, rich in objective poetry, of how the wasp medium was discovered–Of the painter's chromatic tuning-fork–Philosophy of the viscosity of successive overpaintings by which the painting acquires body and the picture acquires a soul which sustains it–Of earthly light from which heavenly light is produced.

"Le temps enflé sera celui de tes disciplines"

S. D. 1947

AND NOW, cease thinking of your delightful and monastic painter's slumbers. Put aside the optical dreams of your araneariums, your erotic reveries of wheelbarrows. Put your amber necklace away in your drawer. For I must now awaken in you only temptations of laziness in order that, by thereby understanding them better, you may go back with me to the limpid fountains of the true scholarly disciplines which you will have to undergo at the beginning of your ninth year. You will tell me that you gladly accept the invitation, since it is in my company that you are going back, although you thought several times you were on the point of beginning to paint your picture. And you will tell me that you understand that I am speaking figuratively, since it is given to no man to go counter to the laws of time and return to the age of nine, which is what I wish you to do now.

I shall answer that you are greatly mistaken, and that time is so flexible and so relative that even while continuing to do the things which correspond to your present age you will always be able in a certain measure to take up afresh those which you should have practiced at a time which now seems lost, since it has disappeared from your day-to-day reality, but which is still within you, since you have lived it, and perhaps even more virginal and I dare say more malleable than if you could really go back to it, since at the moment when you were living it you did not make use of it, you did not touch it, as you should have done.

Do not be discouraged, therefore, and consider that if this book is above all addressed, rather than to yourself, to your pupils who are the painter's true sons—for every true painter must have pupils—you must nevertheless try out each one of the secrets of this book for yourself, for each one is intended to operate a small or a great miracle in your own work, marking it with the highest prerogatives of honor.

A fundamental truth in your painter's apprenticeship is that you must learn to draw before you even touch your brushes. Yet Secret Number 19 of this Dalinian treatise will teach you he contrary, namely, that you are going to begin to paint long before you know at all how to draw.

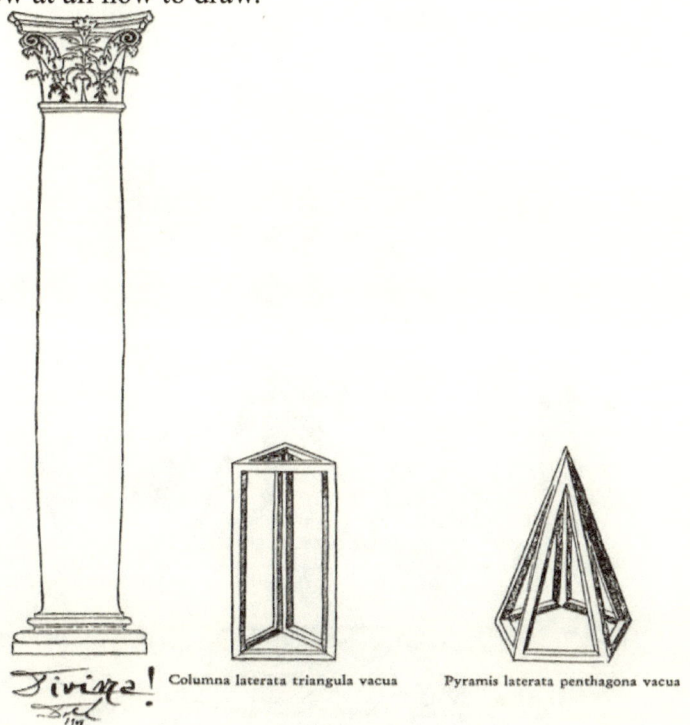

The first discipline of the painter is to make washes, first with India ink diluted with water, then with wash colors and gummed water, of geometric planes and solids, which are first to be traced from other model drawings, and later drawn by rule and compass with India ink, then their shadows washed, in monochrome to begin with, and then in polychrome. Thus from the very beginning, over tracings for which you may be completely ignorant of the science of drawing, you will wash the shadows and the modulations of simple geometric bodies, working up to the point of copying columns, pedestals and moldings, always after the immortal archetypes of Palladio and Bramante.

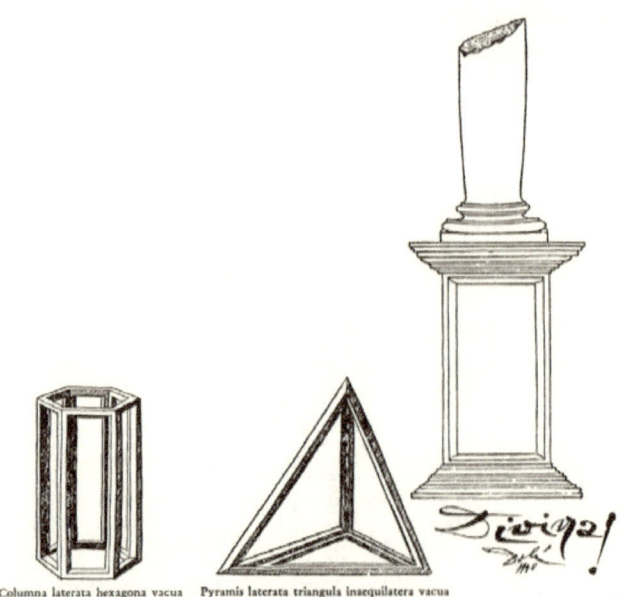

Columna laterata hexagona vacua   Pyramis laterata triangula inaequilatera vacua

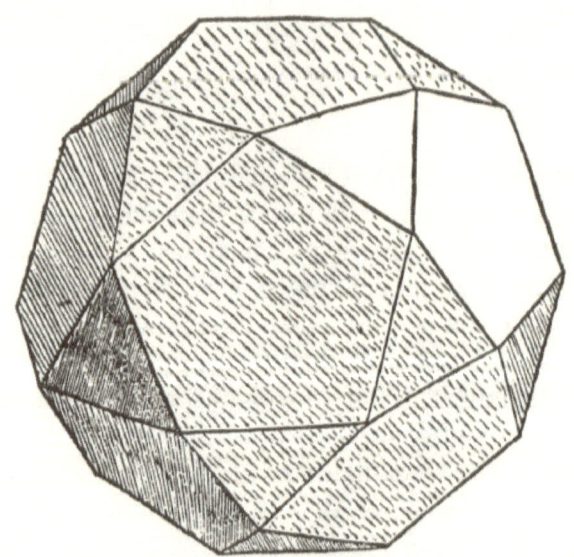

Dodecahedron abscisum solidum

For the first art with which the painter must make himself familiar is before and above all architecture. Never music, which is the enemy of painters, and injurious to them. Architecture will be for you a very superior "frozen music," since it addresses itself not to the ear but to the noblest organ, the eye. And in the optical solidity of architecture your sensibility will quickly distinguish, without anyone's teaching you, what is rhythmical and what is musical to your eye, for it is of rhythm and of melody that all the forms which you are to utilize are composed. The washes, for the practice of which you need not yet know how to draw, constitute the severest discipline that exists for a painter, for it requires an extreme dexterity, since the slightest negligence in the spreading and shading of your colors will cause these, as they dry, to make a "break," that is, an interruption impossible to eradicate, so that when you are through you will be able to count every one of your slips and errors, and you will also be able to know objectively when your work has been successfully executed.

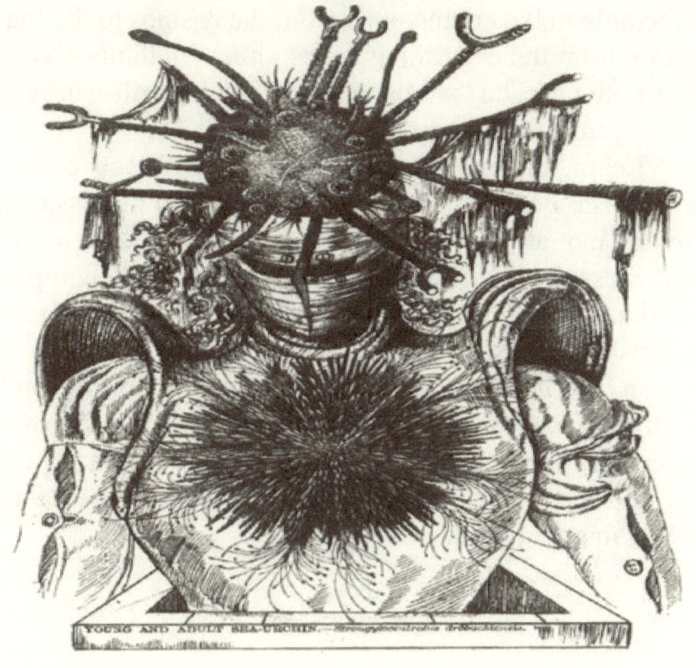

I learned to wash at the age of eleven, for this, together with drawing, is a required course in the Romanones plan for the Spanish baccalaureate. I was one of the worst students in washing, and the difficulty which it gave me caused me to work at it very stubbornly, to develop a passion for it, until I mastered it much later. I will tell you that a severe course in wash-drawing constitutes the best and the most rigorous discipline possible for a young painter, and that I look to the good wash-executors to win the future battles of the arts as in the army one looks to those who have gone through St. Cyr or West Point. Washing will give you the feeling for that high aspiration which lined with angelic wrinkles and pentagons the face of Mantegna, "the passion for not going beyond the line," the inexorable consciousness of limits. Know that the whole rest of your life will be for you nothing but drawing limits, reducing, substantializing, essentializing, impoverishing yourself! To pass from the much to the little, from the complex to the particular, from the innumerable to the enumerable, from the cosmos to the logos, that is to say, from the everything to the almost nothing—but what an almost nothing! The "almost nothing" which will win or lose the battle of your life as a painter.

Learn, therefore, coldly, but spiritedly and courageously how to wash. For this task requires a cold and dispassionate state of mind and at the same time a bold and extremely ardent decisiveness, for which reason I have just so aptly compared it to the military art. In my judgment it was in the period of Louis XIV that wash drawings were executed with the most military precision, and it is for this reason that I wish to bring you back to this dazzling and radiant epoch of mastery, so that you will begin to trace and then to wash a few plans, architectural elements, plane or solid, in the manner which they practiced, and this is how you must proceed.

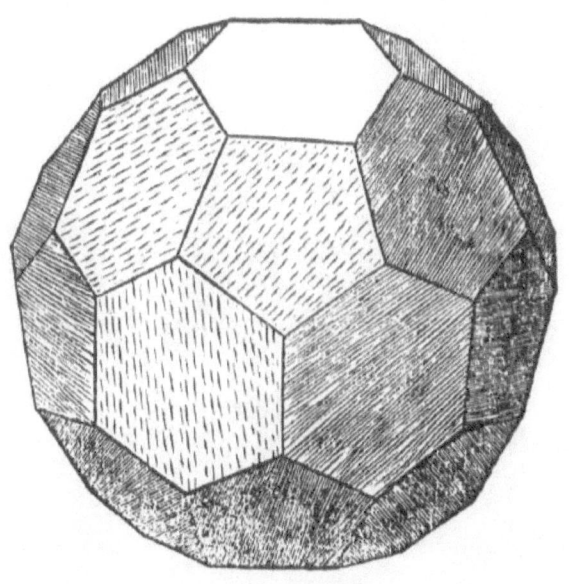

Icosahedron abscisum solidum

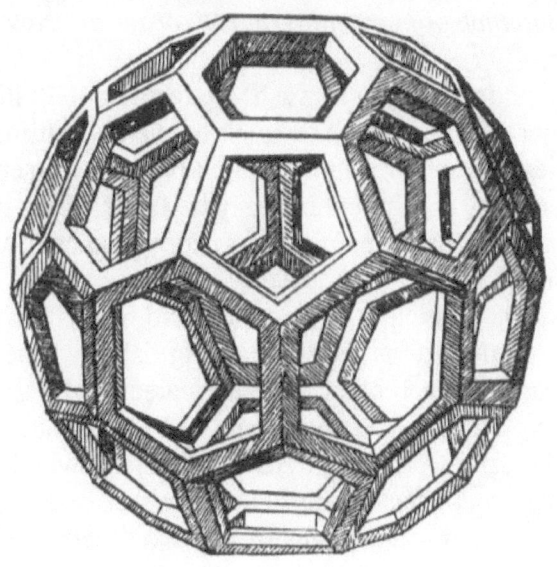

Icosahedron abscisum vacuum

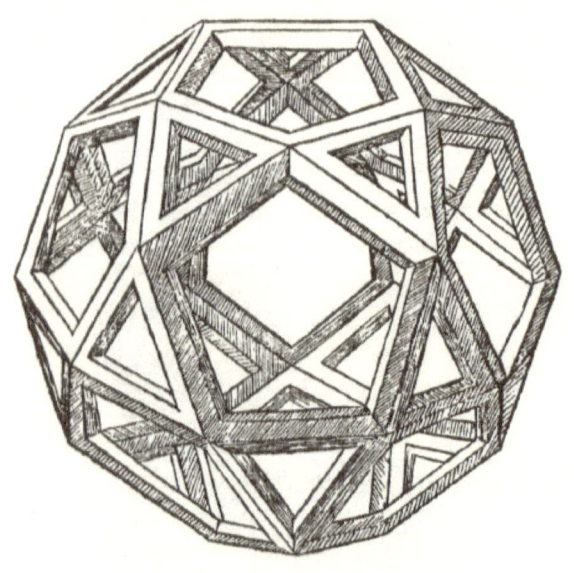

Dodecahedron abscisum vacuum

Of the manner of marking a plan in order to draw it from the original.

Before undertaking to wash a fortification Plan, or whatsoever other plan it may be, it must be clearly outlined: one ordinarily copies it from an original which has already served, or which is old, or dirty, or where there may be faults which must be corrected. However it may be, in order to copy it so as to wash it, this is the manner in which to proceed:

Take the plan which is to be copied and place it on a sheet of paper of the same size as that of the original. To fasten these two sheets of paper to each other there are persons who join them with pins, which puncture the sheets and are thus undesirable. It is better to make use of pincers of steel or of brass, which can be tightened together by means of rings as securely as one may wish, and which are attached to the edges of the two sheets of paper to keep them firmly together. These pincers are to be extremely flat and even, and so made that no matter how hard they press together the sheets of paper they leave no impression upon them.

The two sheets being well joined and spread flat on a large carton placed on the table, one begins by pricking the angles or the points where the lines cross and cut one another upon the Plans. These prickings are performed by means of a very small needle set into a small stick for a handle. It pierces through the two Plans. There be Engineers who do not esteem this method, and who hold it to be better to indent the Plans gently, so that the point used for this may be merely impressed upon the other sheet of paper which is beneath.

Whichever manner you may use, after you have marked the points of the entire original work, you detach your copy, removing the pins or the pincers which you used to join these. And the sheet of paper being entirely covered with pin holes or impressions, one then draws from one point to another lines similar to those which are traced in the original. These lines are first drawn with the pencil of which the point is so divided as to form a double line. The drawing being completed in pencil one then covers the lines with India ink, which finishes the work in respect of its features only. In following this procedure, one incurs no danger of error in copying a drawing. For should it occur that one draws lines with the pencil which are not necessary, having taken one point for another, the error is easily corrected by effacing these same lines with soft bread crumb. Even should the work not appear soiled, it is nevertheless necessary to use this before washing the same. For after one has drawn all the lines with India ink, and after the ink is dry, one then rubs the entire drawing with crumb of white bread. This crumb must be not too fresh, for in this case it would adhere to the paper as one rubs.

Of gummed water to prepare the colors, and the precaution that must be used in grinding these.

Since the colors which have much body are those which most require to be gummed in order that they may adhere to the paper after they have been applied, use must also be made of gummed water, which is prepared in the following manner:

Take gum arabic of the clearest and free from impurity of the size of a nut, which you will bray rather coarsely in a marble mortar. Place this gum in a glass vial which contains approximately six or seven ounces of water. Stir the water and the gum every three hours with a small wooden spatula. Once the gum is dissolved, this solution is to be used to grind the colors which require it. But in order that you may know them, here they are in their order.

Gummed water is to be used to grind lamp black, white lead, lemon yellow massicot, golden massicot, yellow arsenic (orpiment), realgar, yellow lake, ocher, *cendres bleues,* ultramarine, cinnabar, red oxide of lead (minium), lake, carmine, red chalk (hematite), red brown, *vert distille, vert de vessie,* verditer, raw umber and bister. Some require more, others less.

The colors are ordinarily ground on a marble stone, and to clean it one must rub it with sand and water; which renders it extremely clean. If it has been used for grinding color with oil, which has since hardened, one must, after scraping away the thickest part, rub it with sand moistened with oil of turpentine. If the marble has had oil but freshly used upon it, it will suffice to rub it with bread crumb. Some may prefer to treat it with soap, etc. Thus, the marble being clean, one takes the color one wishes to use, the size of a fair hazelnut should suffice, which one grinds rather coarsely; adding thereupon a small quantity of plain water, the color is reduced to a paste, and it is ground until it is extremely smooth. One may know when it has been sufficiently ground by taking a small amount with the tip of the finger or with a brush and passing it over the fingernail. If it seems granulated and rough, it requires more grinding; otherwise not. If in grinding the color it should dry, it must immediately be moistened with plain water. And when one wishes to remove it from the marble, which is done with a horn or an ivory edge, one adds gummed water in order to secure the color to the paper when it is used. One grinds it immediately with this gummed water, and thereupon removes it from the marble with the edge, rather than with a knife, of which the iron would darken the colors, and places it in a saucer or a shell, to be treated in advance as I shall now show.

Of shells and saucers in which to keep the colors.

After the colors have been ground, they are placed in shells or saucers. The shells are to be treated in the following manner. One takes a certain number of shells which one soaks for three or four days in fountain water. They are then boiled in a pot full of water and dried. They are now ready to receive the color which you wish to put in them. You place different colors in several of these shells, which you keep, and which you must protect from dust.

Lacking these shells, saucers or bowls of ivory or boxwood may be used with even better results. But those of ivory are infinitely cleaner, and the color appears in them more purely. These saucers are steady when one places them on a table to work with them; whereas the shells, if the table is shaken ever so little, will rock in all directions and may even tip over, thereby spilling the color, if it has been diluted. All these accidents may be remedied by using saucers having the following shape. They are round, hollow within, and flat outside. Their diameter is one and one-half inch, their thickness at the bottom, which is flat, is no more than the thickness of a line, and the edges the thickness of three lines, or a little more. If they be made of wood, they must be made a little thicker; but if they be of ivory, the dimensions which I have already specified will suffice.

The manner of using the colors which are in the saucers.

When you are disposed to work you must have all things in readiness to this end. You place yourself in front of a table, then, which must receive its light from the left side only of where you are posted. On this table must be set out all the saucers in a row, at the end of which must be a glass half full of water, on the top of which will be your two brushes resting by the middle across the top. At the foot of this glass, at a distance of a few inches, you must place your ink stand within easy reach of your right hand. This ink stand must be provided with two or three good pens of different degrees of fineness to make lines whether thick or slender. The space of the table which is between the saucer and your stomach will be occupied by the plan, or drawing, which you wish to wash. And to the right of the plan you will have another piece of white paper which will serve to determine if the colors are too light or too strong; which is done by applying the color upon it, with a brush, which you wish to use on the plan. Between your knees you will hold a clean white cloth which will serve to wipe the brushes, or your fingers, should they become stained with color. The plan being already traced by black lines which have been drawn with india ink, or ink made with lampblack, you cover your plan with a sheet of paper so as not to soil it, and you leave exposed only the space which is to be washed. You even cover the saucers if necessary so that the dust will not tarnish the colors.

All things thus being ready, and the color which you wish to use being dry, you dip the brush which is lying on the glass into the water in the glass and apply the brush to the color in the saucer which you hold in your left hand. After having passed the brush several times over the color it will easily dissolve, having been well gummed. You take some of this color and assay it on the paper which is beside the plan, and you see if it is sufficiently thick, or sufficiently light. You apply it to the point which you wish, adding more water to the saucer if it is too thick. You then apply your color entire if you are not to shade it as Column A shows you; or, if it is to be shaded, as Column C shows you, you apply just a little of it as it is marked in Column B. Color B being still fresh, with the other brush which is at the other end of the handle of the first brush you blend Color B as delicately as you can in the white space of this Column B. And thus Column B becomes like Column C. You will do likewise with all the other colors.

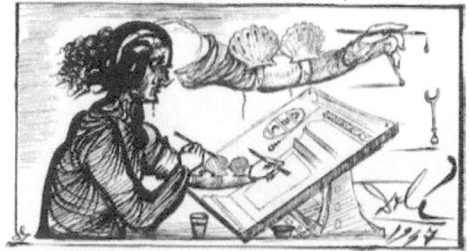

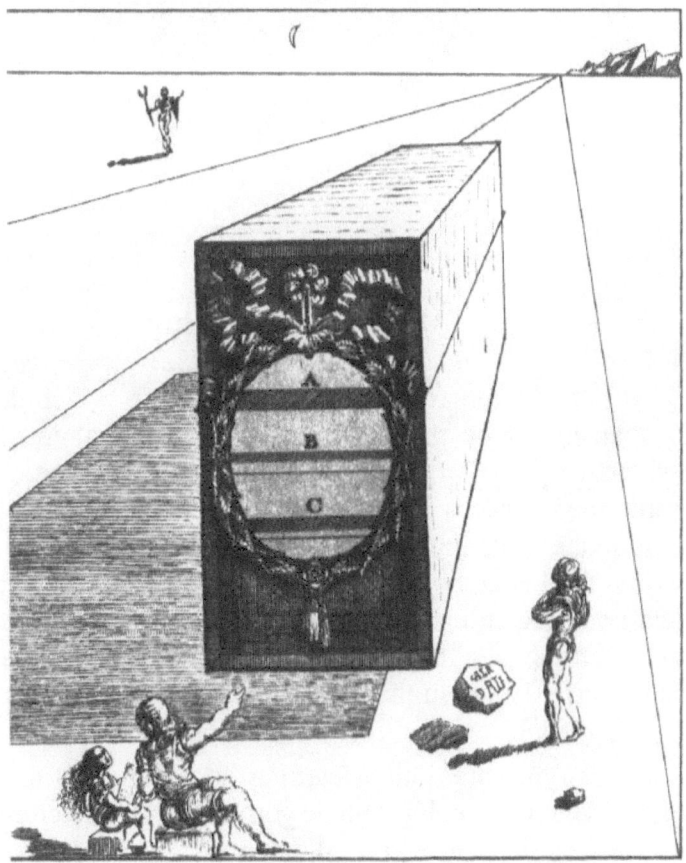

As most novices are not accustomed to manipulating a brush, they will have some difficulty in the beginning and may feel quite incapable of achieving a satisfactory result. In order to accustom themselves they will have to combine several of these Columns B, reducing them to C. Having done this they will soon acquire the necessary skill. One day of habit and patience will enable them to accomplish their undertaking.

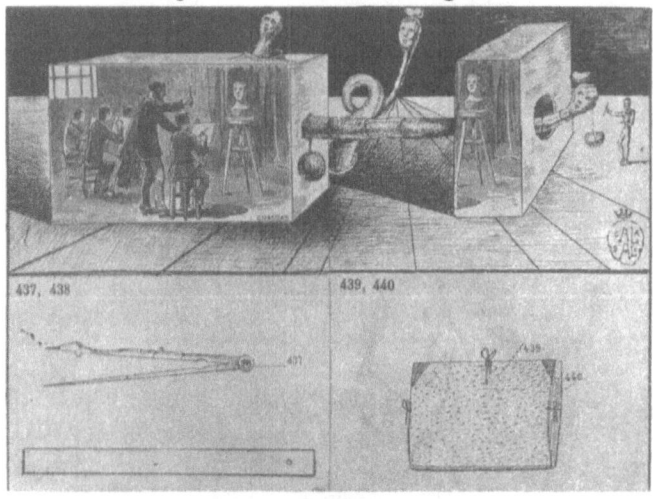

It must be remarked that there are colors which dry more easily than others on the paper. Thus the more gummed colors will shine longer after they have been applied. Moreover, the most gummed paper will be found to be the best, and one is not likely to make spots in the wash. It is therefore necessary that for this work the paper be very white, smooth, fine of texture and well gummed. A little practice will enable persons with the least aptitude for the slightest task to overcome this first and last obstacle; and it is herein that the whole essence of wash-drawing consists.—*

Thus you are daily learning to wash the images of geometry which are being taught you and of architecture which are being edified for you. You are, so to speak, being uninterruptedly nourished by these two Supremely edifying sciences. Simultaneously, or at some point of your progress in this study, you will have to begin to learn the science of drawing. And I cannot claim it as a secret when I tell you—in spite of the fact that it is not frequently said nowadays—that the best way to learn to draw is to have a good drawing teacher. I shall be telling you somewhat more when I affirm that even if he is a bad teacher, this is better than having none at all, so true it is that four eyes see more than two. This is a case in which the truth and discernment of the teacher's eye count less than his disinterestedness in seeing what your lack of disinterestedness prevents you from seeing. For you, in your stubbornness, will struggle for hours in order to convince yourself, with a thousand sophisms and subterfuges, that your error is correct, whereas to other, impartial eyes, your defect will appear obvious, for it awaits only impartiality in order to jump forth like a flea held prisoner beneath the anxious, unjust and sweating finger of your prejudice.

But if the assistance of a drawing teacher is not a secret, I shall immediately announce to you my Secret Number 20, which will teach you the most effective way to learn to draw without errors. The method of beginning to draw directly from nature and without the intermediary of pictures is the right one, and also that of working first from plaster casts after the antique before going over to the living models. Here is my method for learning how to draw: the plaster model is placed behind a glass marked into squares, and facing a mirror in such a way that what you will see and draw will be its reflection. And in this reflection, of course, the image of the object will be reversed. In some cases the model may advantageously be placed upside down. The reason for this reversal is that when you copy your model in this way, the preconceived image of its "intellectual representation," the conventional cliche which its associations have formed in your mind, which constitute such a hindrance to the beginner, disappears as by enchantment, and after very few sessions of practicing this method all the vices of infantilism which persist so stubbornly among apprentices in drawing will vanish. After having drawn your model in reverse, draw it again lying down, on the same scale—that is, filling the same number of squares. Put your model back into its vertical position, and in this normal position you can then correct your two drawings. Also when you draw, whether directly or in reverse, make an abstraction of what the object you are copying represents, see only forms before you, without giving them any kind of name, and preferably, instead of outlining two legs, try rather to reproduce faithfully the empty space that separates them. Thus I always recommend placing two plasters next to each other, framed by a rectangle, also of plaster, in order to draw above all the outlines formed by the empty spaces of the background. Likewise every figure must be begun with the big toe, and it is a grave mistake to begin, as you must never do, with the head. But this exercise must be done without any squared guide, and only when you have begun to master the problem of proportions. This corresponds to the troubling moment when, abandoning the scholastic coldness of the plasters, you begin to use the living, warm molds of flesh and blood which you have been looking forward to, the tingling anticipation of which has filled your professional reveries.

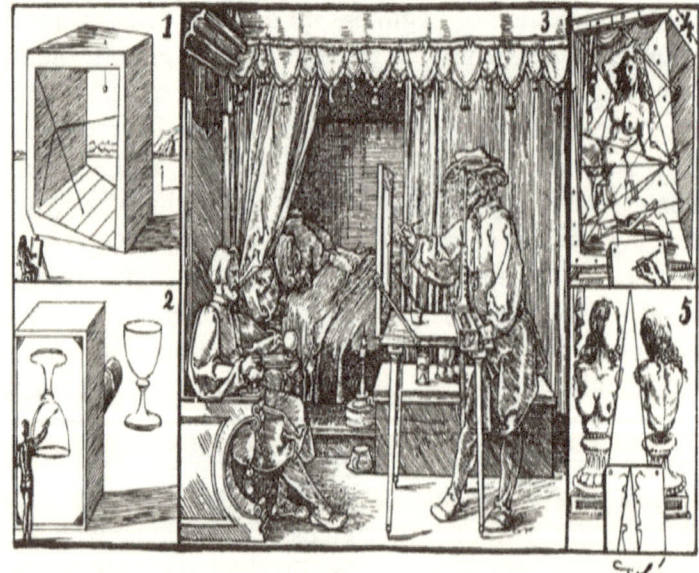

FIG. 1 *assymetric cage to place the models.* 2 *Gigantic dark chamber to trace the inverted figures.* 4 *Harmonic cage for models.* 5 *Triangle of empty spaces.*

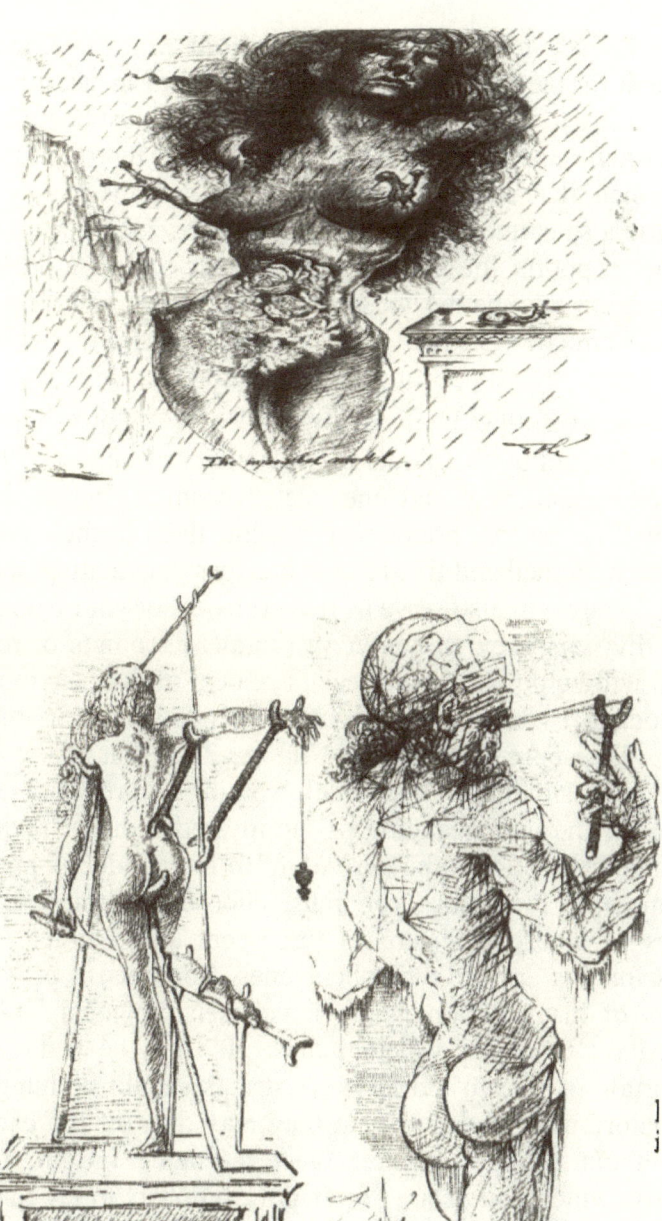

I shall tell you that this itch of your imagination is excellent for the painter and that it opens, so to speak, the appetite of the desire to paint, to such a point that you must begin by using nine crutches, so that you will not be dazzled by too much flesh. Learn then, that Secret Number 21 of drawing the nude from life is to use a substitute for the squares that served you as guides, as abstract supports for the copying of your plaster models. Now that you are eliminating those abstract crutches you will have to use real crutches, so that your models, *especially* your models, may begin by supporting their anatomies on them. These crutches, which may be of various dimensions and which may be readily utilized by the model to the number of nine,[*] will give to the body astonishing and unexpected postures, but at the same time will act as true crutches to support them in their poses and keep them pinned and fixed like butterflies "meditating upon their flight." They will also serve as real crutches for your eye, for with these divisions they will offer you numerous points of reference which will help you to place each accident of their anatomy as in a melodic network, a kind of lyrical appendage to their attitudes.

The apprentice's Secret Number 22 is that of the drawing of the geodesic lines of his model. Nothing will reveal itself more useful for the understanding of the mysteries of the nude figure than the knowledge to be derived from the assiduous practice of this method. Preferably you must choose a plump model, the curves of whose flesh are as turgescent as possible. The best poses for this are the recumbent ones. You need a provision of strings of black cotton which have been previously soaked in linseed oil to which venetian turpentine has been added, in a proportion of five to three. These strings should be hung up the day before using them, so that they may drip off the excess oil, but without drying altogether. Once the model is lying down in the pose which you desire you begin cautiously to lay the strings on the model's body in the places where you wish a clearer indication of the forms. The curve which these strings adopt will naturally be the geodesic lines of the surface which you want made clear. You may then draw your nude, but especially these geodesic lines which, if they are in sufficient quantity, will suffice—even should you efface the nude—to imprint its absent volume.

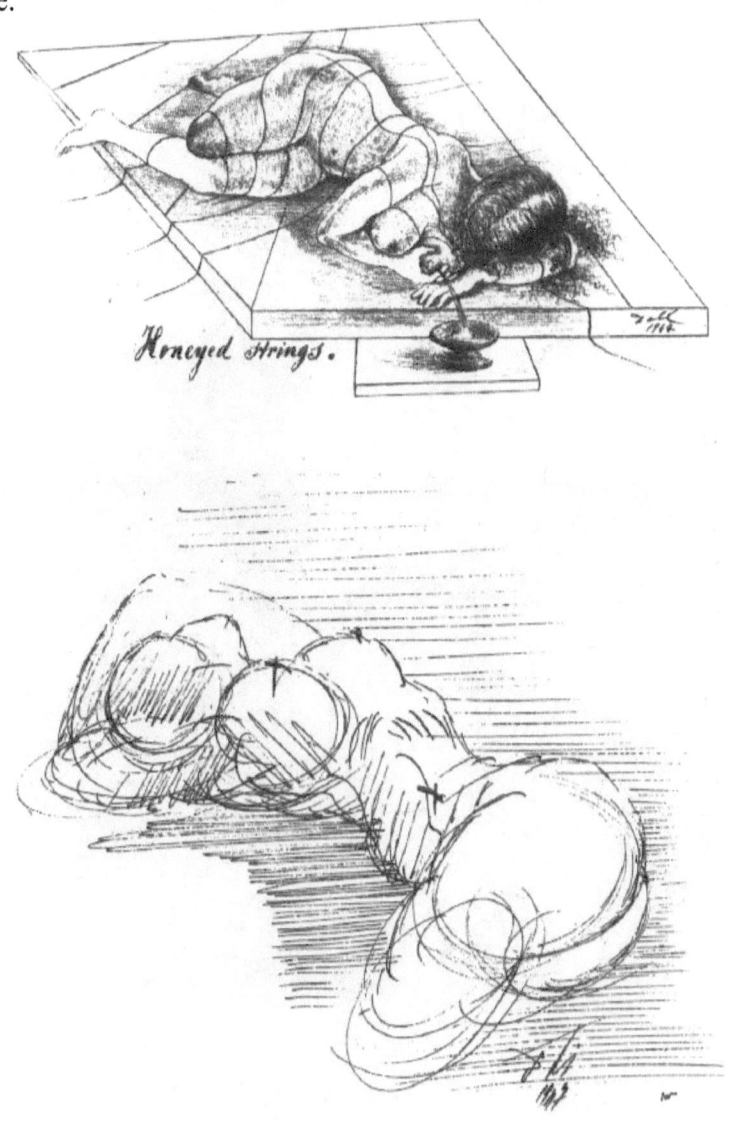

In the same manner, pentagonal cages and other derivatives of these obtained by tautly drawn strings can form networks singularly propitious to exercises in drawing. By degrees you will discard all your glasses, squarings, crutches and other paraphernalia and your drawing must attack directly the unencumbered and total nakedness of your model and of the string, naked as a worm, at the end of which a mere suspended ball of lead will mark the force of gravity of your situation.

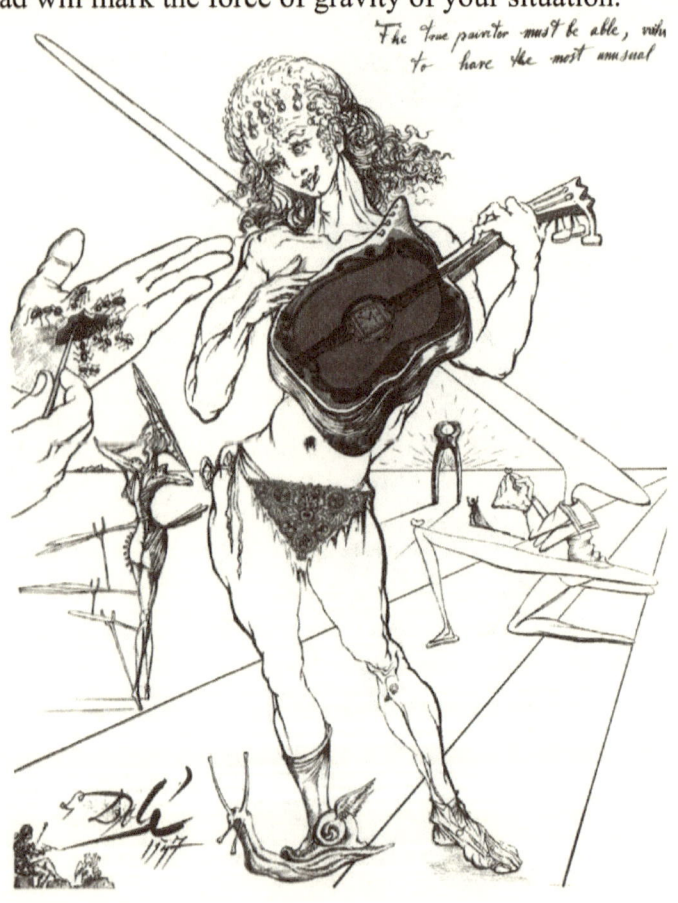

The true painter must be able, to to have the most unusual

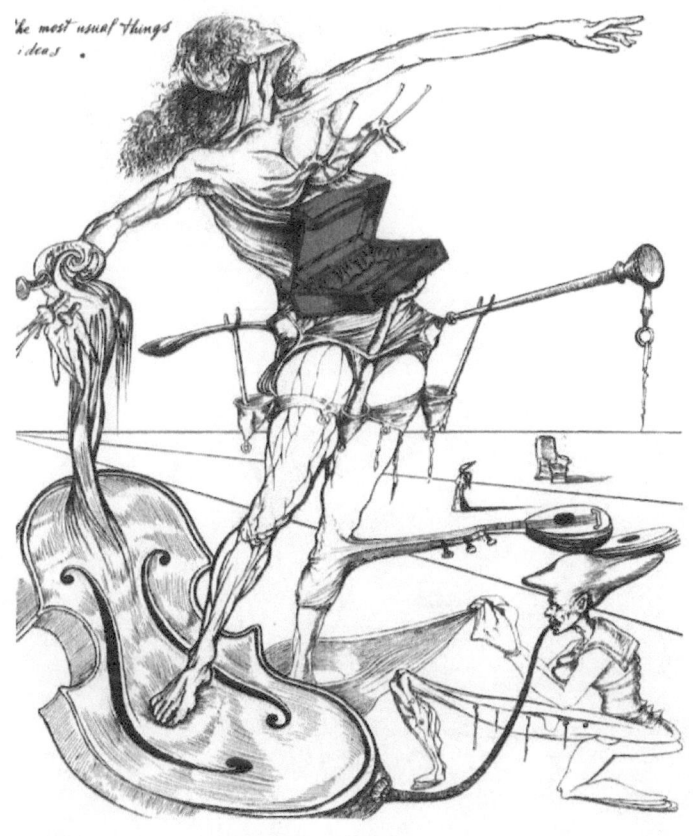

By the time you have acquired proficiency in drawing I advise you in turn to undress completely, for it is necessary for you to feel, as you are drawing, the design of your own body, as well as the august reality of the contact of your bare feet with the floor: for the man who knows how to draw and who, charcoal in hand, is able at last to draw what he wants, feels himself to have become a kind of god—and sensations of that kind I very strongly advise you to experience in a state of total nudity, rather than clothed. Know this as Secret Number 23.

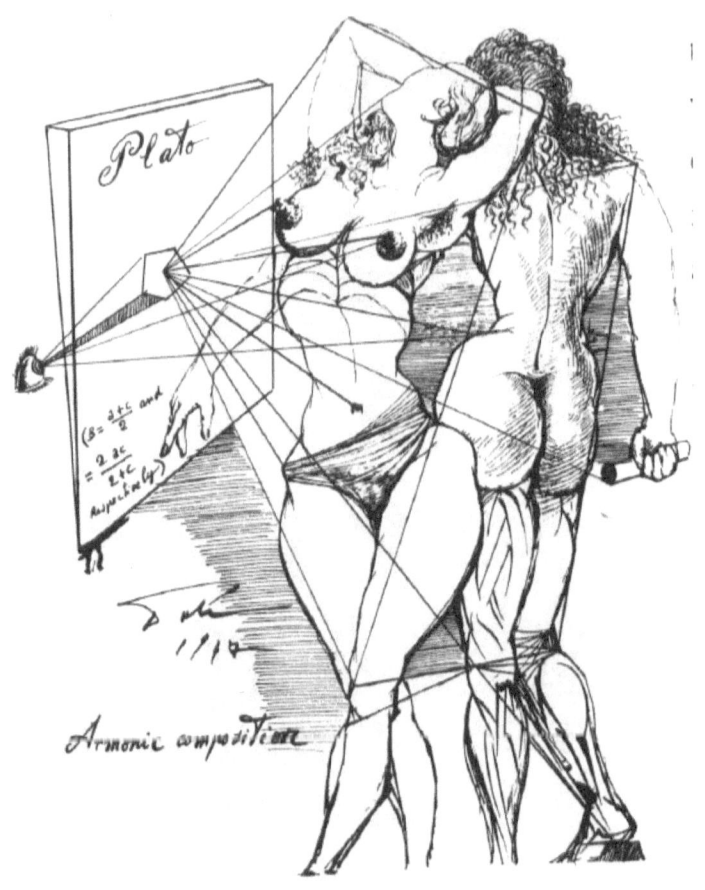

You may be certain that it is when you have learned to draw that the moment has come for you to learn anatomy. Mr. Ingres was a mortal enemy of anatomy and, in this sense, the mortal enemy of Benvenuto Cellini who professed a fervent passion for it. And just as Ingres recommends to the student to go ahead and copy masses without concerning himself with what is beneath, with whether the hump in question is a chin or an elbow, and would therefore have had no hesitation in approving of my

Secret Number 20 of drawing the model in reverse with as little understanding as possible, so the fiery Benvenuto who, on the contrary, would not hear of drawing any form of the human body without knowing exactly what lay under it in the way of muscles, and especially of bones, would just as surely have categorically disapproved of the Dalinian method. Yet in this I am superior to Ingres and Cellini, for unlike them in their partiality, I assure you that both were just about equally in the right. You must begin to draw with a total disregard for what you are representing, but when you have achieved mastery in placing the things that you see in the real space in the presentation of your drawing—then comes the moment to begin to know what is lodged in each of the parts, so that in knowing it, and only through the imponderables which this knowledge will vouchsafe you, you will be able to add the spark of truth which your too blindly academic drawing runs the risk of not having. When you know how to draw, but only then, the use of snapshots in certain cases may be valuable to you. You must realize that a camera is rigid and mechanical and your eye on the contrary is soft and full of an inventive whimsicality which the poor lens in no wise possesses. Hence if you are anxious to execute a pose or a foreshortening having great truth, I recommend to you rather to project, as the ancient masters did, unusual shadows of your models on the walls, quickly tracing the outlines with the help of two or three of your pupils at a time. After a reflective choice you will easily be able to fill in the body of these outlines with the corresponding muscles and shadows from life, using the same models.

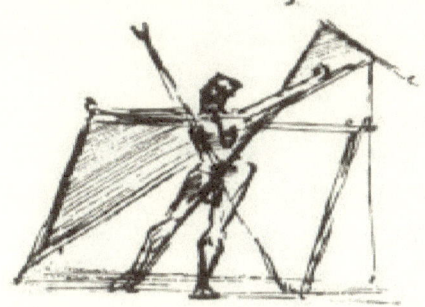

But I must leave off here on the subject of drawing, which deserves a treatise by itself. Remember only that the whole lofty morality of your work depends on knowing how to draw well, and that Mr. Ingres wished to inculcate into you deeply this patrician idea, engraving it with the sharp point of his severe and juridical pencil when he wrote, in order that you should always remember it, that "drawing is the probity of art."

And now, since I am quite disposed to consider you, as you assure me you have become, a past master in the art of washing the most subtle architectural elements, of placing your figures in space according to the laws of perspective, and since you tell me that you already have resolved a subject in your mind which you want very much to paint, I shall accede to your entreaties.

Let me tell you forthwith that I want you to paint your first work on a gesso-covered wood panel, nonabsorbent and as smooth as possible—which is the most difficult surface to handle, but which at the same time will enable you to attain the highest degree of perfection. I shall assume that your panel has had the best of preparation. I shall not go into the making of the painting materials and tools, for this is to be the subject of a special treatise.

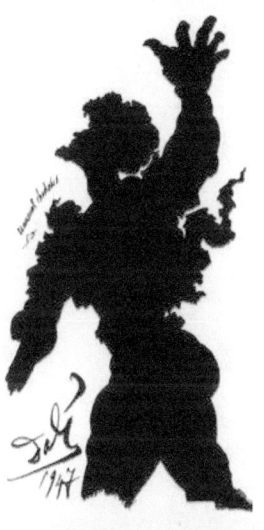

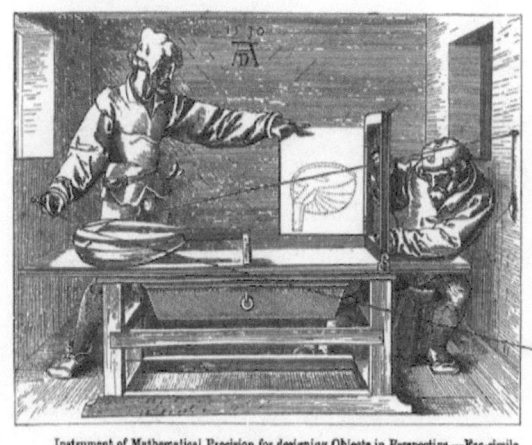
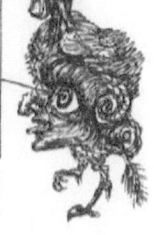

Instrument of Mathematical Precision for designing Objects in Perspective.—Fac-simile of a Wood Engraving from Albert Dürer's Work, "Institutionum Geometricarum Libri Quatuor" (Parisiis, ex officina Christiani Wecheli, 1535, in folio).—In the Library of M. Ambroise Firmin-Didot, Paris.

First, do not fail to keep ever present in your mind that the most fanatical cleanliness is, and must remain, insufficient to your task. Thus it is that I recommend to you, to begin with, not only that your studio be built in such a way as to receive the best light, but also that the center of the platform on which you work be as isolated as possible from dust or floating particles. Your panel must be washed with water, using a hard brush which at the same time does not streak. Let the gesso panel dry and rinse it once more with distilled water. Before you proceed to trace your drawing on it, you must let it dry a minimum of three days, after which you will transfer your tracing to it according to the following directions, which constitute Secret Number 24.

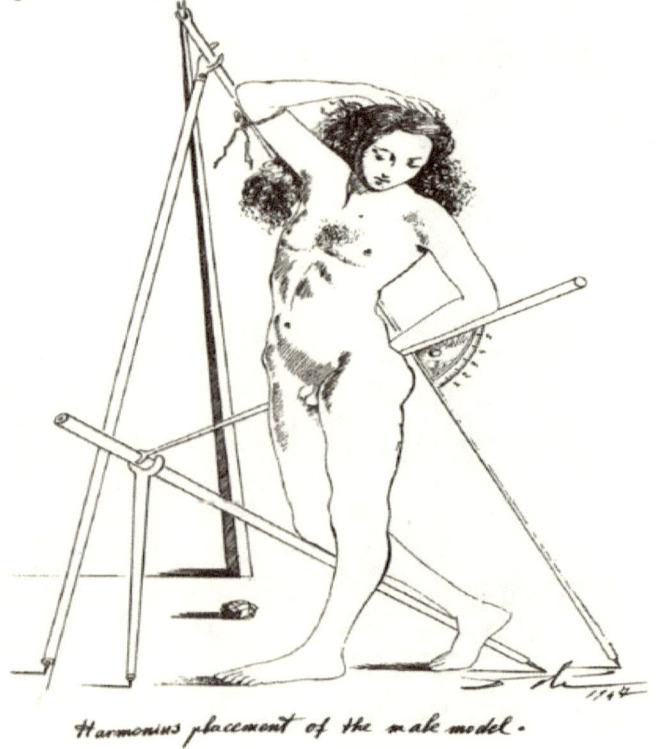

Harmonius placement of the male model.

For this you will proceed as do the engravers to transfer their tracing to their copper plate. In other words, you will engrave your drawing by means of a needle or other extremely fine point on a sheet of cellophane of the right size. Then you will daub your tracing with oil paint, a mixture of zinc white and burnt umber—a color which dries the fastest of all the colors in your palette and excellent for this, but solely for this, since in my Instrument of Mathematical Precision for designing Objects in

Perspective.—Fac-simile of a Wood Engraving from Albert Dürer's Work, "Institutionum Geometricarum Libri Quatnor" (Pariaiis, ex officina Christiani Wecheli, 1535, in folio).—In the Library of M. Ambroise Firmin-Didot, Paris. Secret Number 30, I shall give you the reasons for banishing it wholly and without exception from your palette. With the white and the burnt umber you will make a tint just sufficiently perceptible to enable you to see clearly the finest details of your tracing. This paint must be applied without any varnish or drier, so that your tint will penetrate the indentation of each line engraved in your cellophane. Thus you will easily be able to rub the latter's surface in order to clean it, without fear of removing the paint deposited in the lines of your engraving. Once it is clean, you must even rewipe the whole two or three times with a flat buffer slightly moistened with ammonia in order to remove the oiliness which might remain on the surface. Having done this, you apply the face of your tracing to your panel laid out horizontally, and using an engraver's roller you press it as you would to obtain a printing of an etching. Otherwise you can rub your tracing by means of a spatula smoothed with a light oil and go over your tracing with a gentle pressure until you obtain a complete transfer. This method is the only clean way of obtaining a perfect tracing of the most detailed drawing executed directly in oil paint, without the foreign bodies of charcoal or pencil, the particles of which constitute an annoyance and a hazard to your subsequent work. You know already that the use of carbon paper for the transfer of tracings intended for an artistic painting is sacrilegious, but since those who tell you this conceal the rest, know that charcoal, and especially lead pencils, are also bad. In your picture there must be only pure color and its appropriate media. Very good india ink in solid form diluted with water creates a gray which is very satisfactory for preparing the drawing on the panel, but as one cannot trace directly with this ink, you will first have to transfer your drawing with powdered lead and then go over every line with india ink. Do not forget to wash your panel again after this has been completed, in order to remove the powdered lead, and then let it dry for at least a day before beginning to paint.

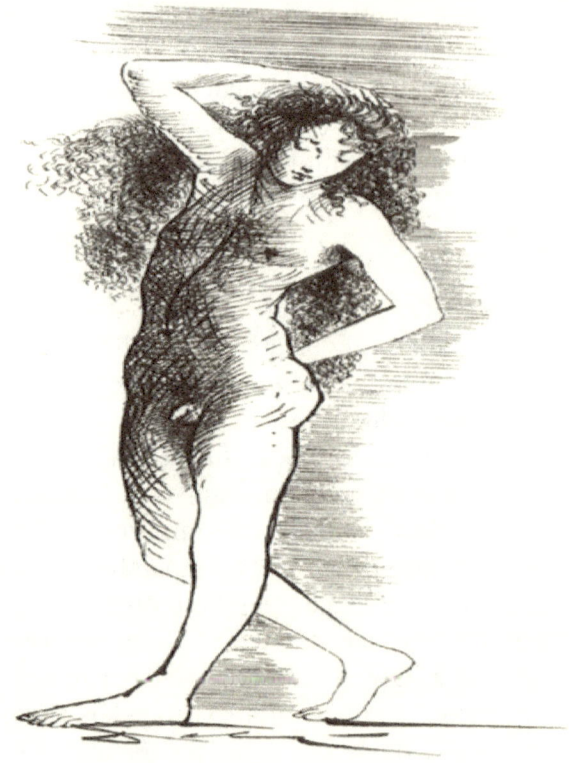

After your rigorous discipline in wash drawing, oil painting which you can handle wet without haste will at first appear to you an easy matter and will procure you a great deal of satisfaction. But I warn you immediately that to paint well means always obtaining a painted surface which completely covers your panel with the most homogeneous and continuous coat and with the least possible thickness. This will give you plenty of trouble and worry, to such a point that at the beginning it will seem to you impossible to succeed. For I shall ask that after each session you examine the surface which you have painted against the light, that is to say, with a lamp striking it with its rays as obliquely as possible. Then you will be able to observe, with discouragement, how irregular, harsh and clumsy the coat of matter you have spread on the panel is, bristling with hairs and a thousand foreign bodies, and how much more smooth and noble it was before you touched it. When, on the contrary, you know how to apply your color with science and art, your surface will become more smooth and burnished and clean after you have worked on it than before. Thus it is in examining your work each evening in a grazing light that you may and must judge the progress you are making in the unity and continuity of your matter.

Since you are so fortunate as to be able to read this book, in which nothing that is given as a secret is to be found written anywhere else, do not be astonished if I now declare to you— and this is Secret Number 25—that the two most beautiful and useful colors that exist are white and black, and that the true nobility of the art of every colorist depends on the knowledge of how to utilize these as the basis of your pictorial work.*

After your West Point of wash drawing, I therefore advise you to devote six months to executing monochrome paintings from plasters, for which you will use solely your two blacks and your two whites. In this connection I must teach you one thing which is not a secret to any painter, but which will immediately become one as soon as it is told you by me. It is in fact known that the bright parts of your picture corresponding to the light must be painted with more matter than the dark parts corresponding to the shadows, to such a point that the latter can never be sufficiently thin and immaterial, whereas for the others I will allow you to add as many layers as you wish, even to obtaining a thickness sufficient to be considered "impasto." Well, I shall give you now the name of a unique color and I advise you—this being Secret Number 26—always and without exception to mix in more or less perceptible doses for every kind of shadow some Naples yellow, which is the atmospheric color *par excellence;* to use this color whenever your shadows are invaded by air and even by breezes, if you are painting a landscape.* And you must also know that the most beautiful yellows are obtained by spreading aureolin over Naples yellow.

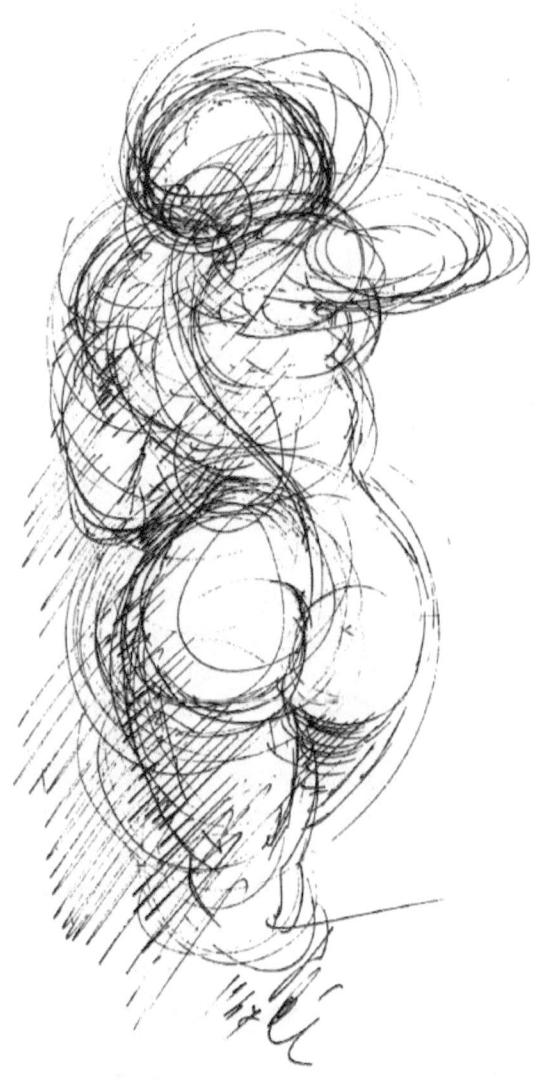

Hence the six months which I will allow you in order that you may experience for yourself the virtues of black and white. In this connection, here is what you must know. *Blanc d'argent* dries very promptly and covers very homogeneously, and these are always the properties that you must seek for building your foundations. Whereas zinc white, more subtle, but infinitely more luminous, must always be applied as final coatings and over the *blanc d'argent* for everything that is to be glorious— a smile, or the down of a swan. On the other hand, your blacks will dry most slowly of all the colors and their whole virtue resides therein. Respect this in them. For know that in painting, the blacks are the most transparent colors, not from the physical point of view but in regard to the subtleties of their nuances. Thus it is that great colorists like Velasquez did not hesitate to use it to paint their most celestial and exquisitely pure flesh tones. The tonality of ivory black is imperceptibly ivory, and the tonality of blue black is cold, with an imperceptible blue tinge. Likewise with your whites: your silver white is warm and your zinc white icy.

The coloring of the good painter is based wholly on the rhythmic and melodic utilization of the warm and cold tonalities. Know then that one can already know if you are a great colorist, and in fact it is the surest way of knowing it, by having you execute a painting solely with whites and blacks in a single color, which is called monochrome, or camaieu painting.

As the first painting that you should practice is camaieu painting, before you are initiated to the other mysteries, know that a necessary condition of all painting is that it should dry naturally. A picture is not a door which must dry fast so that people's hands and clothes will not stick to it. Here is my secret: never use in painting driers of any kind, for Secret Number 27 is that the virtue of painting is that it should dry slowly and evenly.

As for the blacks, the ivory black you will use for the under-painting, and the blue black as you do the zinc white, for the song. This has never been said, and you may count it as Secret Number 28 of the good colorist. For you may even glaze with blue black on a camaieu painting painted *a la prima* with the two blacks, and the new grays thus obtained will be diaphanous. Whereas in proceding contrariwise, that is to say by glazing with ivory black on blue black, your grays will be dirty and pasty.

That is your problem as a colorist—to paint in camaieu, and to make blue tones appear without blue, solely by the play of the airy values of your Naples yellow, which you will utilize in certain warm parts of your shadows, which will give the illusion of bright, warm yellows in the luminous parts of the "impastos" of the silver whites. If you can become a master in this exercise, which is no longer—notice!—camaieu painting, but Dalinian painting, you may tell yourself that you know how to paint!

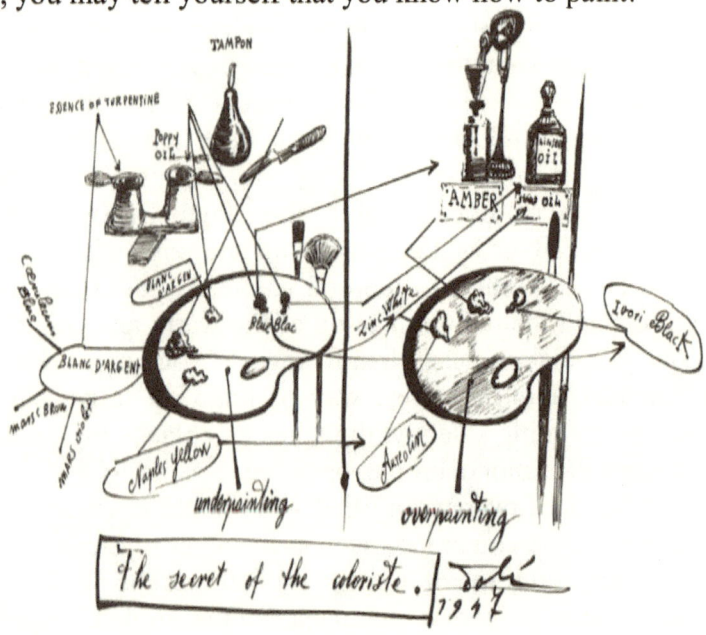

I must tell you now what media you must use for mixing your whites and your blacks, for it is essential that each of these extremely personal colors be treated in its. own special way. But before slipping into the viscosity of the oils, listen to the great secret of the painter's Achilles callosity.

A number of painters consider as a great secret the manner and order in which they place the colors on their palette. I shall tell you that such secrets exist, but that your instinct must find them for you, for this depends wholly on the degree of classicism or of romanticism of the work which you are destined to accomplish. If you are a classic, a rigorous and immutable order in the placing of the colors will be of great aid to you. For, being an enemy of every kind of surprise which might disturb the rules, you will thus be able to find each "local color" and even each intermediary nuance always exactly in the same place. So that it has been claimed that painters, for hours on end, did not need to glance at their palette for an instant: the well-trained hand would find, in its precise place, the shade that it required and thus the eyes, not having to be distracted, could look uninterruptedly at their picture without for a moment relinquishing their hold on the prey of their model.

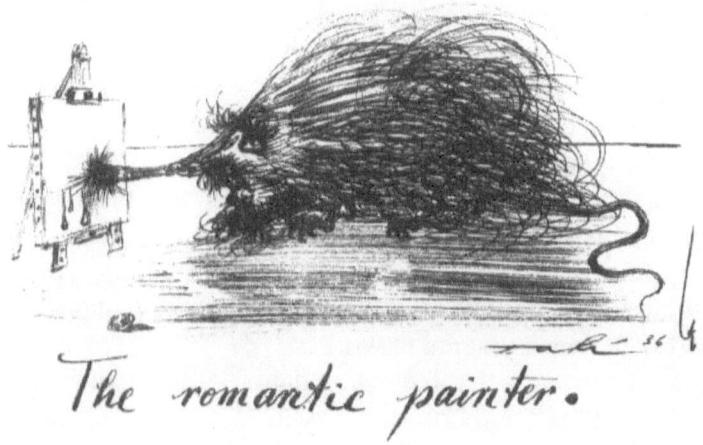

The romantic painter.

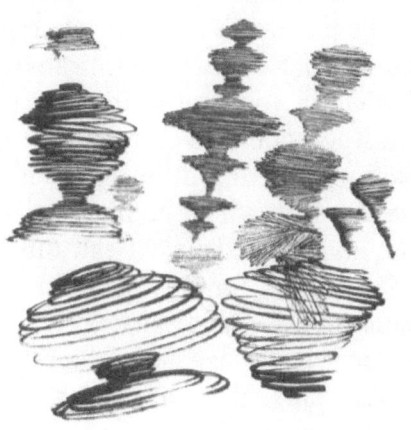

But let us suppose that your palette is furnished according to your own harmonic principles; and that the wood of this palette has been carefully chosen for its slight tendency to form a concave, which is necessary for the propitious flowing of your juices. This palette, moreover, should preferably be oval, and provided with a mobile lead counterweight which will enable you to eliminate its weight, as it were, by balancing it. For you must tell yourself repeatedly that when you begin to paint, nothing must hinder you, just as when you are preparing to sleep the slightest defective posture must be a thousand and one times perfected before you surrender yourself and the god Oniros has the right to possess you wholly. Likewise, then, before allowing yourself to be possessed by painting, find your exact position. You must know already that at one of the extremities of your palette there is a hole through which you must pass the thumb of your left hand to support it on your wrist or on your arm. Of the four remaining fingers, three must be used to hold your brushes, and the little finger to hold the stick which is to support the right hand with which you are to work.

Learn now that the manipulation of the maulstick is Secret Number 29 of this book, for it is in fact more decisive than the manipulation of the brush itself, since the manipulation of the latter depends on the former, and it is this stick—as Archimedes so well understood, since like his own lever this resting point is a fulcrum outside the space of your picture—by means of which you can move the world which it constitutes. In order to initiate you to this new secret I must tell you that every painter develops a slight callosity at the last joint of the little finger of his right hand, which is the precise point on which he must daily rest his hand for a period of hours on his maulstick. I call this callosity the Achilles callosity of the painter, for it is the vulnerable spot where the painter's craftsmanship is exactly localized. When the moment arrives at which you wish to execute outlines of a great sureness and finesse—silken hairs, the scintillating touches of acanthus leaves, etc.—you will proceed thus: first you will daub the exact spot of your callosity with a little fresh pitch and you will use a twig of elder, hence extremely light, having a slight flexibility. Your callosity daubed with pitch glued to your stick will suffice to make the latter follow the movements of your hand to whatever point you wish. But in order to give the maximum of suppleness to the movements of your stick, so that it will seem to you to be really magic—since you should be aware of it only by the single useful resting point which you keep glued, with the pitch, to your Achilles callosity—I must tell you this: instead of holding your stick with the little finger of your left hand, it should be attached to the latter only by means of a cotton string (several strands preferably) from which it is suspended. By this device every encumbrance and the possibility of jerky movements resulting from the immediate contact of both hands with the stick are eliminated, leaving only the single ideal resting point which will circumvent the least trembling or hesitancy of your hand which, under these conditions, will be able to execute lines of a delicacy which to others will appear superhuman. All those who do not know this Dalinian secret will continue to struggle like knights of the Crusades to win the battle of lances of their stick—with which, as I have just revealed to you, the more obstinacy and tension you apply the worse it will be, and if you are not careful you will puncture your canvas! Since the solution is exactly the contrary, let your stick hang, and let it follow you in blind obedience, suspended at the end of the little finger of your left hand and glued to the fulcrum of the Achilles callosity of your other little finger.

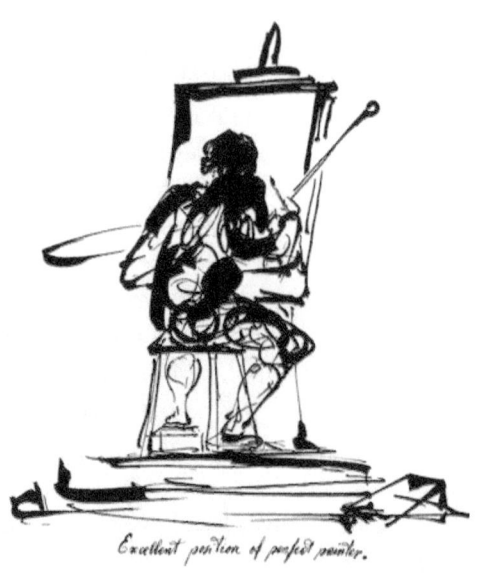

Excellent position of perfect painter.

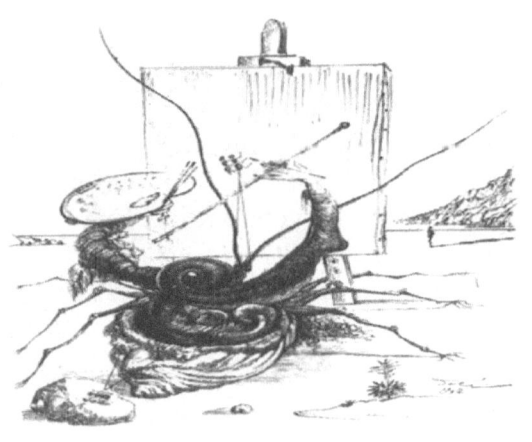

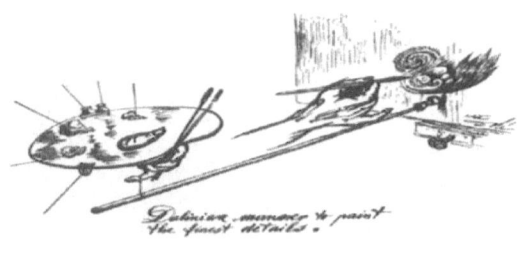

Delicious manner to paint the finest details.

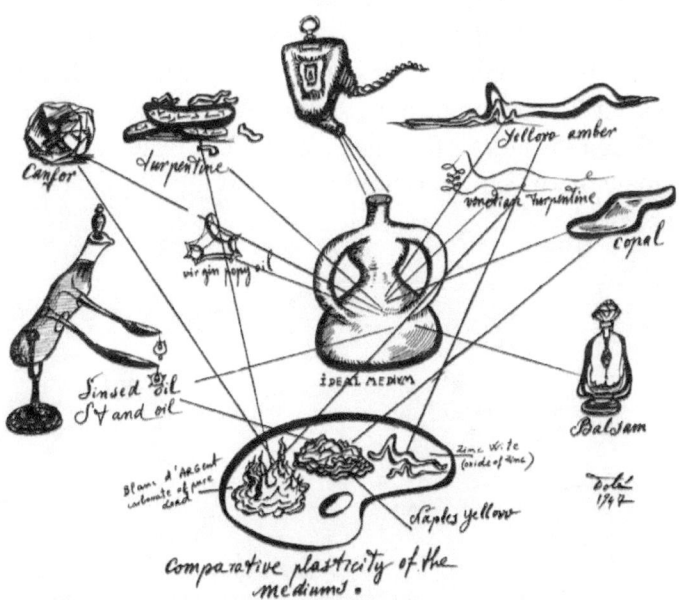

Comparative plasticity of the mediums.

To return now to your colors, I wish you to know that you must mix your silver white with linseed oil. With your zinc white, on the other hand, you will be able to achieve the most limpid and delicate shades only by always mixing it with poppy oil. If you want later to cool your ivory blacks painted with linseed oil, it is with walnut oil that you will achieve your most savory new coats of blue black.

When you begin to paint you may do so on a perfectly dry canvas or wood panel. Or else—and this I prefer—you can moisten it lightly with the same medium with which you are going to paint. This is best done with a perfectly clean finger, so that with its pressure you remove all surplus moisture, for your surface is best when, appearing practically dry, it nevertheless remains a little sticky. When you wish to continue to paint on a piece which is already dry, you must also first moisten it in the same way, in order that the fresh application will become consubstantially incorporated into the previous one. But in this case the best procedure is to use the same medium with which you are going to paint, except that you will have specially kept aside a part of the latter in a separate and open flask, protected from dust' by a small roof of oiled paper, so that in thickening, its viscous virtues become more subtle. This is the moment for you to reflect on this Dalinian maxim: "The magic of the craftsmanship of oil painting depends on the physical coefficients of viscosity."

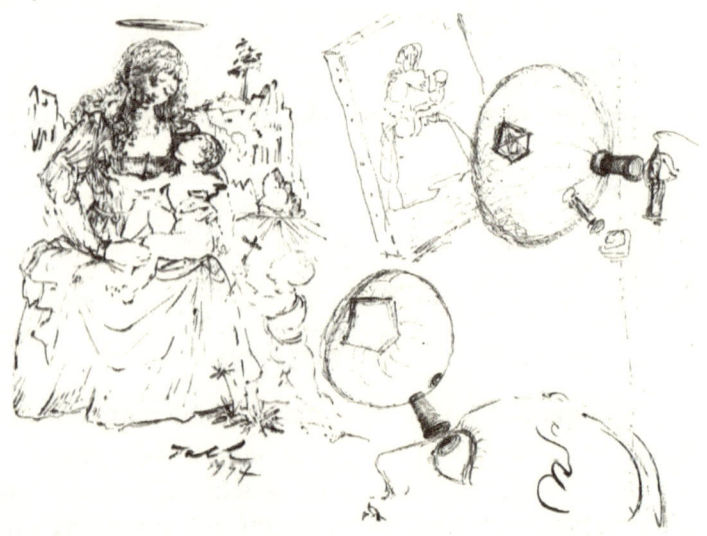

Five rules for the use of white

Since white is the essential base of your picture, this is what you must know:
1. Use silver white to begin your under painting.
2. Use zinc white to finish your overpainting.
3. In between, you may use an excellent mixture composed of three parts silver white to two parts zinc white.
4. Since zinc white is the most luminous, you must use it only mixed with the most colorless of all oils, carnation oil.
5. With silver white, you may add a minimum of very pure essence of turpentine to linseed oil.

Before continuing to guide you in your navigation through

these viscous matters of oil painting, and in order that you will not remain glued from the outset with your pots and your painter's brushes to your painter's canvas like a fly to its flypaper, I must inform you that your picture must be a steady and prudent progression from the most lean to the most fat. This means that the foundation of your picture must be poor in matter, both physically and chemically, and that with each session you must augment the viscosity and enrich your matter, to the point of opulence if that is your inclination. For if you begin the picture lean, you can always add more fat and viscosity, but on the other hand, if you begin with fat substances, you will presently find yourself with your hands and your feet stuck in a premature treacle which, like the lime used for catching birds, will prevent you from taking any further step. Learn at the beginning, therefore, to avoid martyrdoms of this kind, for those countless painters who remain glued to their colors during the slow and interminable agonies of their gluttonous painters' lives suffer a cruel martyrdom indeed. Be careful, then, to avoid this trap of premature viscosity which threatens you with such a frightful painter's death, and do not forget that in spite of all your precautions it is probable that you will not be able to avoid, by successive reworking, using too much fat and, so to speak, overworking the gall-bladder of your painting.

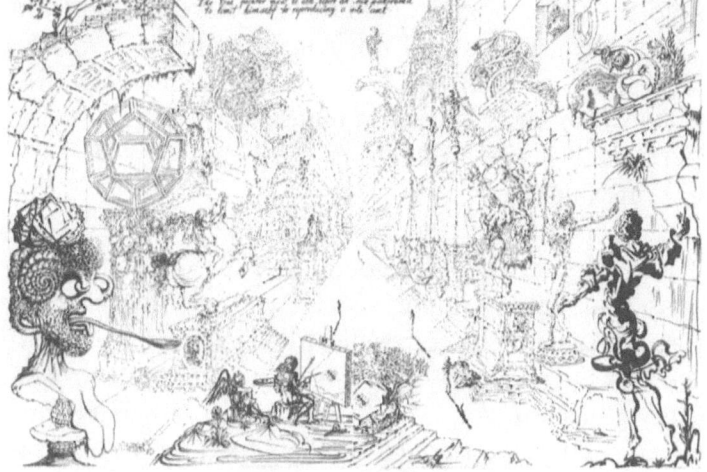

This overworking, if you do not quickly remedy it, may produce a chronic malady in your painting, and an unequivocal warning of this will be given you by a little physical phenomenon. When, at the moment of moistening with your finger the surface which you are preparing to repaint, the latter breaks out into tiny drops, refusing to allow a homogeneous moistening, this means that your picture is giving you warning. "I can't take any more," it sighs. "I am saturated with fat!" When this happens you must rub the surface in question with a raw potato, and this will suffice, as if by miracle, to restore a clear complexion to your piece, which will then let itself be moistened normally, and on which you will be able to continue to paint. Nevertheless take the precaution to rub your potato through a fine silk rag, and in addition wash the surface with water, letting it dry thoroughly, before rewetting it with your medium to resume your painting, which must previously have been varnished with retouching varnish.

As in this book I shall not repeat to you the things which may be learned elsewhere, I shall not inform you, for instance, that Naples yellow is so called because it is extracted from the lava of Vesuvius, or because of this or that; or that copal varnish is a fossil resin; or that spirits of turpentine is a solvent and that its redistillation, etc. If in addition to being a painter, you are also a great chemist, this will do you no harm. It involves the risk, nevertheless, of distilling and solarizing your head in which, as you know, so many spiritual quintessences must be calmly folded and refolded in the oil lamp, in the hump or in the humps of the camel of your head.

Tell yourself, therefore, that there still exist in our day sufficient good colors and good oils to produce masterpieces, and unless you have a quite special aptitude for chemistry, busy yourself rather with the practical and rational means of utilizing them. This is not to say that you should not do constant research in the subject if you wish. But let this research remain on an experimental plane parallel to the course of your works, which you must paint with your feet solidly on the ground, using rather the experience of the failure of your experiments than their success, which I advise you at least to keep in quarantine before hastening to introduce them with too much enthusiasm in the monotonous stream of your pictorial technique, in which the surer and more devoid of surprises are your means, the more astonishing miracles you will realize.,

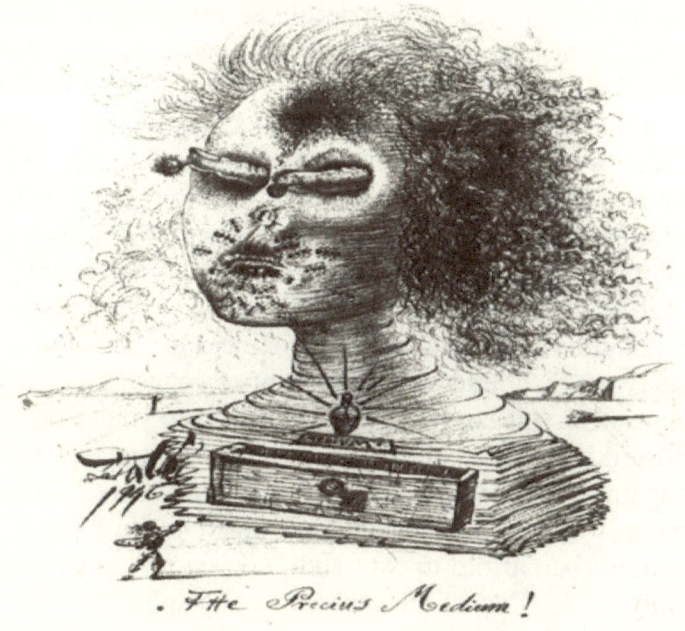

. The Precious Medium!

Thus if on the one hand I advise you and heartily encourage you to buy every week everything you are humanly capable of unearthing in the shops of paint dealers and of those obsessed by the honeys of painters' media, however chimerical they may be, to the point of transforming a part of your studio into a veritable alchemist's den, I advise you on the other hand, and with an equal amount of discouragement, to touch all this alchemy and pathophysics only in order to try and test everything, for perhaps the medium which you thought would be ideally suited for immaterial glazes will turn out to be just what you needed to stiffen with viscosity and at the same time vaporize the spiderweb of one of your precious aranneariums! Make,. therefore, a sharp division between your experiments and your work; and paint the latter with the simplest and surest means, let your quantities of bottles of varnish, of resins, of solvents and siccatives serve you only to confirm the law. Thus your studio must be equipped with everything for your experiments. But in your work I forbid you to use siccatives, essences or varnishes of any kind, with only some very special and precious exceptions which I shall presently enumerate. Dryers you must use on your painting under no circumstances whatsoever, for if you paint well you must never feel the need to have your picture dry faster than it is normal for your colors mixed with your oils to dry. The virtue of painting is never to become impatient for one's piece to dry. On the contrary, the great luxury must be considered by you to be that prerogative which is unique in oil painting: to be able lengthily and without haste to continue to model and to shade in the wet, a prerogative which, after the West Point of your disciplines of life, will appear to you heaven itself. Banish from your desires, then, that absurd haste for your piece to dry. Again, your picture is not a door against which you are afraid of soiling yourself in passing, and your work of art, which is destined to nothing less than immortality, can afford to wait and to dry slowly, and must of all necessity do so. For all the cracklings, the splittings, the turning yellow or black and other even more disastrous accidents have their origin in the physical and chemical inequalities and disharmonies provoked by the *agents provocateurs* of premature desiccations.

Before inviting the colors, your friends, to the ballroom of your palette, begin by drawing up the list of the colors you will not invite, and remember in this connection that witty and lapidary epigram uttered by the Count of Grandsailles, "Balls are given for those who are not invited." Know, then, immediately, the names of the colors which you must ban from your palette by a kind of tacit and silent excommunication and the reasons why you must exclude every unfaithful color, every color, that is, which is not permanent, or which, mixed with the others, is a constant cause of litigation ending in spoiling the relations of good harmony between them and also in the end casting a shadow over the sparkle and luminosity of your picture.*

Exclude bitumen from your palette unless you wish, by mixing it with lacquers, to obtain a crackling comparable to a seismic phenomenon, for your cracks may by this means attain the width of several millimeters. As categorically as bitumen, you must totally exclude burnt umber, and this because of its seduction, its falseness and its perfidy; its seduction, for it attracts by its beautiful greenish tinge, a tinge which it will lose after a time, leaving a dirty blackish residue; its perfidy because this color will always perfidiously and irremediably reappear, discoloring all the successive coats, no matter how thick they may be; and its falseness, finally, because being of the whole palette the color which dries fastest, even when it mixes without any intimacy with no matter what other color, it will immediately succeed in influencing it in its desiccation, to the point of fixing it and rendering it recalcitrant to the most assiduous and solicitous efforts of your brush. Know this as Secret Number 30.

List of Colours Unsuitable for Artistic Painting*

COCHINEAL CARMINE
CARMINE LAKE
ROASTED MADDER-LAKE
REDWOOD LAKE
CHROME YELLOW
LAQUE DE GAUDE
BROWN PINK
INDIAN YELLOW
STRONTIANE YELLOW
SCHWEINFURT GREEN
CINNABAR GREEN

GREEN LAKE
MALACHITE GREEN
MINERAL BLUE
PRUSSIAN BLUE
ENGLISH SKY BLUE
ZINC YELLOW
YELLOW ANTIMONY
RAW SIENNA
TERRE VERTE OR VERONA EARTH
GREEN OCHRES
EMERALD GREEN
PARIS GREEN
SCHEELE GREEN
VIOLET LAKE
RAW UMBER
BITUMEN
EGYPTIAN MUMMY
IVORY BROWN
BURNT UMBER

    After the burnt umber I advise you only rarely to invite terre-verte (or Verona earth), if you cannot get along without it, because of the frivolous and ephemeral smartness of its presence, and if you do not decide (as you ought to) to cut off all relations with her, for you must be without pity for all colors that age badly. You may without too much danger remain faithful to the old friendship you have for the glamorous name which burnt Sienna bears. It is natural in its essence, and it cannot be said that it turns black, for when it darkens it always does so toward brown, hence it forms a good patina.

    If, however, you do not care for the imponderable and, for that matter, the unpredictable element involved in cultivating these relations, you may replace your burnt Sienna with Italian earth. And I do not think that from the point of view of the name you run the risk of losing a great deal. You do not even have to move out of the same country.

    Now that you know the weaknesses and the treacheries of

certain colors, and what you must beware of, I shall teach you the excellences of those on whose generosity and fidelity you can count.* First your great and faithful companion-at-arms, in defeat as well as in victory, will be your blanc d'argent, for this color must be involved, from second to second, in everything that you do, especially at the beginning, in the foundation of your picture called the "underpainting." This is Secret Number 31. I have already pointed out that this color is adept at building everything that is solid, and it is thus that it is destined to assure, so to speak, not only the permanence but the indissoluble sacramental marriage with each one of the other colors. The zinc white you will use very sparingly, even in glazing over your solid blanc d'argent, and thus it will remain incomparably clean, and it is with this color that you will achieve the most absolute whites in your picture. It is the ermine, the swan and the cloud, the ultrapure image which only the retinas of painters can conceive outside of their terrestrial and celestial wailings and gnashings of teeth.

Extra Secret

List of Permanent Colours Which Can be Used with Confidence*

BLANC D'ARGENT—Possesses the secret of terrestrial and celestial opacities.
It is the Jupiter of colours.
LIGHT (ENGLISH) RED
MARS RED
VENETIAN RED—Possesses the secret of everything

that is biological.

It is the Adam and Eve of colours.

INDIAN RED

PERMANENT MADDER-CARMINE

MADDER LAKES

ROSE AND RED (Unroasted)

BURNT SIENNA

MARS ORANGE

CADMIUM (in Orange and Yellow shades) —Possesses the secret of solar time. It is the Chrones of colours.

MARS YELLOW

AUREOLIN—To be used for everything that is to shine. It is the gold and the god Mercury of colours.

TRANSPARENT YELLOW

ITALIAN EARTH

PURIFIED YELLOW OCHRE

VERONESE GREEN—Possesses the secret of everything that is born from the sea. It is the Venus of colours.

CELADON GREEN

LAMORINIERE GREEN

LIGHT OLIVE GREEN

"MARIE COLLART" GREEN—Possesses the secret of everything that is vegetal and humid. It is the river-nymphs of colours.

COBALT BLUE COERULEUM BLUE

REAL ULTRAMARINE

GUIMET'S BLUE

COBALT VIOLET

MARS VIOLET

BROWN OCHRE

MARS BROWN

TRANSPARENT BROWN

CASSEL EARTH

BLUE BLACK

IVORY BLACK

Secret Number 32 is that of all the reds the most excellent

is Venetian red, for with none other will you be able to obtain so much fineness, subtlety and infinitesimality in the imponderable of nuances. Also none of these imperceptible modulations will change, for the permanence and fidelity of this red will stand every test. You must love Venetian red so much that your passion will leave you no room to love Indian red which, in spite of its merits of permanence and its natural beauty, can tell you nothing new after all that Venetian red has taught you. Venetian red is an opaque color with a unique capacity for covering, therefore you will use it especially for the under-painting, to model and solidly build your foundations, mixed with blanc d'argent. Blanc d'argent, Venetian red and blue black are the three virtuosos and the surest colors for preparing in "monotone" the basis of your flesh colors.

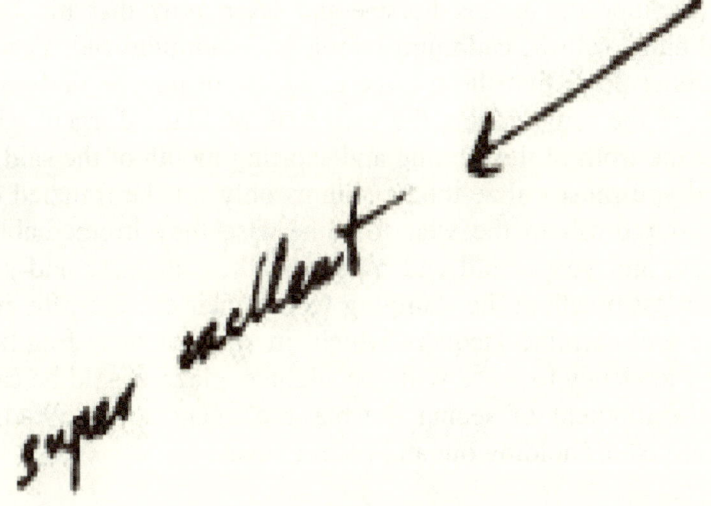

A la guerre comme a la guerre! Thus in your pictorial war destiny has willed that the colors of Mars should be not only those offering a more sustained capacity for endurance, but those capable of the highest feats of heroism and sacrifice, for at the same time that they hold their ground fanatically, to the point of rendering it impregnable, they are prepared to give their last drop of light to save a fortified place besieged by enemy colors. Secret Number 33 is that you must therefore without hesitancy give the rank of captain to your Mars yellow, to your Mars orange and your Mars violet, and do not fail to notice how this last, especially if he appears parsimoniously, that is to say for the feats of arms of your brushes, which must be signalized by acts of bravery, will make himself loved for his courage by all the yellows and all the younger battalions, that is to say, by the greens.

    The Marshal of all the greens, as you now learn from Secret Number 34, is the Veronese green, which you may and you must consider as the generalissimo of your whole palette, and when all the arms of heaven and earth seem to you insufficient to dominate the retreats and adversities of your picture, it may be that your hope will revive by the simple fact of watching the gallantry of your Veronese green, seated proudly, straight and almost upright on his horse—and learn now that his horse is cadmium yellow, cadmium lemon and cadmium red. For Secret Number 35 is that these three colors form but the body and the legs of the same gallop, the gallop of the blanc d'argent which is like the froth of the panting and snorting mouth of the said horse. And you must utilize the cadmiums only for the frenzied dashes of your brush in the wet, for otherwise they irremediably turn black, and you would end by seeing them agonize and give up their last breath at the stamping feet of their enemies, the madder rose and carmine lacquers which, in spite of their fragility and their tendency to crack with the slightest glaze, would be capable, at the moment of seeing the blanc d'argent and the cadmiums disunited, of holding out and getting the better of these.

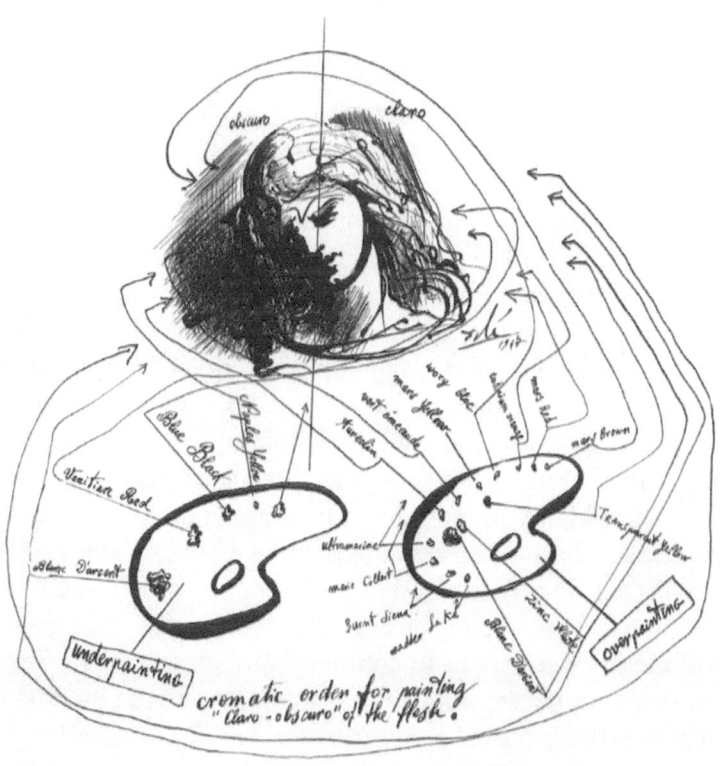

Give a deep and respectful bow to olive green and to Marie Collart green. In both of these you can have confidence, and you can confide to them your most intimate secrets. These two superlative greens excel in their diplomatic gifts and it is to them that you will have to have recourse for the difficult missions in which the spirit of conciliation and the subtlety of your dialectic must replace the brutal and categorical offensives of force which, you must know as Secret Number 36, will be represented for you by vermilion—of an exceptional quality it must be, however, in order to hold up. If it comes from China or, better still, from Germany, you may then count it as an unbeatable color. Yet with this color you must be on your guard, for vermilion is so strong that the misfortune of the bad example of its vulnerability, of a sudden defeat, might of itself alone suffice to demoralize all the rest of your colors, even the noblest and most aristocratic. You must therefore use vermilion only in extreme and strategic moments when its crucial presence becomes absolutely indispensable. In this connection it will be well for you to reflect on the laurels won by the vermilions in the case of Velasquez and, if you have ever so little the soul of a colorist, you will feel rising from its depths a flash of infinite gratitude for such past glories. On the other hand, Vandyke red will evoke for you nothing but defeats without honor, leading to periods of enslavement of your painting. And because of this I would have you pass it by as you will all the other shameful memories of those companions without glory, the Vandyke brown and the Bargta yellow, which are a veritable cacoscopy of painting which you may deign to use on condition that at the end you do not hesitate to execute them as veritable spies of the other colors, burying them under a thick coat of peach black which, as you know, is made from charred peach stones—a color sufficiently permanent to continue to mark the spot where Bargta yellow, with its accomplice in dishonor, Vandyke brown, will thus remain forever buried.

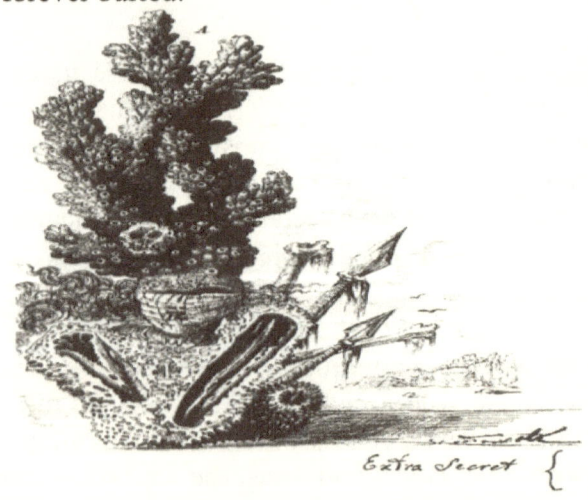

I must now, I feel, try to overcome the sinister mood which I have induced by speaking of these sinister colors, which I preferred to have done with so that I would not have to speak of them again and would feel free to proceed to the discussion of those other colors, so refreshing both for your eyes and for your soul, which are called, and are, the blues.

Immediately and without mincing words I shall declare to you to begin with that I do not feel for ultramarine blue the enthusiasm which it enjoyed throughout the Renaissance and that, in consequence, I shall boldly refrain from considering it, as did Cenino Cenini, the most precious color, which excels in the realm of all the colors. I believe that the high repute enjoyed by ultramarine blue is due above all to its extremely high price, the dearest of all, and to the fact that its source is lapis lazuli. But its disadvantage, in my view, is that the other colors do not thrive in its proximity. Note this as Secret Number 37, and once you are convinced from your own experience that its too new limpidity soils everything that surrounds it, cease to admire it, detach yourself from it little by little, while casting increasingly langorous eyes in the direction of cobalt blue, with which I sense that you will end by living without being able to separate yourself from it, becoming more attached to it day by day as you grow older: cobalt blue which, as you may know from Secret Number 38, the deeper, the more stable it is, the more patiently it is applied, the more it will make you deserving of heaven which, as you should already know, will be vouchsafed you by coeruleum blue, since it is with the latter that you can and that you must paint the most diaphanous heavens. This color has an exceptional adhesive quality and you will be able to blend it with several fan-shaped badger brushes in succession over a period of two days, if you wish. It is thus that you will be able to obtain with this blue surfaces so polished, compact and definitive that even if you compare them to that of an agate, the latter will seem to you but a bad and defective imitation of your sky.

To rest you from the splendors of such skies I am quite willing now to permit you to go and sit, with Secret Number 39, in the severe shade of cobalt violet, but just remember that this honorable color decomposes, like Naples yellow, on contact with iron, therefore you must not touch it with your knife. On the contrary, your knife will be the friend of yellow ocher, golden ocher and *ochre de ru,* which ecstatically lend themselves to being spread on the canvas with it, like butter. Bear in mind that often, for stretches of terrain in which these colors are to be used in the foundation coats, it is precisely with the knife that you will obtain a matter suitably constructed and solid, for it must be as if you could really walk on it.

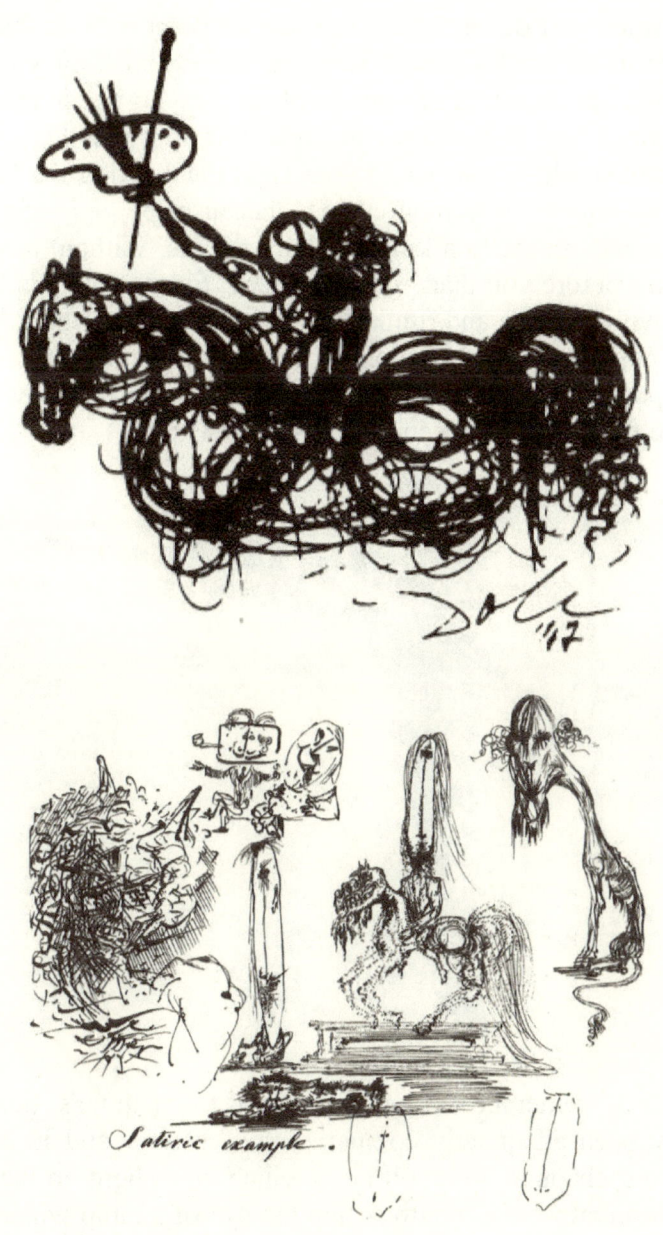

Satiric example.

Walk, then, with firm steps, toward the horizon of the solid distances of your ochers, for the plain chant of colors ends here. Since you do not need, in order to paint well, to have me enumerate others for you, I see you already making your way toward the background of your painting, obeying me in this, as in everything. And as I observe the shield of your palette, your left hand armed with brushes and your right hand lifting the lance of your maulstick, I compare you, because of our frightfully mechanized epoch, to a kind of Don Quixote. Without any other windmill before you than your own head, for the painter's head is a mill which grinds and ruminates the images which the full wind of the plain chant of the colors of the sky turns monotonously on itself, producing as a result that flow of ultra-white flour which is like the flow of light which emerges from a lamp.

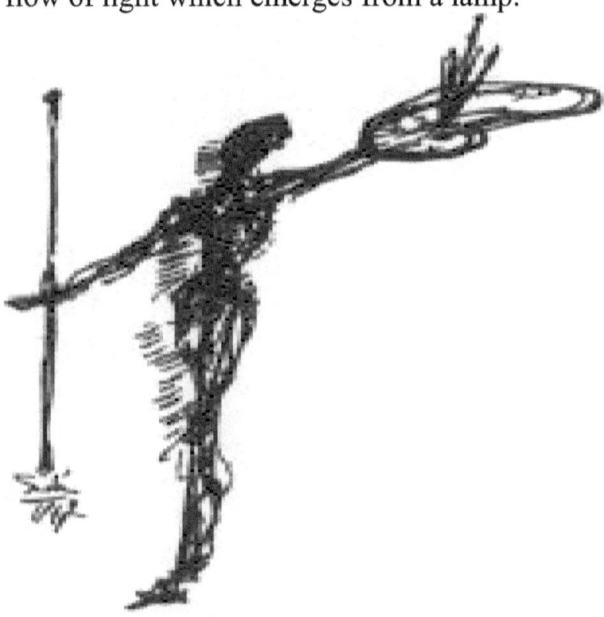

For remember once more that the painter's head has already been adequately compared, successively and in each of these four chapters, to an oil lamp which gives light, to the hump of a ruminant whose mouth is like the eye of a lamp which gives light, to a Bernard the hermit who lives within the shell of your skull, and whose red teeth are the arms of the painter which, like a flame of light, also illuminate the picture. And now to give you even more pleasure, I shall without more ado compare this same painter's head, not to a Bernard the hermit but to a miller who is also, like yourself, a kind of hermit who ruminates and masticates and grinds in the mill of his brain which is the storehouse and attic of reserve images of the camel's hump; in which the grain of intelligence lies piled, that luminous quintessence, that flow of wheat which is the whiteness of the earth with which you are to knead that daily bread of painting, which thus becomes again the prayer which the painter, with his flour which is the terrestrial luminosity of this world below, daily lifts toward the celestial luminosities of the above. For all the mystery and miraculous humble aspiration of the man painter is nothing less than to make light, radiant and divine, with white and earth colors which are dull and sere.

Sleep, sleep, miller, camel of daydreams, hermit of mediterranean depths, oil lamp of man! You are no longer listening to me! You hear only the beat of the rhythm of the mill wings of your head. I should have suspected it before this on seeing your gaze troubled by impatience as I initiated you to the wonders of the colors. Yes, at last you are painting!

And now, while I observe you, I shall summarize for all those who are not yet painting what you are already doing so well, with so much infused experience, how from your flour, your earths, your oils, to the regular rhythm of the mill of your brain, you are creating such a dazzling flow of light with each new touch of each of your novice brushes! Toc, toc! Toc, toc! Toc, toc!

Once you have the definitive drawing which, I wish to suppose, embodies the lines of dynamic symmetry in which the geometrists of the Renaissance excelled, you will have obtained a tracing which has been transmitted to your panel of nonabsorbent gesso, using for this my Secret Number 24 for the transfer of tracings. Also you will have proceeded to spread the first layer of paint which your picture requires, the "imprimatura," and the finest of all the successive layers which your panel is destined to receive.

For this imprimatura you will spread your liquid by means of a silk pad, perfectly semispherical in form, with rhythmic vertical movements, until your color is spread in the most uniformly transparent coat possible, leaving your tracing as sharply visible as before. From this you will gather that for the imprimatura you must choose the most transparent colors. The two most appropriate are burnt Sienna and ultramarine. blue. But in order to kill the too blinding luminosity of such an imprimatura, it will be well for you to add a suspicion of blanc d'argent. The imprimatura is the only layer which it may interest you to have dry quickly. Nevertheless do not, even for this, use a siccative. Avoid also dammar varnish like the pest, for even after several months, depending on the climatic conditions, it may behave unreliably in the moistening processes of your future applications of paint. The medium which you must use for your imprimatura must be as lean as possible, and should therefore have as a base a superior rectified turpentine to which you add some copal varnish in the proportion of one ounce of the latter to five of turpentine. This formula for the imprimatura, due to Mr. Taubes, appears to me basically excellent, especially if one add to it Secret Number 40 which I call the "veil-imprimatura." To produce this quasi-miraculous effect of the veil-imprimatura, for the excellence of which you will be able to thank me a hundred times only after you have practiced them, since they are like the breath of life of your future picture, you must proceed thus.

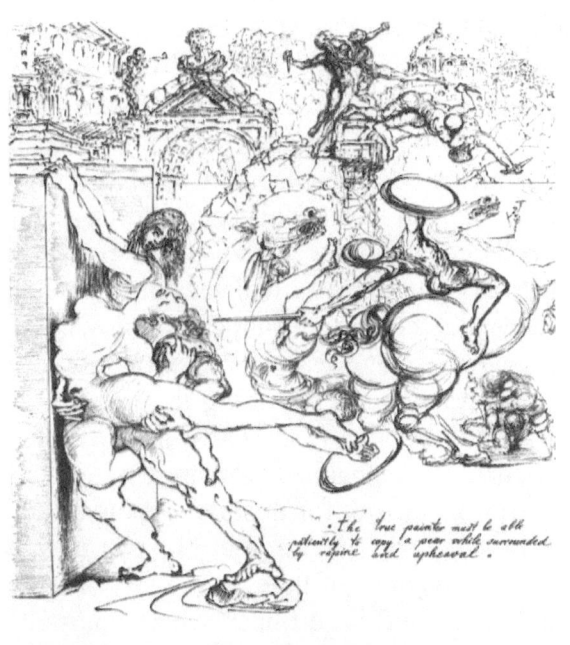

The true painter must be able patiently to copy a pear while surrounded by rapine and upheaval.

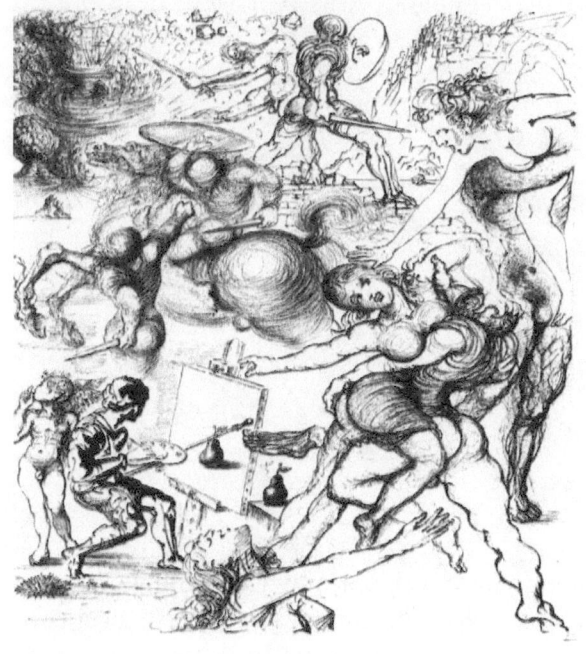

You will add to your medium two ounces of "yellow amber" diluted with aspic oil, and the moment when the imprimatura —which you have been able thanks to this new minimum of viscosity to spread in the most humanly imponderable manner possible—seems to you almost dry, with a clean silk pad, which has been moistened the day before with aspic oil, you will proceed anew to rub in the parts where you with to bring out the light, and you will see emerging before your wonder-filled eyes modelings so subtle that it will affect the whole future development and leave its traces in your work. But this extremely important secret regarding imprimatura must still be completed by going through to the canvas in the light parts, to which the somewhat too mechanical monotony of your pad might give an effect of boredom. But for this grave moment of creation neither pad nor brushes will suffice you. For you must use your very fingers, and not even all of these, but a single one, and this single one must be your left little finger, which you will use as a pad, letting it be manipulated, as if it were dead, by your right hand.

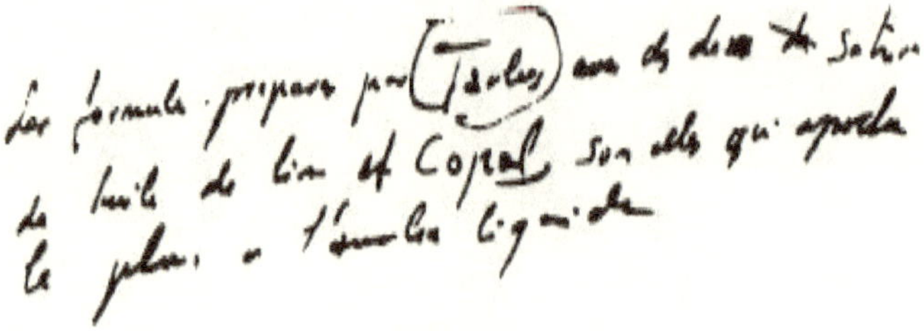

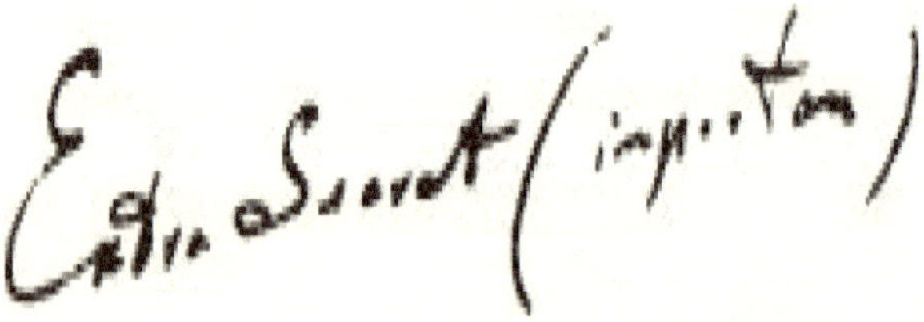

[handwritten note]

But here you must learn what medium corresponds to these last touches of your little finger in the last accents of light in the veil of your imprimatura. Your little finger must be treated with a teardrop of pure resin as it flows from a pine, as follows: knead this tear between your little finger and your thumb until you have formed a solid little ball which no longer sticks to your fingers. Your little finger then will be endowed with a sharp adhesive power while being dry at the same time, which will pick up at the least contact, as though it were magnetized, the parts of the veil of your imprimatura of which you wish to accentuate the high lights.

The object of your imprimatura is to create before your eyes a suspicion of the vision of your painting, a breath, a veil of what you desire, so that you may the more surely progress toward the complete weighty objectivity of its future .realization. I find most horrible that process, of romantic origin and consequences, consisting of obtaining imprimaturas by the savage manner of capriciously wiping with a rag, in order to gratify one's vanity and resort to accidental effects to stimulate the imagination and through a paranoiac interpretation to discover figures and azure landscapes almost finished, which merely need to be completed. This method, which is an amusing experiment, to be practiced as an imaginative and hallucinatory rather than a technical exercise, must be excluded from the rigorous sovereignty of the masterpiece. Pliny relates that Protogenes, enraged at his inability to paint the foam of the sea, furiously tossed a color-soaked sponge against the wall and that the splashes admirably realized what he so conscientiously and vainly had tried to achieve. Rather imitate Dali who needs no mad dog, who successfully renders sea foam, and then in turn paints the sponge itself. But if you cannot imitate me, since you have told yourself several times on reading me that I am inimitable, I do not categorically advise you against giving vent to such outbursts of creative anger from time to time. For that matter, you cannot avoid them, for your painter's craft is often so despairing and exasperating that it leads to painter's rages, which are of the most impulsive. I permit you therefore, since so illustrious a painter as Protogenes did so, to throw your sponge in fury when you are beside yourself. Throw it, nevertheless, against the wall or against a picture not yet begun rather than against the one which causes your despair, for a later repentance will not mend the damage, and follow this wisely Daliesque advice: instead of continuing the splash of the sponge, copy and patiently paint your sponge, the image of your anger, by way of penitence. After which I assure you that in recompense you will successfully master your foam.

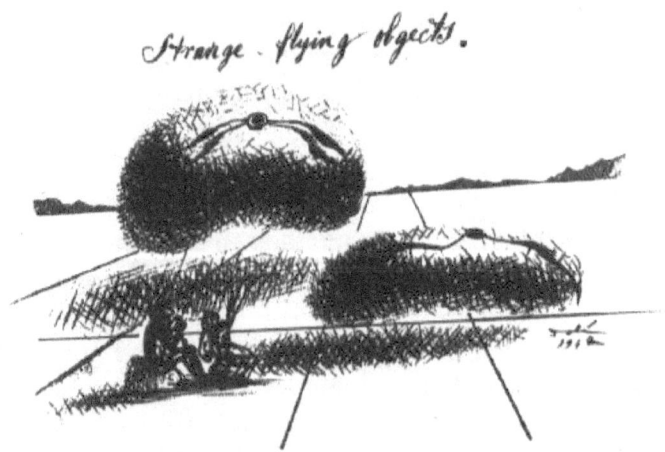

Wonderstruck as you are before the veil, the mirage, the

breath of your picture, so vague that you alone can as yet believe in it—but this only if your imprimatura is successfully realized, and you adore it, for otherwise do not continue your picture and begin another—the moment has arrived to paint it, to render real and visible for all what the imprimatura represents for you alone. This new coat of paint with which you are to cover the first, that is to say that of your imprimatura, is called the under-painting. Remember this: painting well is never correcting, but on the contrary completing. This means that having started from the almost invisible veil of your imprimatura, your picture must become progressively visible until it finally bursts forth, without ever retrogressing, from the pale to the deep, from the vague to the precise, from the monochrome to the polychrome, from the lean to the fat and to the opulent, from the opaque to the brilliant and the dazzling. Thus if the successive layers of your picture were to be filmed, from your imprimatura, your underpainting, your successive overpaintings and glazings, up to the last touches and the last varnishes, one would see in the film of your picture something like a vision which, beginning as an almost impalpable mist, would gradually materialize without discontinuity and in a progressively visible manner, like a photograph that was being very slowly developed. At each new session, therefore, you must make your coats more intense than the previous ones, and never the contrary, for the darker layers would sooner or later have the tendency to reappear through the lighter ones, a phenomenon known as "*pentimento,*" pitilessly soiling all your color relations and revealing shamelessly to all eyes your most ignominious "repentances."

If you want to correct, then, that is to say to paint over with lighter tonalities a part which you had too impatiently or adventurously overdone in intensity, you will first have to smooth out your "repentance" by means of powdered pumice and your finger, to the point where it is so thin and smooth in body that it will appear to you just like a new veil. Then rub it with the famous potato, rinse with water, let dry, and when at last it is moistened with liquid yellow amber you will be able to repaint over your "repentance" with a lighter tonality, and you may be sure that it will then remain secretly buried forever. I say, "famous" potato, and I repeat it. For I consider it almost impossible, without the virtues of the raw potato, to bring an oil painting to its successful completion, so irreplaceable it is; just as, if it is true that excellent gums are being manufactured for "erasing," there is not a single one that can be compared, for "modeling" with vine charcoal, with the honest and antique crumb of white bread—always kept from the day before. Sieur Gauthier de Nimes of the king's court explains minutely in his treatise on water-painting the unique virtues of human urine, especially a child's, for grinding cinnabar when it is in the stone. All those who have known the workshops of Parisian etchers and engravers know also the imponderable virtues of this precious liquid mixed with nitric acid, with which etchings are cut. In the same order of things, learn that human saliva is irreplaceable for painting water colors on ivory, and that only the slaver excreted by the snail is superior to it. Onion and garlic are excellent to add mordancy if rubbed on the parts which are to be repainted.

All this should suffice to convince you that the magic of painting is an essentially "natural" magic, and that just as your best colors are those formed from natural earths and not by artificial chemical mixtures, so it is in things that most commonly surround your mediterranean daily life that you will find the secrets of the miraculous virtues of your media.

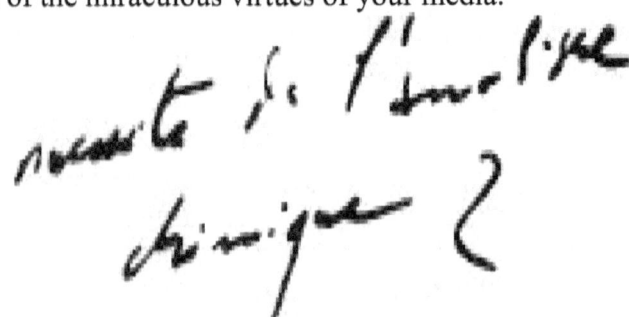

And so I must tell you now about the "wasp medium,"

which is Secret Number 41 of this treatise. But as this medium has a special application in the spreading of the second coat of your picture, with which you will build and consolidate like a mason the veiled visions of your imprimatura, you must first know what in substance and in essence is your underpainting.

The underpainting you will execute with the brushes called " *paletines,* " because they are flat, square or slightly elongated, with which you will paint with the parsimonious movement already described in connection with this brush. Your mission in the underpainting is above all to cover and to model. Consequently it is preferable to use monotones as neutral as possible, and to spread them as evenly as possible. You may blend your underpainting at the end of each session to even it, and you may also, once it is dry, smooth it with pumice stone, but I advise you to do both. And remember this: never will the surface of your underpainting be sufficiently homogeneous. For even if you desire later—as is necessary—to distribute the richness and importance of your matter according to the subject, you must, in order to be able to be master of this divine prerogative, have the most absolute smoothness in your underpainting as a starting-point. For paradoxically, the most divine element in painting is when you accomplish the miracle of spiritualizing by manipulating that indescribable thing which connaisseurs call the fine matter of a painting, without which the latter is like an idea without a body. And in plastics you must know this profound truth, that it is the body which gives soul to ideas. All the painters who know their craft who have seen my under-paintings have been unable to understand how I can cover so homogeneously and at the same time so smoothly.

First you must know that blanc d'argent is the base and the body of underpainting, and after this Venetian red and coeruleum blue. The painter who, without experience, uses the transparent colors destined to the layers of the overpainting and the glazing to build his underpainting can paint till he goes mad and his hair turns white without success. But even the exact knowledge of the physical properties of each of your colors for the underpainting will not suffice you. For here, as in everything that is to follow, to the very completion of your picture, the medium is perhaps the quintessential thing.

Thus I shall leave you to shift for yourself with your colors, for this depends on what you want to do. If you are a born colorist, you will, after feeling your way for a time, find solutions of your own which are the only ones that can serve you. But the media are something else. For even though you will daily have to adapt them to your needs, the things which are about to be described are things which I doubt that you could find for yourself, for I myself can only thank heaven for having accidentally discovered them.

For your underpainting you need a lean medium. Remember this essential precept: the underpainting must acquire the semimatness of a terra-cotta Tanagra having a slight luster. Its matter should be such as to make you desire to paint over it richly. And here is the formula of Dali's "wasp-medium": you prepare the basic medium out of equal parts of poppy oil, walnut oil and rectified turpentine. For five parts of this mixture you add one part of the following: yellow amber dissolved in aspic oil, in which some wasps have been soaked. To prepare the latter you place a small funnel of wax paper in the mouth of the flask in which you wish to contain the mixture, obstructing the neck of the funnel with three dead wasps, which must have their stings intact. You then pour your amber diluted in aspic oil into the funnel, enough to cover the wasps completely. The liquid should flow into your flask very slowly, drop by drop. You then mix it in the proportion already given with your mixture of oil and turpentine. The slower the operation is carried out the better it is. Therefore instead of pouring your solution of amber in aspic oil directly into the funnel it is better to let this flow out drop by drop from another flask into the funnel, which should be exposed to the rays of the morning sun during the hottest summer season. Rather than doubt the efficacy of my medium, I suggest that you try it. Nothing could be simpler.

Here now is the objective story of this discovery. I was

twenty-nine years old and I was painting my first basket of bread during the three months of June, July and August with poppy oil and walnut oil mixed without any varnish or turpentine. During those three months I did not remove this mixture from the little white bowl which contained it. The quantity was very small, and each day it grew a little thicker and more viscous. Every day through my open window the sun beat down on my little white bowl for over an hour. One morning I found a large wasp drowned in it. The color of the oil shining in the sun mingled with the wasp's yellow and black stripes fascinated me, and I did not remove the wasp from my medium.

From that moment on I began to notice a quality which I had never before experienced in the ductility, which was honey-like, and in the homogeneous fusion of my colors. Applying these became a pleasure inexplicable in itself. I immediately attached a feeling of superstition to the virtue of my wasp, and for nothing in the world would I have been willing to remove it from its inhumation in the oil, and it remained there until the picture was finished and signed.

Nevertheless, recognizing in myself a certain propensity for fetishistic fixations of this kind, I was convinced that this pleasure was suggestive, having a delirious character, and I attributed my satisfactory results rather to the natural thickening of the small quantity of the medium employed and also to the exceptional heat of that summer. Yet I spent a whole winter of nightmares, trying a thousand different combinations, without succeeding in recapturing the beatific state of my wasp medium. The following summer I tried the same proportion with the same daily exposure to the sun. I was painting a similar subject. In vain! I had to go through another winter of despair before I would yield to the tyranny of my obsessive chimera which my reason refused to countenance: to plunge another dead wasp into my oils. And this happened again accidentally, one Sunday as I was having coffee (for every Sunday, at my parents' house, we had coffee with a glass of yellow chartreuse), when another large wasp came and stuck itself at the bottom of my small glass.

Immediately I turned my glass upside down, thus imprisoning the wasp, and I ran upstairs to my studio room where, in great excitement, I plunged it into my medium, and for two long hours of revery I experienced the voluptuous emotions of a Nero as I watched it agonize. Thus in giving its life for my painting, this wasp redeemed it of dryness, which was its single sin, so that to this day I am mindful of the principle of the coefficient of divine viscosity, which is the enigma of organic matter (on which I shall write a separate treatise) and which was revealed to me by a wasp descended from heaven to sacrifice itself and thereby sweeten my life as a painter.

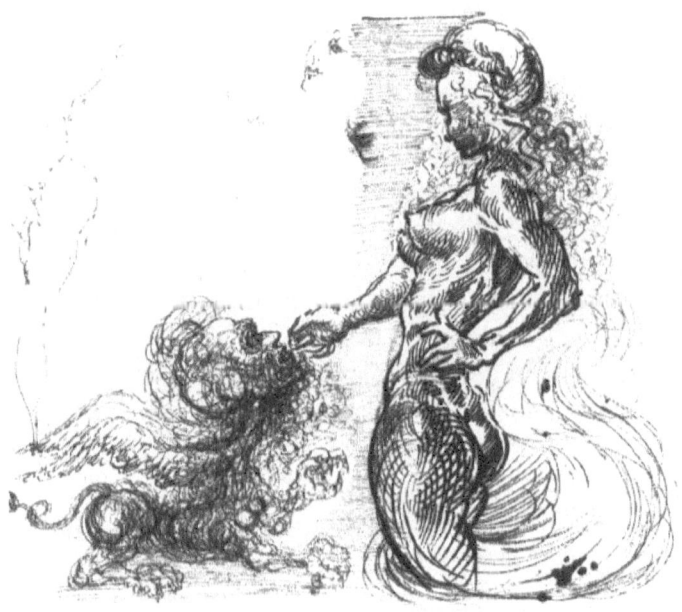

And the sting of this wasp was a precursor of that of the love of Gala-the-bee, the honey of my life as a man.

But before you begin, over your underpainting, to work your successive and infinite overpaintings up to the final stroke, I must initiate you to Secret Number 42, which also derives from the wasp.

During the three long months when I was painting my first basket of bread, I became so accustomed to looking regularly and intermittently at the stripes of my wasp illuminated by the sun that I found I could no longer do without it. I tried to analyze introspectively the reasons for the fondness which my eye had developed for these stripes, and after a number of experiments I arrived at this discovery: during the long painting sessions the eye needs to look from time to time at a small striped or spotted object. If these spots are in contrast with the coloration of your picture, glancing at them periodically will greatly help you in revaluating the chromatic relations of what you are painting. Looking constantly at one set of colors, without any object of contrast to strike your retina from time to time, you would otherwise—and this is no exaggeration—find yourself sooner or later painting "blindly," that is to say, without a constant consciousness of your color values which should at every moment communicate to your eye the savor, the salt and pepper and sweetness of each color. Take my word for it, therefore, that just as many people do not even know whether they dream in black and white or in full color, so painters, and you yourself, while employing all sorts of colors on the canvas, very often do not even see them because the vicious habit of your long sessions tends gradually and dangerously to drain these colors of their life and sparkle and to neutralize them. So keep your painter's eye constantly awake to the slightest murmurs of the tones, semitones and infinitesimal subtones, by the very simple and efficacious Secret Number 42, which is the following: Obtain two good-sized sea shells of the kind called cowrie shells which are adorned with little brown spots, like leopards. On the spots of one of these, with the tip of your brush, apply in as sharp relief as possible some Veronese green. Do the same to the other, but instead of Veronese green use a deep cadmium orange. When you are working on your picture with salmon red or even ochers, place next to the container holding your medium the cowrie shell spotted with Veronese green. And when, on the other hand, you are working in grays shading toward the cold and violet colors, place next to your container the cowrie shell pricked with cadmium orange. By so doing you will notice, at the end of a single session, how the scales of your picture, without having cost you the slightest effort, as if by magic, have suddenly become sharper and more refined, for you have already realized that the cowrie shells in question are for your eye what the tuning fork is for the ear of a piano tuner. Therefore do not refuse yourself the use of my two fundamental cowrie shells, thanks to which your eye will see truly. And, painter that you are, you must be the most just and the most judicious of men, for it is you who must be able to say that this is white and that black. In justice I tell you: be now the supreme judge of the hierarchies of matter, for we are going to consider the absolute monarchy of the latter, the reign of which begins in the third layer of paint which your picture will require, and which is called overpainting.

The king of overpainting is linseed oil, which will reign by heredity to the end of the civilization of your picture, at the close of which there will be a regency period, of which you have already guessed that the hereditary prince of the linseed oil is the solution of yellow amber in aspic oil, with or without wasps, a regency which terminates at the moment of the coronation, in all the splendor of the pictorial ceremonial of the overpainting, of the linseed oil. This linseed oil which may be obtained almost as supple as that of poppy, and as thick as honey, you must increase in thickness with each new overpainting.

Understand here the philosophy proper to the use of media, for the precise formulae you must find for yourself in each new circumstance, according to what you want or need to do, and these circumstances, happily, never repeat themselves exactly alike. For here—know this for always—you must govern both with authority and diplomacy that mysterious domain of the coefficients of viscosity to which I have already alluded. Even as for the viscosity of peoples, every inflexible and mechanical rule is false, and if you resort to it rigidly, as in a military dictatorship, it is the viscosity which in the end will get the better of your power, and you will end your life as a painter its prisoner and its slave. I repeat to you therefore that each new over-painting must be more viscous, but also more liquid. For essentially every true overpainting must proceed by "transparency" achieved by means of the round brushes, each time more long and more thin, and according to their proper movements as already described. To your bleached linseed oil you may add poppy oil to lighten and walnut oil to add snap or sun-thickened linseed oil or stand oil to give it body.

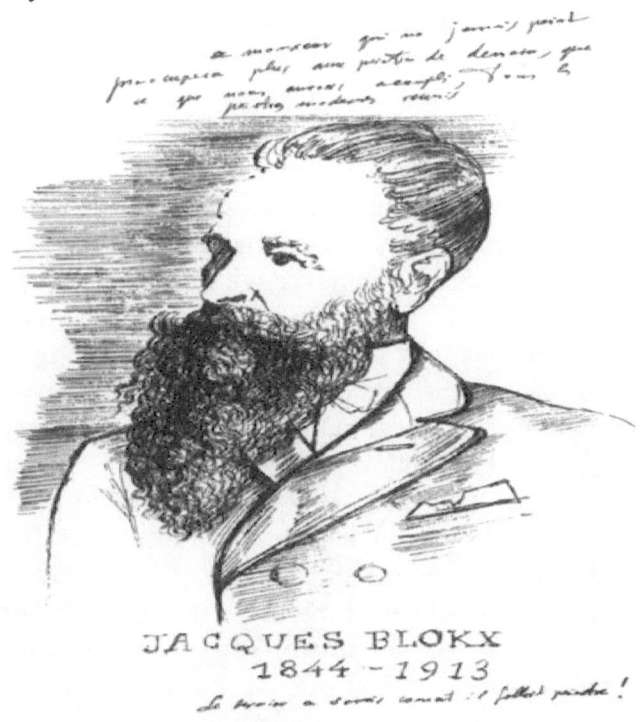

JACQUES BLOKX
1844 - 1913

At this point I must put my hand on my heart and confess to you sincerely that my whole experience of thirty-five years as a painter has convinced me that it is an error to mix with the precious oils of your overpainting any kind of varnish or solvent whatsoever, and that the sole really precious vehicle which for the first time in this book I permit myself to call "sublime" is the yellow liquid amber according to the formula arrived at by

Jacques Blockx, which you dissolve in your oils at the beginning of your overpainting in the proportion of one drop of amber to five of oil, and which you augment progressively up to the end of the picture. At this point, instead of varnishing it with mastic or other harmful substances subject to pulverization, you will do so with pure liquid amber, which has the unique advantage of integrating itself completely and as by a consubstantial consequence with your last overpainting without ever needing to be removed even if it should become necessary to repaint over it.

You have already noticed my insistence on the consecutive order of your layers which is required in order to obtain a fine matter. But do not suppose that I am tired of repeating it, since this consecutive order is the one which you must follow with equal rigor for the chromatic progression and juxtaposition of your picture. Here it is most essential that you know that each new overpainting must be achieved with different colorations and that they must be the colorations which are most suitable and which you most want to superpose on the preceding ones. You must decide this at least one day in advance, for the best moment to prepare your palette is at night, before you go to sleep, so that it will be ready for the following day.

What you must keep ever-present in mind is that if you superpose two layers with the same tonalities the result will be of a frightful opacity, pastiness and absence of luminousness. On the other hand, if you find each time the best color to lay on the bed of the other, this bed will thank you for the pleasure of the virginal splendors which you offer it, for it has a horror of flesh vitiated by repetitions. For example, if on flesh tonalities with a basis of Venetian earth you put a new coat of Venetian earth, the result will be dirty and without sparkle. If, on the contrary, on the Venetian earth you use burnt sienna your new color will become more clean and luminous than before. If you continue your third overpainting with the same burnt sienna you will again make your piece dirty and pasty, but if you proceed next with your ochers you will be surprised to see that your painting instantly lights up with a new and added brilliance. You know now that a new overpainting with the same ochers would ruin this limpidity which you have progressively achieved. Therefore lay your new overpainting over these with pale cadmium, and I promise you that if at the next overpainting, and with the aid of barium yellow, you do not see pure gold shine at the tip of your brush it is because no matter what you do, you decidedly will never be able to learn the lesson of Secret Number 43—that is, you will never succeed in making gold with painting. And, painter, I recommend to you from every point of view to be rich rather than poor, in the gold of the honey-oils of light and in that of the golden section, both of them having divine proportions, the one in the viscosity of matter and the other in the geometry of the spirit. Yes! I will allow you to use in small doses that supreme fusion of the corpuscular pigments of terrestrial light with Venetian turpentine, but you must mix it with your "sacred oils" only at the end of the life of your painting, which is the moment when it is about to pass into immortality.

Since I have already spoken to you so much about the body and the matter of your picture it is time that I should now deal, in the next and final chapter, with its soul. For it is the soul which sustains your picture. But as I have already told you so philosophically and so profoundly, it is with the body that the soul forms ideas, and in the particular case of the geometry which will rule the monarchy of your art it is the bodies of the five omnipotent solids, which I shall proceed to describe to you.

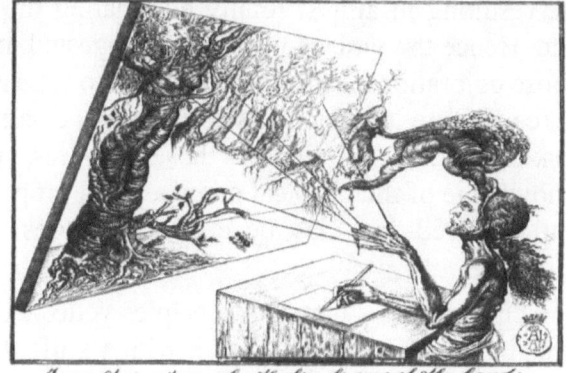

Inspiration entering by the five fingers of the hand.

* Sieur H. Gautier de Nisme: L'Art de laver ou la Nouvelle Manière de Peindre sur le papier ... Brussels,1708.

* 1. Crutch long enough to fit under the arm and brace the model by extending diagonally.

2 Crutch to support the bended knee.

3 Crutch to extend from the Achilles tendon to the thigh of the same leg.

4 Crutch to support the wrist of the left arm.

5 Crutch to hold up the chin.

6 Crutch to extend vertically from the left armpit.

7 Crutch to support the left hand and resting on the left calf.

8 Crutch to support the waist.

9 Crutch for between the legs.

Each crutch is provided with a prong to hold it in place on the wooden platform used by the models. The crutches may also have divisions painted in black and white, thus giving the artist useful points of reference.

* Let us visit one of the most impressive and complete collections of modern art. I was struck, as I took in the great exhibit room as a whole, by the horrible prevailing effect of the coloring that emerges from all those paintings. This is due above all to the monstrous conception of color dating back to impressionism, resulting in almost totally eliminating the blacks from the palette. Hence the violaceous, blued, congested, herpetic aspect of all those colorations, especially the flesh tones, each one of which evokes, before anything else, the most disagreeable varieties of skin disease. Obviously these pictures, painted without any knowledge of the physical and chemical properties of colors, have all changed and may be cruel caricatures of their authors' intentions.

* Inasmuch as metal is harmful to Naples yellow, you will have to bear this in mind and never work it with a knife. But this precaution does not suffice, for as the hairs of the brush are set in

metal, which may touch the paint, it will be necessary to have special brushes to be used only in applying this precious color, brushes of which the hairs are bound by hardened and varnished leather.

$\overset{*}{\text{–}}$ See table page 141.

$\overset{*}{\text{–}}$ List taken from Jacques Blockx, *Compendium of Painting* corroborating twenty years of my own experience.

$\overset{*}{\text{–}}$ See table page 143.

$\overset{*}{\text{–}}$ From Jacques Blockx, *Compendium of Painting*.

CHAPTER FIVE

Why the painter's hand has five fingers–The number five never occurs in the mineral kingdom–Unique properties of the five solid bodies and why there cannot be more than five–Piero della Francesca's egg–Eve's apple, Newton's apple, William Tell's apple, Columbus's egg–The crown of milk–Of the spiritual virtues of the skeleton of the sea urchin–Luca Pacioli's *divina proporzione*–Of the utilization of the golden section in perspective–How to determine the golden section–Manner of constructing a compass for finding the golden section–Of the use of geometric frames–Of the inimitable grace of the curves of vine tendrils–Of the sponge and the cross–The secret of the Angel.

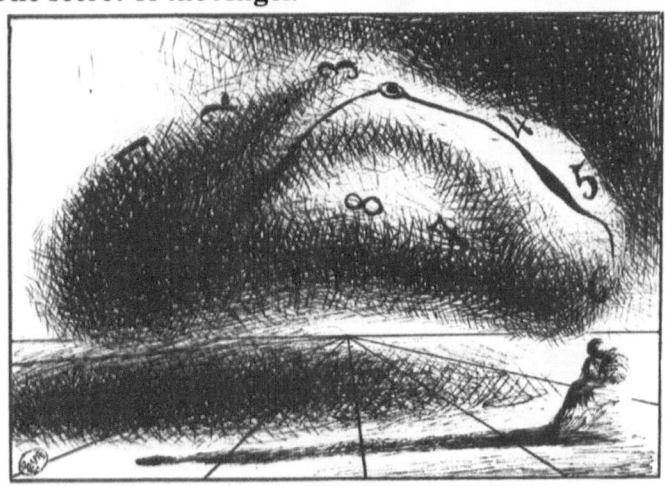

DES INFLATA
(TENEBROSA)

PAINTER, you must now open your painter's hand and look at your painter's fingers. You will see five of them. Count them parsimoniously: one, two, three, four and five—five and not six. Therefore never let that number, five, leave your painter's brain henceforth, for it is essentially the number, not only of your human condition, but also of your cosmogony.

Know at once that among the most inexplicable secrets of nature and of creation is that which rules that the number of five governs the animal and vegetable world, that is to say, the organic world, but that on the other hand never, never does this number of five occur in the mineral or inorganic world. So that if the pentagon must become for you the archetypal figure, since in your painting you must express without discontinuity only the quintessence of the organic, the hexagon on the contrary must be considered by you the prototype of your anti-type, as well as all its derived crystallizations which are the inorganic ones of the mineral realm.

You have thus just understood, in learning this, the profound reason of what your painter's intuition had so surely revealed to you when you confessed to me that you had always detested without knowing why the decorative charm of crystallizations, and especially the congealed, blind, additioned and arithmetical ones of snow. If you do not like them, and are so right in not liking them, it is because your art of painting is exactly the contrary of decorative art, since it is—as you now know—a cognitive art. Therefore know your world, and exclude from your world everything that is outside of the number of five, since you can attain the soul of your work only by the regularity of bodies, and of these there can be only five that are regular—that is to say, bodies of which the sides are regular planes equal to one another. These are the tetrahedron, the cube, the octahedron, the dodecahedron and the icosahedron. In this order they can be enclosed in one another, and all of them can be inscribed, with their points touching it, within the sphere. Consequently you must use only them and their derivatives, which are in infinite number and so complex that most of them can be represented to the human intelligence only by the imagination. Thus, since I believe you when you assure me that you are not lacking in imagination, I shall permit you to consider with me for a moment this august phenomenon: that the architecture of the soul of man may be governed only by the absolute monarchy of the solid body of the sphere.*

Now that you still have present before your eyes the corporeality of the solid sphere and that, having opened your painter's hand, you have counted your own fingers, the organic law of your pentagonal world, I ask you once more to lift your painter's head toward the sky and to observe the celestial vault. But not, this time, in order to consider the color of its azure, so transparent and hard that by common accord we were pleased to liken it, at the beginning of this book, to an agate, but rather in order that you try to render its form sensible to your spirit in relation to the human condition of the solid sphere of your world, and to see that you find yourself exactly beneath a perfect cupola, and thus beneath another monarchy.

Now, and without your ceasing to look fixedly toward the center of this cupola, in which it almost seems as though the celestial shell is opening above you, I ask you to withdraw nimbly and respectfully toward the left side reserved for painters and geometrists. For perpendicularly to the center of the shell, with mathematical exactness, is the spot reserved for the Virgin Mary, that is to say for the queen of heaven. From this moment on I wish you to breathe regularly, but ever so lightly, so that you may observe with the maximum of attention and veneration the divine and human mystery which Piero della Francesca painted for the glory of the centuries. In the august silence which now fills this celestial vault which I have asked you to contemplate and which, thanks to the painter, you have just seen before your wondering eyes materialize and architecturalize itself in the form of a decorative shell from which hangs, by a thread, a dazzlingly white egg, bright as a star suspended gravely, virtually and vertically above the head of the Virgin Mother. This egg is one of the greatest mysteries of the painting of the Renaissance, and it was written that its secret should be Number 44 of this book, for I shall now tell you what Piero della Francesca probably did not know himself. For only modern morphological science permits us to approach such knowledge and such mathematical exactness, which the artist's brain often attains as inevitably as the sea urchin elaborates its intricate geometries. Without ceasing for a second to look at this egg, follow my discourse which, in spite of its speculative elevation, is one of the clearest that have ever been formulated —you can take me at my word—and which will be concise from beginning to end.

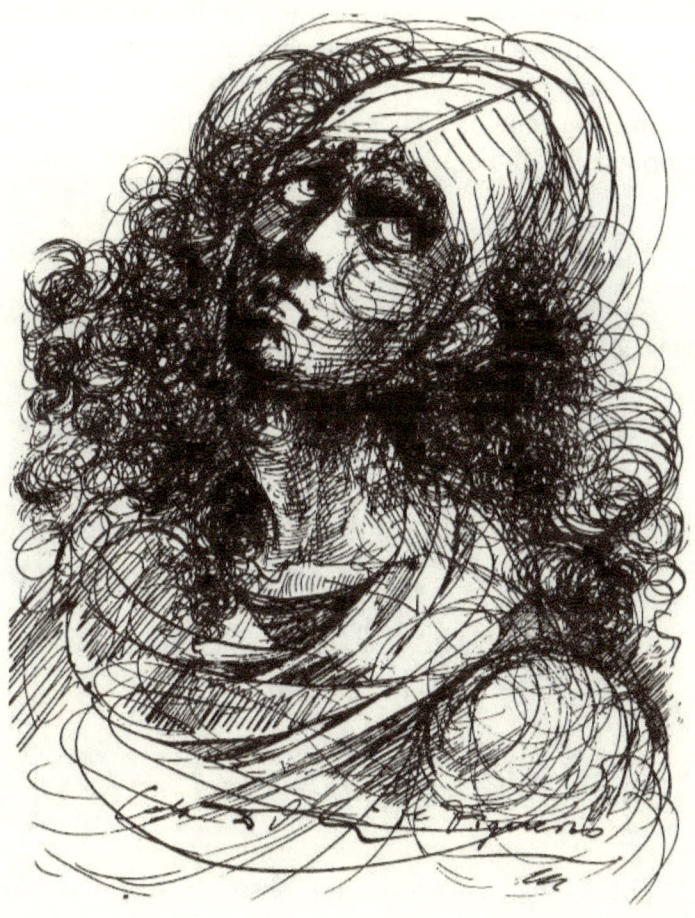

This egg which, as you have already understood,

gravitates beneath the vault of heaven like a world, is gravely suspended over the head of the Virgin Mary, of the Queen, which is the head over which is suspended the greatest weight of gravity, since it is around her that everything, gravitates, that the world gravitates, and the gravity of such a weight placed on her head has, as a consequence and visible symbol, the crown which is maternal since the weight of the solid sphere of the world weighs, not only on the royal head but also on that of all other royal heads of heredity to come. For all that falls on the head of the queen falls also on all the others, past and future, as on a round and limitless recipient filled with the calm and biological lake of the maternal and royal milk, and of which only its architect can determine the contours, since these can be only ideal, as properly corresponds to all that is without limits and thereby absolute.

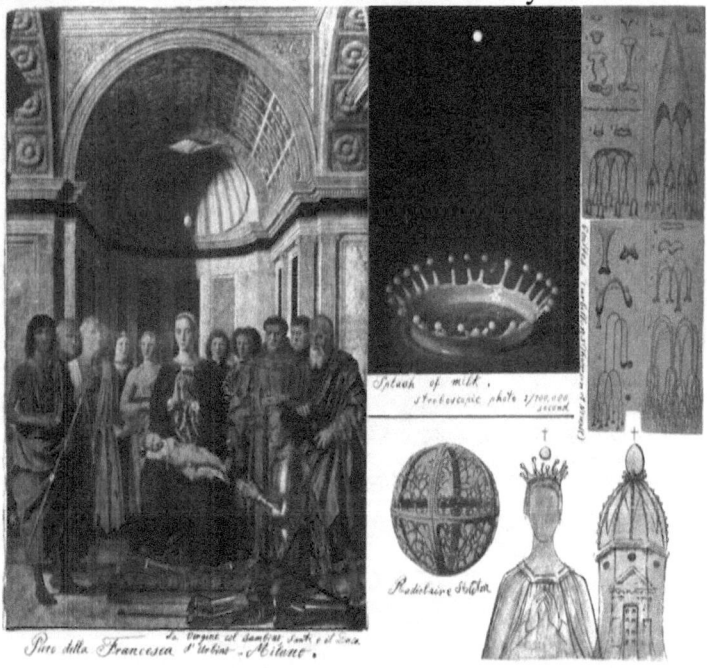

Milk that is white and absolute like the allegorical whiteness of ermine itself and on which the entire weight of the sphere of the world is destined to be placed, forming at the moment of contact and as a physical result the splash which is the crown itself, which thus can only be formed of ermine, that is to say, of milk, and this so completely that the gravity of this world which weighs in the virginal womb of Mary to the point of rendering her heavy, gravid, pregnant with her pure conception, can be rendered visible only on the summit of her majestic head, which is the supremely "visible head," that of the queen, who from that moment "sees" herself crowned—even as certain pentagonal plants are in their turn crowned, growing a vegetal crown at their summit at the moment of flowering. Do not forget this trinity: world, ermine and crown—object, element and effect of your painter's cosmogony—which you will find throughout the "aesthetic monarchies" which have not ceased to rule the civilizations of our occident.

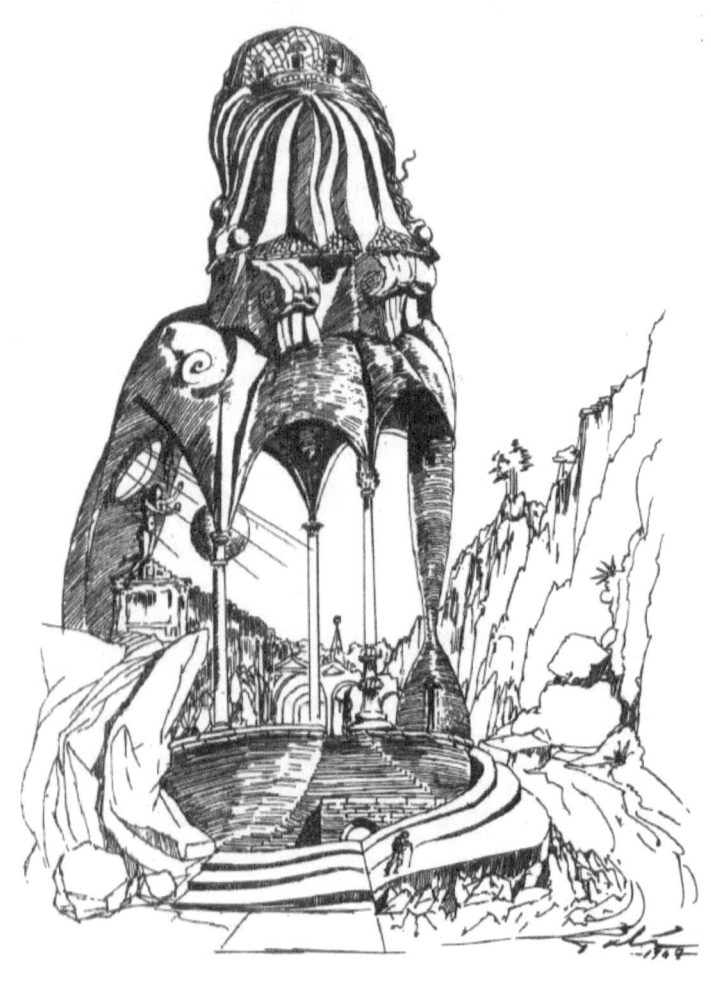

Remember now that the gravity of the world is already exercised in the apple upheld by Eve's hand, like a veritable sword of Damocles suspended over the entire progeniture of humankind, and doubt not that this apple of Eve is the same which, falling on the brow of Newton, caused him to discover the physical law of the force of this very gravity, and that again it is this same apple which you will see later placed in perilous hereditary balance on the head of the son of William Tell himself. Later again this apple of the world becomes an ultra-white egg, that is to say a new world, at the moment when Christopher Columbus discovers the new world, the moment of the unity of Spain over the reign of the Catholic kings, which is essentially, as you know, the maternal reign of Isabel the Catholic.

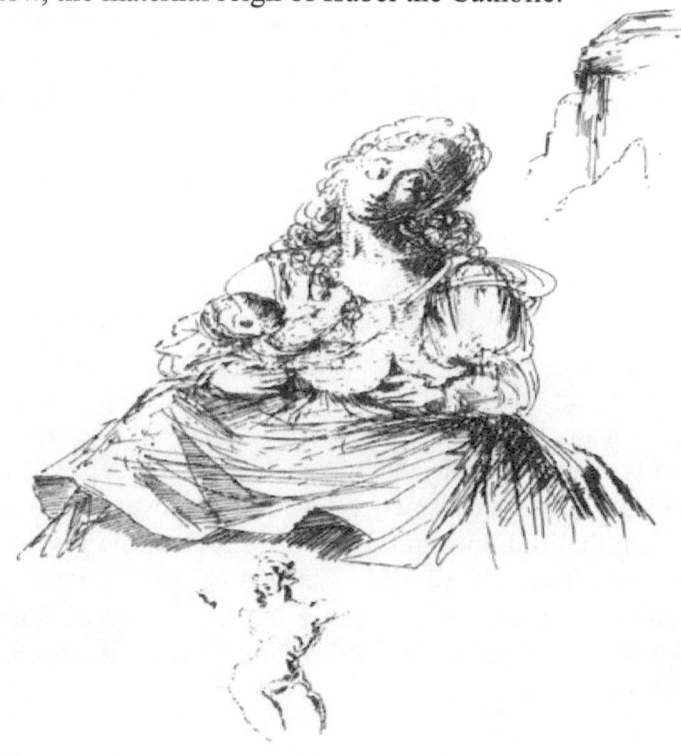

It is thus, and not otherwise, that you must understand that the unity of the egg of Columbus merely continues in a Catholic sense the same unity as that of the force of gravitation of Newton's apple, still pagan and sylvan, and you will have understood this in observing the egg appear, hanging by a thread, attached to the shell of the cupola of heaven and suspended thus over the head of the Virgin Mary. Reflect on the fact that that moment is the tenderest moment, the most biologically acute, of the geometric and architectonic discoveries of the Renaissance, the moment when creation is on the eve of its total accomplishment in perfection, hence the moment of the pre-coronation. For the coronation is close at hand and it occurs when, everything being in place, ordered and perfectly carried out, one adds to the whole, that is to say to the achieved diversity of the whole, and at its summit, an attribute of unity to crown its universality in Catholic fashion, like the ball of the world surmounted by a cross and placed on the culminating crowns of perfect cupolas, or in an even more perfectly Catholic fashion when, on the most perfect of these cupolas, as in the case of certain ones by the divine Bramante, instead of a ball they appear to us surmounted by an egg.

But as the physical law of gravity is inevitable for humans, open your own eyes to see how the world, however delicately it may be poised on the most perfect and Catholic of architectonic monarchies, has nevertheless fallen vertically of its whole weight, and it is from this material fall that the crown is metaphysically born.

The holy crown which appears before your eyes avid of knowledge as the supreme ornamental achievement is nothing more than the irrational and physical residue of the gravity of the world, the foam of absolute perfection, the material splash, precious and venerable maternal relic; the crown of milk, as it forms when a sphere is dropped on the serene and absolute lake of this same milk.

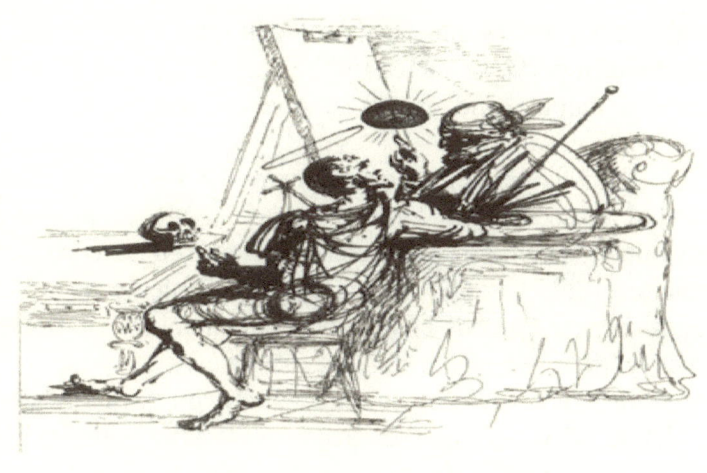

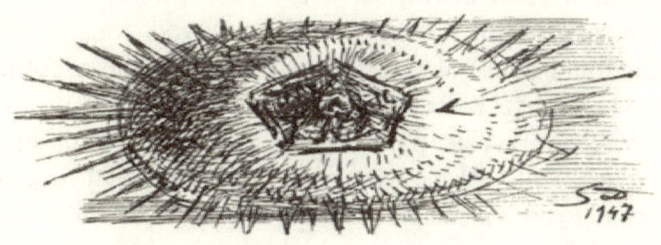

Since, with uplifted head, you are still admiring the crowned summits of the cupola of the perfection on which you perceive and admire the egg of Bramante surmounted by a cross, I shall take advantage of your attitude of ecstasy to enlighten you without wasting a moment as to Secret Number 45, which concerns the aesthetic virtues of that other cupola, and which you will find neither in Vitruvius nor in Pacioli. I am alluding to the sea urchin, in which all the magic splendors and virtues of pentagonal geometry are found resolved, a creature weighted with royal gravity and which does not even need a crown for, being a drop held in perfect balance by the surface tension of its liquid, it is world, cupola and crown at one and the same time, hence universe!

Bow your head, now, toward the depths of those other celestial abysses of the white calms of the Mediterranean Sea and pull out a sea urchin and accustom yourself to considering the entire universe through the geometric quintessence of its teeth, which form a kind of cosmogonic and pentagonal flower in its lower orifice where is lodged its chewing apparatus, called "Aristotle's lantern," and through which you have already formed the habit of watching the progress of your paintings if, as I advised you to do in my third chapter, you have constructed with the sea urchin's skeleton the famous telescope by virtue of which you could judge the degree of perfection of your work. Painter, take my advice: keep ever beside your easel or somewhere close to your work a sea urchin's skeleton, so that its little weight may serve by its sole presence in your meditations, just as the weight of a human skull attends at every moment those of saints and anchorites. For the latter, since they lived constantly in their ecstasies and celestial ravishments, required the presence of the skull which, like ballast, held them to their earthly and human condition; while you, painter, live only in those other ecstasies and ravishments which are given to you, on the contrary, by matter and its viscosity. And you will need that blue-tinged skeleton of the sea urchin which, by its lack of weight, will constantly remind you of the celestial regions which the sensuality of your oils and your media might so easily cause you to forget. Thus the mystic who lives only in the celestial paradise bears in his hand a terrestrial skeleton: the skull of man; while the painter who is an Epicurean—for even if he is often a Stoic in his work, he never ceases to live in terrestrial paradises—must bear in his hand the sea urchin, which is like the very skeleton of heaven. Therefore consider the skull which always appears with anchorites as a simple and typical object of his work. Likewise your sea urchin must figure among the other objects of your studio, beside your hand-supporting stick, your palette and your brushes.

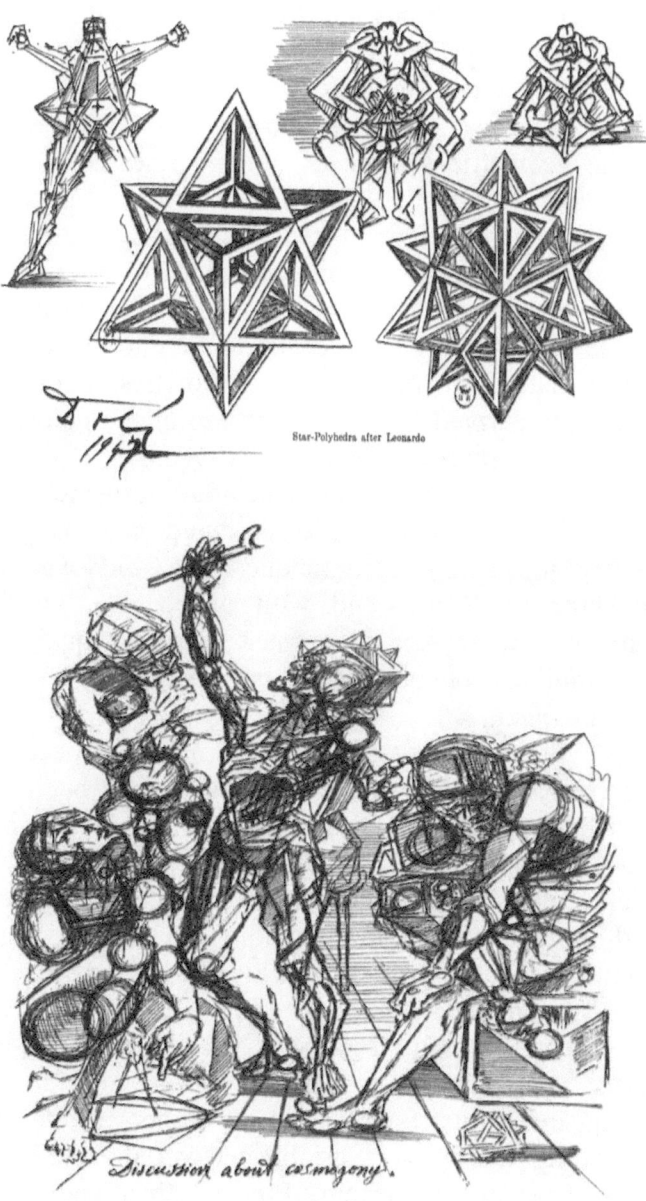

Star-Polyhedra after Leonardo

Discussion about cosmogony.

Since morphology, which is the youngest, the most modern science, which has the greatest future, has in this book just married with royal pomp the most lucid aesthetic geometry of the Renaissance, I tell you here, young painter, YES, YES, YES and YES! you must, especially during your adolescence, make use of the geometric science of guiding lines of symmetry to compose your pictures. I know that painters of more or less romantic tendency claim that these mathematical scaffoldings kill an artist's inspiration, giving him too much to think and reflect upon. Do not hesitate at that moment to answer them promptly that on the contrary it is in order not to have to think and reflect upon them that you make use of the properties, unique and of a natural magic, derived from the wise use of the golden section, and called the *divina proporzione* by Luca Pacioli in his memorable book, the most important of all aesthetic treatises, in which the philosophy of Plato is cured and purged of its primitivistic idealism, a really unique book which was dedicated to the Duke of Urbino and with which you, young artist, especially if you are American, must become acquainted at the very beginning of your studies and have constantly beside you as your bedside book.

But since it is not my intention here to repeat what you may find elsewhere, however excellent it may be, I prefer to continue by unveiling to you a new secret, which bears the Number 46, and which is Dalinian *par excellence:* You wish, for instance, to place objects situated here and there, scattered over a deserted beach, according to the guiding lines. I tell you that you will commit a grave error of primitivism in executing it in the traditional manner. So this is, according to my view, how you must proceed. Simply establish your golden proportions, subjecting them to the contraction given you by the lines converging in infinity, establish points of perspective, just as if your "guiding lines" were established on the surface of the receding plane of the terrain. Proceed thus and know that, however simple this may appear to you, this application in perspective of the guiding lines is wholly original in painting, especially if, in accordance with the "Gestalt theory" you succeed in communicating to it the sense of true configurations and individualized groups. For the eye seizes the most subtle mathematical calculation in spite of the deformations of perspective. I will even go so far as to say that it seizes them *better!* And herein, you may be sure, resides one of the secrets of the melancholy beauty of certain paintings thus conceived.

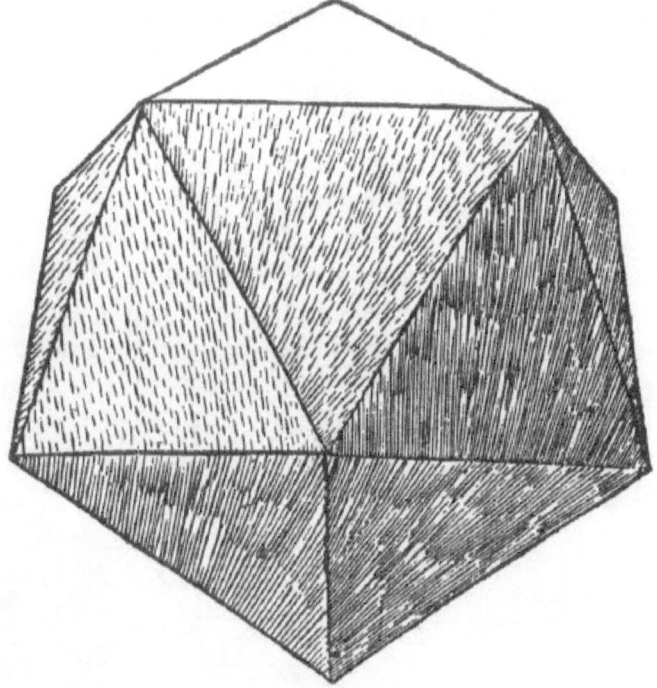

Icosahedron planum solidum

As I do not wish you to spend days and killing hours which you might devote to painting at your mathematical calculations, I shall now reveal to you the secret of a compass—and this is Secret Number 47—by means of which you will be able automatically to find as many golden sections as you wish, without having to have recourse to the painful geometric operation for which you often need an immense compass, requiring that you go beyond the area of your painting, and this is often so inconvenient that your laziness will counsel you at last to get along without such a proportion.

In order to obtain your golden section in the simplest and surest way, begin by drawing a pentagon. From the ends of the base to the top of the pentagon draw the two lines which will form the triangle of the pentagon which, as you must know, is the most perfect triangle which exists. The intersection of the horizontal line drawn between the other two points with either side of this triangle will exactly mark for you the golden section which you wish to obtain.

Take now a slender compass of seasoned olive wood, and with its two points take the exact measure of one of the sides of the triangle. You will then only have to fix rigidly two new branches which join and meet at the intersection which marks the golden section. As this intersection is to remain articulated, any measure which you take with such a compass will determine its golden section. And the fact that such compasses are not currently for sale at paint dealers is but the proof of the lack of geometric rigor of schools of art, and of modern painters in particular.

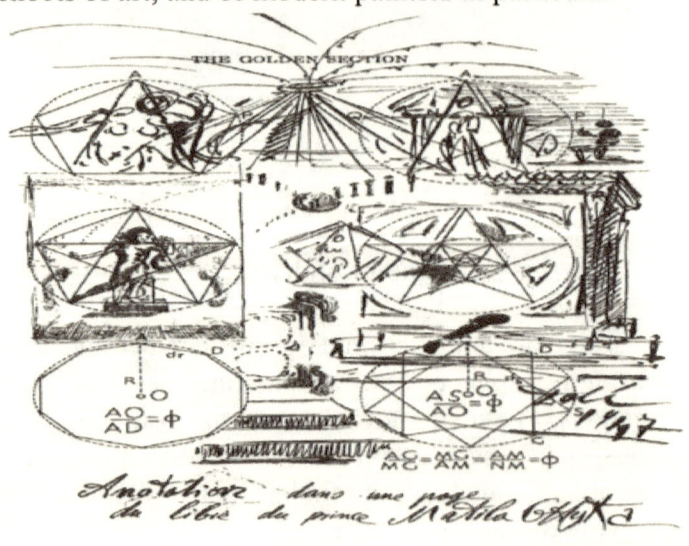

Inasmuch as what is most convincing to you will always be what enters into you most effectively through your eyes, I shall impart to you Secret Number 48. Ask your wood joiner to build for you the following figures out of rectangular strips of very old oak, put together in such a way that they can be easily transported, taking them with you, according to your needs, for your open air sessions with your easel and other tools which you need. These are to be constructed according to the models which Leonardo da Vinci drew for Luca Pacioli—who, incidentally, reports having learned from manuscripts which have since been lost that when Phidias caused to be executed, in the temple of Ceres in Rome, the figure of an icosahedron which was the symbol of water, this figure was a lively subject of speculations and discoveries for the contemporary philosophers and aesthetes, temporarily eclipsing the architectural splendor of the said temple, which, by the way, was excellent from every point of view.

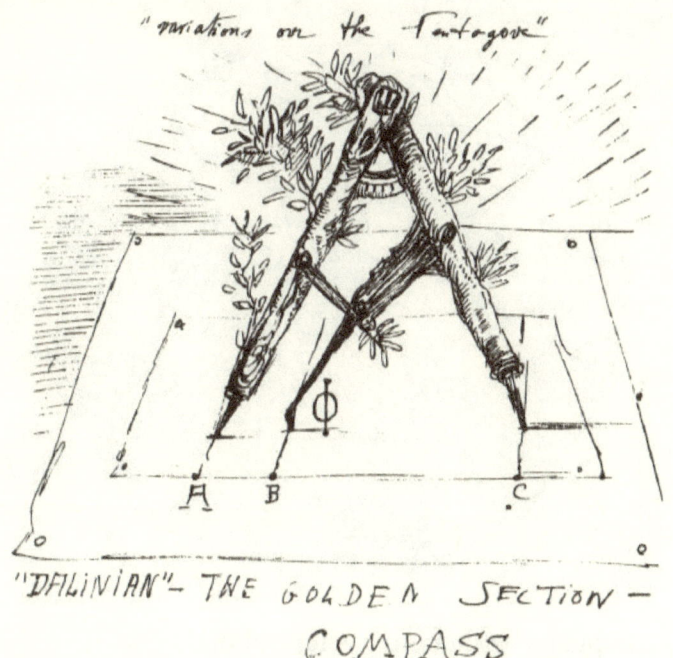

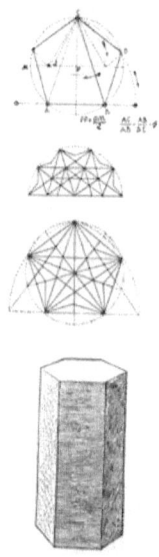

Columna laterata hexagona solida

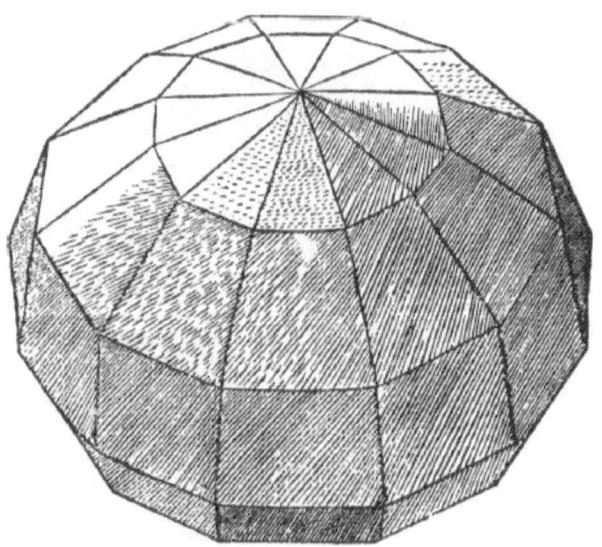

Septuaginta duarum basium solidum

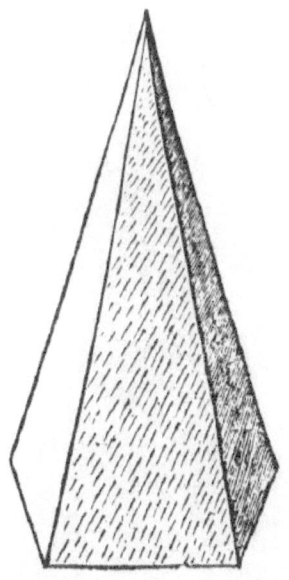

Pyramis laterata penthagona solida

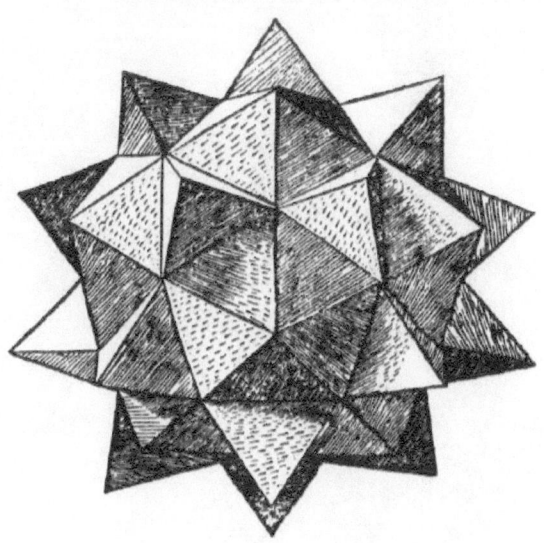

Dodecahedron abscisum elevatum solidum

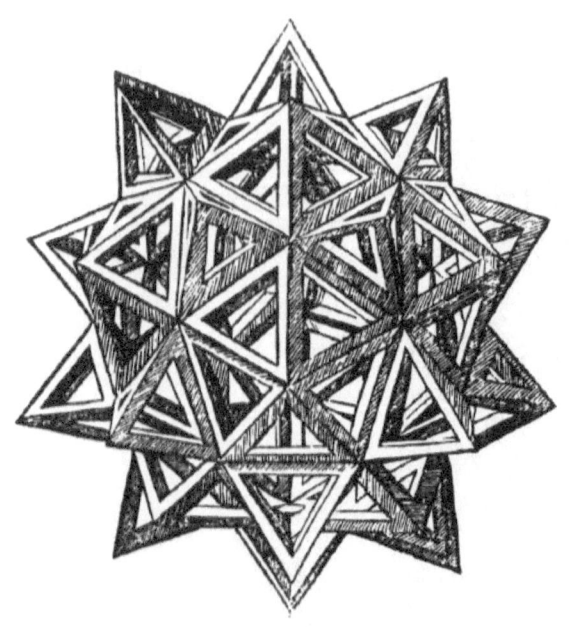

Dodecahedron abscisum elevatum solidum

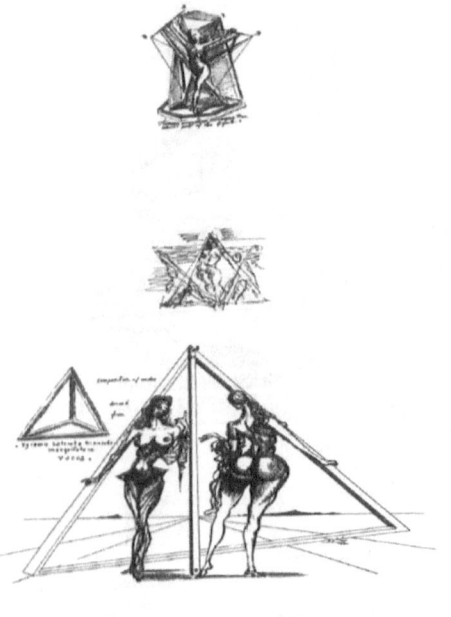

I therefore want your joiner to construct for you an *icosahedron planum vacuum* large enough so that a human figure can stand upright inside it; also an *octahedron elevatum vacuum,* a *dodecahedron planum vacuum,* which as you will remember, is the symbol of the macrocosm, a *columna laterata triangula vacua,* which will be useful for harmonious reclining postures of nude models, a *pyramis laterata quadrangula vacua,* which will be the norm for your seated figures, with its companion, the *pyramis laterata triangula inequilatera vacua,* in which you will easily be able to compose a couple of seated figures.

Only the habit of the presence of these bodies among the objects of your studio will give you a daily familiarity with geometry, and this to the point that if once you try them you will no longer be able to conceive of a painter's studio lacking these pre-established orders, in the empty space of which it will be so easy for you to compose, by placing in them directly your models, your objects, your fragments of landscapes or your skies. They are constructive scaffoldings with which the emptiness of your studio must be, as it were, constantly architecturalized, for they are the materialization of all the problems which your spirit unconsciously, in the antigeometric void, has been blindly seeking to solve, without ever fully succeeding.

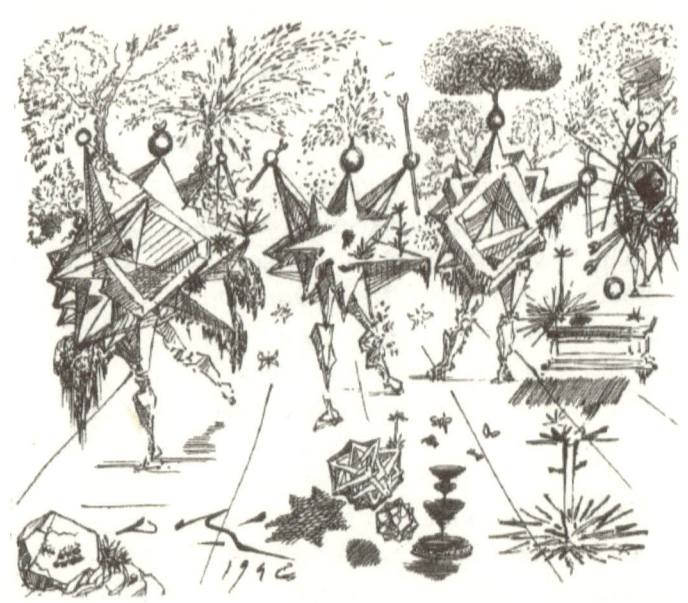

Now that you know my secret regarding the geometries of the straight lines, I shall give you Secret Number 49 regarding the geometry of curves. You must now learn, in addition to the curves of sea urchins, those of spirals and volutes. The archetype of the painter's spiral is given you by the logarithmic spiral which, in nature, can be admired in a great number of shells, and with the most astonishing perfection in the "nautilus" because of its mathematical "gnomonic" growth. But here—and this is the Dalinian secret—I advise you rather to study the curves of certain plants of the pentagonal type, and particularly vine tendrils. For if, in my opinion, the sea urchin is simply perfect, the nautilus seems to me too perfect. While the sea urchin seems rather made by hand, the nautilus attains an almost mechanical perfection.

Here, then, is the promised secret: for the choice of your curves (and this you will not find, either, in Vitruvius), just before the grape harvest, you will cut vine tendrils in profusion and, after having selected them, you will let them fall fortuitously into shallow, perfectly pentagonal recipients containing liquid plaster. Once these have solidified they will give you a series of imprints of a grace truly inimitable and irrational which, outdoing the spirals of the nautilus, will put to shame everything you have seen so far in this difficult and perilous realm of curves which, however decorative you may like them, will be worth nothing if they do not remain biological.

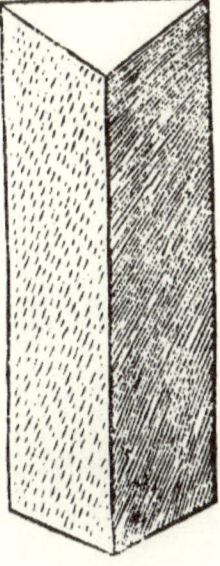

Columan laterata triangula solida

When the moment comes to establish the straight lines according to your needs from the curves contained as samples in your plaster pentagons, I shall ask you to trace in each of these the triangle of the pentagon and to utilize the segments of the imprints of vine tendrils thus cut off and always in harmony and proportion with the measures which the said segments have produced in their triangles. Relations of this kind, because of their irrational similarity to the golden section, I call the "golden vine tendril."

After the golden autumn of your golden vine-section, swear to me that you will never forget the persevering unfolding of the volutes of the fern, which is like the dolphin's head. Make molds of these, too, as well as of the eternal acanthus leaves, which as you know, have never ceased to rejuvenate the ornamentation of all styles, in spite of the fact that too often these styles have copied them by pure routine, their authors having failed to see anew with their own eyes the perennial biology of this leaf unique among all leaves.

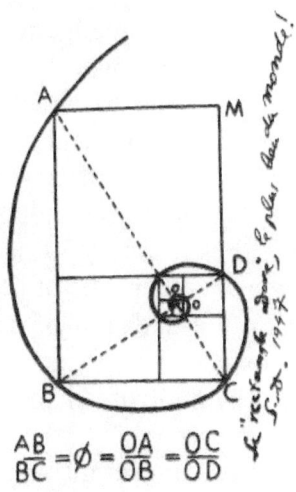

$$\frac{AB}{BC} = \emptyset = \frac{OA}{OB} = \frac{OC}{OD}$$

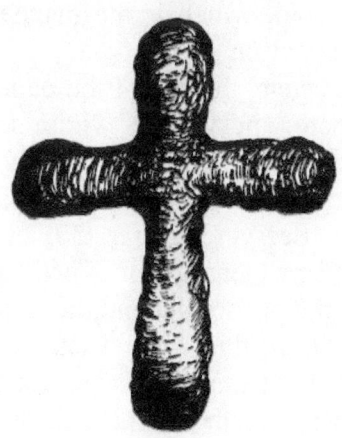

SPONGE SKELETON

Seated as you are now among the most gracious vine tendrils of this month of September of your life, an acanthus leaf budding at your feet from the moldings of the Roman pedestal on which you are seated, I want to beg you to conclude the reading of this book by a short but worshipful meditation on the cross erected at the summit of the balls of the world which crown the most perfect cupolas. Thus I wish you to direct your spiritual exercises of this evening toward the porous and perishable aspect of the sponge, avid by this very fact of absorbing heaven, desirous of being disintegrated. You must understand that the theory of atoms views the world as a sponge of heaven, and you must know that within a sponge, whether it be of heaven or of the sea, there are spicules forming the skeleton of a cross, of that cross toward which once was extended a sponge soaked, not with heaven but with vinegar, as a symbol of all the harshness and bitterness of this world.

In my recent morphological studies the sole cross which I have found was in the interior of sponges. The day you know the world of these sponges as I know it, and especially if you possess the Catholic faith which I myself do not yet possess, you may continue this meditation here just begun and you may do so in the manner most edifying for your soul, which is the manner most suitable to conclude a treatise on painting.

Since Gala—she who sweetens the life of the painter and who is our reality—is always here, and without whom so much natural magic included in this treatise might have made us merit the rigors of the Holy Inquisition, after due prayers, I shall now without further prayer unveil Secret Number 50, which I promised you at the beginning of my clear and brief prologue and which should indeed have been the primordial and the first secret of this book. Secret Number 50 is this: that when you have learned to draw and to paint without mistakes, when you know how to distinguish the sympathies and the antipathies of natural things with your own eyes, when you have become a master in the art of washing and when by your own resources you are able to draw an ant with the reflections corresponding to each one of its minute legs, when you know how to practice habitually your slumber with a key and the so hypnotic one of the three sea perch eyes, when you have become a master in the resurrection of the lost images of your adolescence, thanks to the natural magic of the retrospective use of your araneariums, when you have possessed the mystery and the most hidden virtues belonging to each of the colors and their relations to one another, when you have become a master in blending, when your science of drawing and of perspective has attained the plenitude of that of the masters of the Renaissance, when your pictures are painted with the golden wasp media which were then as yet unknown, when you know how to handle your golden section and your mathematical aspirations with the very lightness of your thought, and when you possess the most complete collection of the most unique curves, thanks to the Dalinian method of their instantaneous molding in dazzlingly white and perfect pentagons of plaster, etc. etc. etc., nothing of all this will yet be of much avail! For the last secret of this book is that before all else it is absolutely necessary that at the moment when you sit down before your easel to paint your picture, your "painter's hand" be guided by an angel.

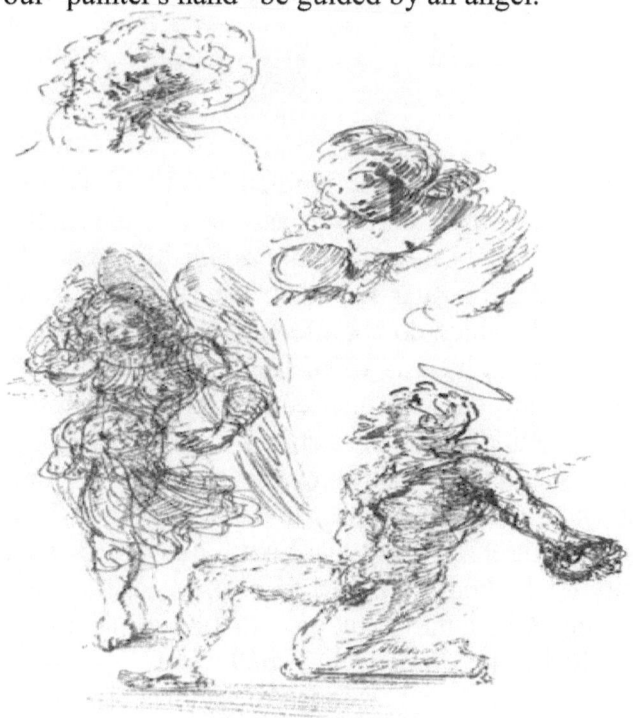

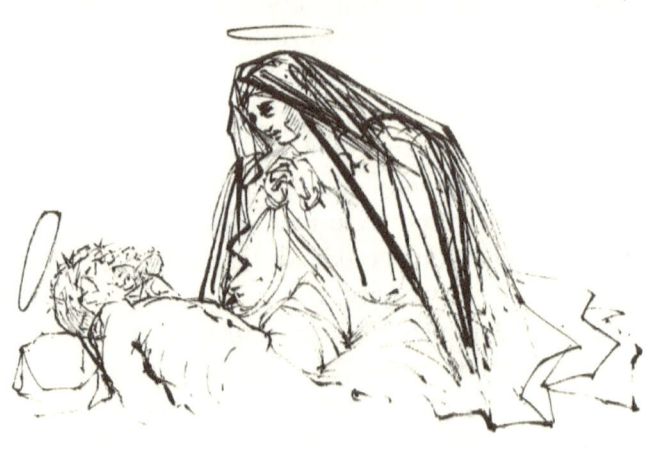

On the Form of Sea Urchins*

As a corollary to the problem of the bird's egg, we may consider for a moment the forms assumed by the shells of the sea urchins. These latter are commonly divided into two classes—the Regular and the Irregular Echinids. The regular sea urchins, save in slight details which do not affect our problem, have a complete axial symmetry. The axis of the animal's body is vertical, with mouth below and the intestinal outlet above; and around this axis the shell is built as a symmetrical system. It follows that in horizontal section the shell is everywhere circular, and we need only consider its form as seen in vertical section or projection. The irregular urchins (very inaccurately so-called) have the anal extremity of the body removed from its central, dorsal situation; and it follows that they have now a single plane of symmetry, about which the organism, shell and all, is bilaterally symmetrical. We need not concern ourselves in detail with the shapes of their shells, which may be simply interpreted, by the help of radial coordinates, as deformations of the circular or "regular" type.

While the sea urchin is alive, an immense number of delicate "tube-feet," with suckers at their tips, pass through minute pores in the shell, and, like so many long cables, moor the animal to the ground. They constitute a symmetrical system of forces, with one resultant downwards, in the direction of gravity, and another outwards in a radial direction; and if we look upon the shell as originally spherical, both will tend to depress the sphere into a flattened cake. We need not consider the radial component, but may treat the case as that of a spherical shell symmetrically depressed under the influence of gravity. This is precisely the condition which we have to deal with in a drop of liquid lying on a plate; the form of which is determined by its own uniform surface tension, plus gravity, acting against the internal hydrostatic pressure. Simple as this system is, the full mathematical investigation of the form of a drop is not easy, and we can scarcely hope that the systematic study of the Echinodermata will ever be conducted by methods based on Laplace's differential equation;[1] but we have little difficulty in seeing that the various forms represented in a series of sea urchin shells are no other than those which we may easily and perfectly imitate in drops.

In the case of the drop of water (or of any other particular liquid) the specific surface tension is always constant, and the pressure varies inversely as the radius of curvature; therefore the smaller the drop the more nearly is it able to conserve the spherical form, and the larger the drop the more does it become flattened under gravity.[2] We can imitate this phenomenon by using india-rubber balls filled with water, of different sizes; the little ones will remain very nearly spherical, but the larger will fall down "of their own weight," into the form of more and more flattened cakes; and we see the same thing when we let drops of heavy oil fall through a tall column of water, the little ones remaining round, and the big ones getting more and more flattened as they sink. In the case of the sea-urchins, the same series of forms may be assumed to occur, irrespective of size, through variations in T, the specific tension, or "strength" of the enveloping shell. Accordingly we may study, entirely from this point of view, such a series as the following. In a very few cases, such as the fossil Palaeechinus, we have an approximately spherical shell, that is to say a shell so strong that the influence of gravity becomes negligible as a cause of deformation, just as (to compare small things with great) the surface tension of mercury is so high that small drops of it seem perfectly spherical.[3] The ordinary species of Echinus begin to display a pronounced depression, and this reaches its maximum in such soft-shelled flexible forms as Phormosoma. On the general question I took the opportunity of consulting Mr. C. R. Darling, who is an acknowledged expert in drops, and he at once agreed with me that such forms are no other than diagrammatic illustrations of various kinds of drops, "most of which can easily be reproduced in outline by the aid of liquids of approximately equal density to water, although some of them are fugitive." He found a difficulty in the case of the outline which represents Asthenosoma, but the reason for the anomaly is obvious; the flexible shell has flattened down until it has come in contact with the hard skeleton of the jaws, or "Aristotle's lantern," within, and the curvature of the outline is accordingly disturbed.

On Spider Webs[*]

This whole phenomenon, of equal and regularly interspaced beads, often with little beads regularly interspaced between the larger ones, and now and then with a third order of still smaller beads regularly intercalated, may be easily observed in a spider's web, such as that of Epeira, very often with beautiful regularity — sometimes interrupted and disturbed by a slight want of homogeneity in the secreted fluid; and the same phenomenon is repeated on a grosser scale when the web is bespangled with dew, and its threads bestrung with pearls innumerable. To the older naturalists, these regularly arranged and beautifully formed globules on the spider's web were frequent sources of wonderment. Blackwell, counting some twenty globules in a tenth of an inch, calculated that a large garden-spider's web should comprise about 120,000 globules; the net was spun and finished in about forty minutes, and Blackwell was filled with admiration of the skill and quickness with which the spider manufactured these little beads. And no wonder, for according to the above estimate they had to be made at the rate of about 50 per second.[4]

On Liquid Amber[*]

In the British Museum there is a manuscript by Theodore de Mayerne, entitled, "Pictoria Sculptoris, Tinctoria, et quoe subalternarum Artium spectantia in lingua Latina, Gallica, Italica, Germanica conscripta a Petro Paulo Rubens, Van Dyke, Somers, Greenbury, Jansen, etc. fol. no. XIX, a.d. 1620, T. de Mayerne," in which the author enumerates the principal methods adopted by the painters of his own time, notably Rubens and Van Dyck. Relating a conversation he had with the latter, he writes:

"He spoke to me about an exquisite white, by the side of which the finest white of lead appears Grey, which he said was known to Rubens."

"Item d'un homme que dissolvoit l'ambre sans le brusler,

de sorte que la dissolution estoit blanche jaune, transparent."
Manuscript p. 155.

On Splashes[*]

In Mr. Worthington's beautiful experiments on splashes,[5] it was found that the fall of a round pebble into water from a height first formed a dip or hollow in the surface, and then caused a filmy "cup" of water to rise up all round, opening out trumpet fashion or closing in like a bubble, according to the height from which the pebble fell. The cup or "crater" tends to be fluted in alternate ridges and grooves, its edges get scalloped into corresponding lobes and notches, and the projecting lobes or prominences tend to break off or break up into drops or beads. A similar appearance is seen on a great scale in the edge of a breaking wave: for the smooth edge becomes notched or sinuous, and the surface nearby becomes ribbed or fluted, owing to the internal flow being helped here and hindered there by a viscous shear; and then all of a sudden the uneven edge shoots out an array of tiny jets, which break up into the countless droplets which constitute "spray." The naturalist may be reminded also of the beautifully symmetrical notching of the calycles of many hydroid zoophytes, which little cups had begun their existence as liquid or semi-liquid films before they became stiff and rigid. The next phase of the splash (with which we are less directly concerned) is that the crater subsides, and where it stood a tall column rises up, which also tends, if it be tall enough, to break up into drops. Lastly the column sinks down in its turn, and a ripple runs out from where it stood.

The edge of our little cup forms a liquid ring or annulus, comparable on the one hand to the edge of an advancing wave, and on the other to a liquid thread or cylinder if only we conceive the thread to be bent round into a ring; and accordingly, just as the thread segments first into an unduloid and then into separate spherical drops, so likewise will the edge of cup or annulus tend to do. This phase of notching, or beading, of the edge of the splash is beautifully seen in many of Worthington's experiments,[6] and still more beautifully in recent work (page 172.)[7]

On Gnomonic Forms[*]

There are certain things, says Aristotle, which suffer no alteration (save magnitude) when they grow. Thus if we add to a square an L-shaped portion, shaped like a carpenter's square, the resulting figure is still a square; and the portion which we have so added, with this singular result, is called in Greek a "gnomon."

Euclid extends the term to include the case of any parallelogram whether rectangular or not; and Hero of Alexandria specifically defines a gnomon (as indeed Aristotle had implicitly defined it), as any figure which, being added to any figure whatsoever, leaves the resultant figure similar to the original. Included in this important definition is the case of numbers, considered geometrically; that is to say, by means of rows of dots or other signs or in the pattern of a tiled floor; all according to "the mystical way of Pythagoras, and the secret magick of numbers." For instance, the triangular numbers, 1, 3, 6, 10 etc., have the natural numbers for their "differences"; and so the natural numbers may be called their gnomons, because they keep the triangular numbers still triangular. In like manner the square numbers have the successive odd numbers for their gnomons, as follows:

$$0 + 1 = 1^2$$

$1^2 + 3 = 2^2$
$2^2 + 5 = 3^2$
$3^2 + 7 = 4^2$ etc.

And this gnomic relation we may illustrate graphically by dots whose addition keeps the annexed figures perfect squares.

There are other gnomic figures more curious still. For example, if we make a rectangle such that the two sides are in the ratio of 1: √2, it is obvious that, on doubling it, we obtain a similar figure; for 1 : √2 :: √2 : 2; and each half of the figure accordingly, is now a gnomon to the other. Were we to make our paper of such a shape (say roughly, 10 in. x 7 in.), we might fold and fold it, and the shape of folio, quarto and octavo pages would be all the same. For another elegant example, let us start with a rectangle whose sides are in the proportion of the "divine" or "golden section" that is to say as 1 : 1/2 (√5 □ 1), or, approximately, as 1 : 0.618... The gnomon to this rectangle is the square erected on its longer side, and so on successively.

In any triangle, as Hero of Alexandria tells us, one part is always a gnomon to the other part. For instance, in the triangle ABC, let us draw BD, so as to make the angle CBD equal to the angle A. Then the part BCD is a triangle similar to the whole triangle ABC, and ABD is a gnomon to BCD. A very elegant case is when the original triangle ABC is an isosceles triangle having one angle of 36°, and the other two angles, therefore, each equal to 72°. Then, by bisecting one of the angles of the base, we subdivide the large isosceles triangle into two isosceles triangles, of which one is similar to the whole figure and the other is its gnomon. There is good reason to believe that this triangle was especially studied by the Pythagoreans; for it lies at the root of many interesting geometrical constructions, such as the regular pentagon, and its mystical "pentalpha," and a whole range of other curious figures beloved of the ancient mathematicians: culminating in the regular, or pentagonal, dodecahedron, which symbolised the universe itself, and with which Euclidean geometry ends.

List of permanent colours which can be used with confidence—*

BLANC D'ARGENT ☐ Carbonate of pure lead obtained by wet process, by precipitating a salt of lead with carbonic acid.

The colour which plays the most important part in painting is, without doubt, white. Various productions have been proposed by chemists as white colours but carbonate of lead has always been preferred, because with great permanency it unites qualities possessed by no other whites. With oil, it forms combinations which contribute to increase the permanency. The experiments I have conducted, have proved that for artistic painting, pure carbonate of lead, or blanc d'argent is indispensable. The ordinary leads are not of a sufficiently vivid white; for the most part they are adulterated, often they are acid, which is plainly deleterious to the colour and oils.

When manufactured under favourable conditions and sufficiently washed, blanc d'argent has no perceptible effect on permanent colours; it is as opaque as the best white leads and covers perfectly. It is recognizable by the brilliancy of its whiteness and its fineness. Ground with oil, it forms a paste which ought not to contain the minutest grain nor have the slightest acid smell.

ZINC WHITE (Oxide of Zinc) — The finest zinc white is obtained by the combustion of the metal in the open air.

I have thoroughly and carefully tested this product, the advantages of which are that it does not blacken on contact with sulphurous fumes, is not affected by the colours in the composition of which sulphur is contained, does not form combinations with oils which tend to produce a yellow tint after it has dried, and finally is not poisonous as are carbonate of lead, and ordinary leads.

But these qualities, which would render zinc white so useful to painters in oil, are accompanied by an essential defect which strictly prohibits its exclusive use.

This defect consists in the fact that oxide of zinc becomes glassy, brittle and very liable to scale off.

Zinc white must not be banished from the palette. It has its value for making up tints with vermilion, China cinnabar and sometimes with certain badly manufactured cadmiums. Its tendency to become brittle is toned down by the addition of these colours.

In the light parts of a picture — skies, snowy effects, flowers and white fabrics — in short, where-ever it is desired that the picture should preserve an absolute purity of tone, zinc white, either pure or mixed with other colours, can be turned to account; but it must then be applied by way of light glazings on a blanc d'argent background.

LIGHT RED (Rouge Anglais) □ Sesquioxide of iron.

MARS RED — Sesquioxide of iron and oxide of aluminium.

These two productions are alike for their permanency; their tint is capable of variation, notably by calcination. Mixed with blanc d'argent the Mars red gives a more delicate shade than the light red. Both possess very considerable colouring powers.

VENETIAN RED — A natural colour tinted by iron, like the ochres, and which has undergone a particular process. Mixed with blanc d'argent the beautiful Venetian red imparts very fine tones of a perfect permanency.

INDIAN RED — Of the same nature as the preceding. A beautiful and very permanent colour, which mixes well with blanc d'argent.

PERMANENT MADDER CARMINE. MADDER LAKES, ROSE AND RED, (unroasted) — Madder lakes are composed of alumina and the colouring principle of the root of madder or alizarine; they are prepared by the wet process. The shade of natural, i.e. unroasted madder lakes varies from pale rose to deep blood-red; some have more purple than others, according to the process of manufacture and the quality of the madder roots employed.

These colours possess the defect of drying too slowly; they have a greater tendency than others to crack, when mixed with siccatives, especially when they are applied en glacis.

There are a dozen different rose and red madder lakes on the panel of Dyckmans. Of these, only two have properly preserved their shade, both in the natural state and in mixture with white lead. Crystallized red lake has offered the best resistance. A specimen of Smyrna purple lake and another of permanent madder carmine have proved very stable in their pure state, but the tint of their mixture with the white has much deteriorated. It should be noticed that dark madder lakes, as also permanent madder carmine, do not preserve their shade when mixed with white.

To sum up: the good madder lakes can be usefully employed, their employment is, moreover, indispensable in certain kinds of painting. Their permanency is indisputable.

BURNT SIENNA — Argillaceous earth, coloured by iron and roasted.

Its shade varies according to the degree of heat reached during roasting.

This colour is certainly one of the most permanent; it enamels in process of time, and with blanc d'argent gives very durable shades.

MARS SCARLET. MARS ORANGE — Calcined oxides of iron and aluminium arising from Mars yellow, the original product.

Like all the Mars colours they possess great permanence, and with blanc d'argent, give tones of great delicacy.

CADMIUM ORANGE AND YELLOW, CADMIUM LEMON, CADMIUM RED. — Sulphides of cadmium.

The most beautiful cadmium yellows are obtained by the precipitation of a salt of cadmium with sulphuretted hydrogen. Those produced by the calcination of a mixture of sulphur and oxide of cadmium do not possess so beautiful a tint; they appear more earthy, and their particles are not so minutely divided.

Some authors pretend that cadmium yellow decomposes and blackens white lead. This phenomenon is, in fact, noticeable when the two substances are mixed in a moist or even dry state; but when they are ground with oil their mixture produces no appreciable reaction. When cadmium is free of uncombined sulphur I have never been able to discover the minutest change in the shade obtained. On the contrary, I have noticed that the incorporation of a small quantity of white lead with cadmium yellows enables them to preserve their brilliancy.

The numerous samples of mixtures of cadmium and carbonate of lead, which are found on the panels of Dyckmans have, after about eighty years, preserved an incomparable purity. Light and middle cadmium yellows and cadmium orange should therefore preferably be employed to obtain with white lead the delicate tints which approach the canary, straw and salmon colours.

MARS YELLOW — Hydrated oxide of iron and oxide of aluminium.

Mars yellow is the primitive colour obtained by precipitating a solution of chloride or sulphate of iron and alum, with ammonia, carbonate of soda or potash in variable proportions. Calcined at different degrees of heat, it yields scarlet, orange, orange-yellow, red opaque brown, transparent brown and violet.

All the Mars colours are notable for an indisputed permanency. They have the advantage of not heightening the tones, like the ochres. They blend perfectly with white of lead and their state of extreme divisibility allows shades of a very fine delicacy to be obtained.

On the experimental panel of Dyckmans, the Mars colours and their mixtures with the white possess a freshness and purity which is really remarkable. Unfortunately, these good colours are rarely well prepared by the trade; their difficult and delicate manufacture demands great care. The result of their costliness is that often less expensive substances, such as the ochres, are mixed with them to the injury of both their beauty and their permanency.

AUREOLIN — Double nitrite of cobalt and potassium.

Since 1879, I have been experimenting with this salt, the permanency of which seemed to me to be doubtful. I am now positive that it can be classed among the permanent colours.

Aureolin is a product of the laboratory, which can only be obtained in its perfection after much trouble and care. In its dry state it is of citron colour and remains quite yellow after having been ground, when it is well prepared. When the contrary is the case, the oil, in moistening it, gives it a brownish aspect.

All dark aureolin should be rejected because it heightens its tone to such an extent as to lose its primitive shade or become brownish.

Aureolin can serve to glaze the colours, but its principal use is that of being blended with Veronese green and other oxides of chromium, which will be mentioned later on. It is preferable to light cadmium, because the tints it furnishes are more transparent, warmer, more luminous and also more durable.

Aureolin is a valuable acquisition for the palette. It is the only colour capable of replacing Indian yellow and woad-lake (laque de gaude), the instability of which is well known.

TRANSPARENT YELLOW — Nitrite of cobalt, potassium and alumina.

This colour possesses the same qualities as aureolin, but its shade being paler, it is useful for composing delicate green tints with Veronese green.

ITALIAN EARTH — Hydrated sesquioxide of iron, alumina, and silica.

Several earths or ochres exist which are known under this name. As a good colour it is not often found; it is transparent and of a beautiful golden yellow-brown. Its mixture with blanc d'argent yields very pure and very durable tones.

It advantageously replaces raw sienna, which has the defect of becoming brownish.

A sample of Italian earth from the celebrated firm of Rowney, in London, is on the above-mentioned panels of Dyckmans, and has undergone no deterioration since 1847.

VERONESE GREEN (Vert Emeraude). — Hydrated oxide of chromium.

Is obtained by the calcination of a mixture of bichromate of potash and boric acid.

This superb colour possesses such permanency that a comparison of the specimens on the two panels of Dyckmans reveals no perceptible difference. The mixtures of Veronese green and white lead which have been exposed to the sun, have preserved great freshness, they having even acquired a refinement of shade greater than those deprived of light.

Veronese green is the most durable pigment on the palette.

CELADON GREEN — Anhydrous oxide of chromium, pulverulent.

The colour of this green resembles that of willow leaves. With white, it yields very delicate tones.

LIGHT OLIVE GREEN. "MARIE COLLART" GREENS — Hydrated oxides of chromium and alumina.

LAMORINIERE GREEN — Anhydrous oxide of chromium and aluminium.

In my first edition I described Veronese green as the only green colour admissible in artistic painting; since that time the study of various oxides of chromium has caused me to change my opinion. I find that those calcined at a high temperature are all equally permanent. In the course of my experiments, I conceived the idea of combining alumina with the oxide of chromium, and my researches have led to the discovery of a series of green colours of varied shades. I have adopted those which seem to me the most useful.

The light olive green advantageously replaces green earth or Verona earth, which has the defect of blackening. It is semi-transparent, and suitable for delicate flesh tints.

The principal quality of the "Marie Collart" greens is not to deaden the white. They can be employed in the shaded portions of flesh-studies.

Lamoriniere green is velvety, without having too great a brilliancy. It can be made use of in the varied tones of landscape painting.

All these greens have been rigorously tested. Light and the mephitic gases have no effect on the compounds of chromium and alumina. Like Veronese green, these can be mixed with other colours.

COBALT GREEN or RINNMANN GREEN — A combination of oxide of cobalt and oxide of zinc.

This colour is manufactured in two different ways. The inventor, Rinnmann, obtained it by precipitating a solution of nitrate of cobalt and nitrate of zinc by means of carbonate of potash, and calcining the precipitate at the required temperature.

This process has been modified, as the product it yielded was of inferior quality. At the present time the best cobalt greens are prepared by calcining a mixture of oxide of zinc and nitrate or sulphate of cobalt in varying proportions, according to the tint which the colour is required to possess.

The different cobalt greens which I have made

I think that this change of shade is due to the colouring matter becoming more compact during drying.

Cobalt green appears to be superfluous, because by mixing ultramarine and a little blue-black with Veronese green, a permanent tint is obtained which is similar but much more beautiful.

COBALT BLUE (Thenard Blue) — Aluminate of cobalt.

A very permanent colour, which mixes well with blanc d'argent. Several shades exist in commerce; the deepest are the most stable.

COERULEUM BLUE — A combination of oxides of cobalt and pewter.

This colour, which is extremely useful to the landscape painter, possesses the property of not changing its shade under artificial light. When used with white it furnishes permanent nonvioletish tints approaching sky blue.

ULTRAMARINE — True ultramarine, derived from lapis lazuli, is certainly a permanent colour, but its exorbitant price has practically caused its complete abandonment.

GUIMET'S ULTRAMARINE — Guimet, at Lyons, was the first to discover, in 1872, the method of artificially manufacturing an ultramarine, the beauty of which equals that of lapis lazuli.

The superfine blue of Guimet is the best adapted for artistic purposes. It is of a very rich tint, blends well with blanc d'argent, and has absolute permanency.

Ordinary ultramarine is composed of alumina, carbonate of soda, and sulphur.

COBALT VIOLET — Arseniate of cobalt and magnesia.

My personal investigations have proved that this beautiful colour has a complete permanency. It can be mixed with madder lakes, permanent carmine, cobalt blue and ultramarine blue. The shades it furnishes with blanc d'argent are comparable for their purity and brilliancy to those of Veronese green.

Cobalt violet decomposes on contact with iron. *It should therefore not be touched with the steel palette knife.*

MARS VIOLET and MARS BROWN — The same qualities as the other colours of this name.

CASSEL EARTH — Lignite or decomposed wood.

The colour is a fine very deep brown, very transparent, very permanent in the pure state or when mixed with browns, blacks and lakes. *I have noticed that Cassel Earth fades when mixed with blanc d'argent.*

BLUE BLACK — Calcined vineshoots.

IVORY BLACK — Calcined ivory.

These two blacks are equally permanent; their shades differ appreciably as much in their natural condition as when mixed with blanc d'argent.

Blue black imparts to the white shades a trifle more blueish than does the ivory black, and is more suitable for skies.

Mixtures of ivory black and white occasionally tend to heighten the tone; blue black, therefore, should be given the preference in the composition of certain tints, the value of which might not increase without injuring the effects sought after.

Besides the colours just described, there are still some which can be employed without danger, but in conditions of purity which should be determined; others, like vermilion, should be avoided in mixtures. I am making these colours the subject of a special paragraph in order to more particularly direct the attention of my readers to them.

I can only be thankful for having been scrupulous and severe regarding the admission on the palette of certain colours of which I was in doubt. After further experience extending over several years I cannot but maintain my previous opinion with the exception, however, or cobalt-green which I have definitely placed amongst the permanent colours.

VERMILION — Sulphide of mercury.

When this colour is perfectly prepared and applied with a thorough knowledge of its effects, it preserves a portion of the brilliancy of its shade; it is rarely found of good quality and the generality of the vermilions sold rapidly deteriorate. China produces the best and most permanent vermilion. I have learnt from an unquestionable source, however, that that country does not export vermilion of extra quality. England and Germany supply vermilions that sometimes are exceedingly good.

Among the specimens of this colour to be found on the panel of Dyckmans, only one, of German origin, is well preserved. All the others have contracted a greyish tint after their exposure to the light.

ROUGE DE POUZZOLE — Same composition and identical qualities as Venetian red.

VAN DYCK RED — Oxide of iron.

This colour is obtained by the calcination of sulphate of iron at a fixed temperature. It possesses great permanency. It is often prepared by means of burnt ochres; for this reason I advise Mars red in preference.

BARYTA YELLOW — Chromate of barium is obtained by precipitating a solution of chloride of barium with neutral chromate of potash.

This colour, which has been under my observation since 1881, has preserved all its purity; it enamels like madder lakes. Being absolutely innocuous, it can be mixed with white and other colours.

NAPLES YELLOW — Calcined mixture of carbonate of lead, tartarated antimony, alum and salamoniac in indefinite proportions.

Naples yellow, when well made, is permanent; it can be mixed with blanc d'argent.

The varied products now found in the market under the names of yellow ultramarine and Naples yellow, leave much to be desired; as a rule, they fade in a short time. They ought therefore to be tested before being used.

Naples yellow deteriorates in contact with iron; consequently it must not be applied by means of the steel palette knife.

Naples yellow has far too high a repute and, in my opinion, does not merit the importance which many artists attach to it. As it can only be mixed with a few colours, it presents little real utility; the tints obtained by means of cadmium yellows and blanc d'argent seem to me preferable because of their great permanency.

The shades of Naples yellow are also approximated to by mixing Italian earth, a little Veronese green and blanc d'argent.

Some authors declare the genuine Naples yellow to be extracted from the lava of Vesuvius. Others affirm that this colour was first manufactured at Naples. Having positively learnt that Italy imports Naples yellow manufactured in France and Germany, I considered it needless to further pursue investigations. I had commenced to discover the exact source of this colour.

YELLOW OCHRE. GOLDEN OCHRE. OCRE DE RU. — Clayey earths coloured with oxide of iron.

The ochres are durable colours; they can be ranked among permanent colours. Nevertheless, to be of useful service in artistic painting, they must be properly purified by dilution and slowly dried in the open air, for if not they will heighten their tone in the course of years.

BROWN OCHRE. OCRE BRUNE MATE. — Same remarks as the above.

BURNT OCHRE — The permanency of burnt ochres is generally very great. Their stability depends upon their purification. Their tint is never as fine as that of Mars colours, and they do not produce the same delicacy of shade when mixed with blanc d'argent.

VAN DYCK BROWN. IRON BROWN. — Obtained by special calcination of sulphate of iron.

Like Van Dyck Red, they are often made of ochres or earths. It is therefore better to employ Mars Brown, which is superior in every respect.

PEACH BLACK. CORK BLACK. — Carbonised peach stones, carbonised bark of cork-oak.

The permanency of these two substances is sufficiently great for them to be included amongst the colours suitable for artistic painting.

BARYTA YELLOW and VAN DYCK RED and BROWN, which are found on the market in an infinity of varieties, cannot be exactly determined as to their permanency. I eliminate them from my list of permanent colours in order not to lead the artist into error.

[*] I use the term "monarchy" in the aesthetic sense in which Luca Pacioli used it. For even though as a form of government monarchy has often produced very harmful results, in aesthetics the monarchy of spheres is primordial.

[*] From D'Arcy W. Thompson, *On Growth and Form*, pages 944, 945 and 946.

[1] Cf. Bashforth and Adams, *Theoretical Forms of Drops*, etc., Cambridge, 1883.

[2] The drops must be spherical, or very nearly so, to produce a rainbow. But the bow is said to be always better defined near the top than down below; which seems to show that

the lower and larger raindrops are the less perfect spheres. (Cf. T. W. Backhouse, *Symons's M. Met. Mag.* 1879, p. 25.) For the small round droplets in the cloud tend to cannon off one another, and remain small and spherical. But when there comes a difference of potential between cloud and cloud, or between earth and sky, then the spherules become distorted, one droplet coalesces with another, and the big drops begin to fall.

[3]Cf. A. Ferguson, On the theoretical shape of large bubbles and drops, *Phil. Mag.* (6) xxv, pp. 507-520, 1913.

[*]From D'Arcy W. Thompson, *On Growth and Form,* pages 386-7.

[4]J. Blackwall, *Spiders of Great Britain*, (Ray Society), 1859, p. 10; *Trans. Linn. Soc.* xvi, p. 477, 1833. On the strength and elasticity of the spider's web, see J. R. Benton, *Amer. Journ. Science* xxiv. pp. 75-78, 1907.

[*]From Jacques Blockx, *A Compendium of Painting*.

[*] From D'Arcy W. Thompson, *On Growth and Form,* pages 389 and 390.

[5]*A Study of Splashes*, 1908, p. 38, etc.; also various papers in *Proc. R. S.* 1876-1882, and *Phil. Trans.* (A) 1897 and 1900.

[6]Cf. A Study of Splashes, pp. 17, 77. The same phenomenon is often well seen in the splash of an oar. It is beautifully and continuously evident when a strong jet of water from a tap impinges on a curved surface and then shoots off again.

[7]We owe this picture to the kindness of Mr. Harold E. Edgerton, of the Massachusetts Institute of Technology. It shows the splash caused by a drop falling into a thin layer of milk; a second drop of milk is seen above, following the first. The exposure-time was 1/50,000 of a second.

[*]D'Arcy W. Thompson, *On Growth and Form,* pp. 759-762.

[*]From Jacques Blockx, *A Compendium of Painting*.

www.ingramcontent.com/pod-product-compliance
Lightning Source LLC
Chambersburg PA
CBHW020639220526
45464CB00001B/214